N

Lound
Herringfleet
Flixton
Gunton
Oulton
LOWESTOFT
BECCLES
BUNGAY
Mettingham
Barnby
North Cove
Gisleham
St John
Ilketshall St Andrew
Ellough
Kessingland
Flixton
Ilketshall St Margaret
Redisham
Benacre
Homersfield
S. Elmham or 'The Elmhams'
Ilketshall St Lawrence
Wrentham
Mendham
Rumburgh
Westhall
Frostenden
Covehithe
South Cove
Wissett
Sotherton
Wangford
Redgrave
Fressingfield
Linstead Magna
Chediston
Henham
Easton Bavents
Market Weston
Hinderclay
Wortham
Hoxne
Wingfield
Linstead Parva
HALESWORTH
Wenhaston
SOUTHWOLD
Hepworth
Rickinghall Inferior
Brome
Cookley
R. Blyth
Walpole
Blythburgh
Walberswick
Wattisfield
Rickinghall Superior
Mellis
EYE
Stradbroke
Cratfield
Thorington
Thornham Parva
Horham
Wilby
Laxfield
Heveningham
Dunwich
Walsham-le-Willows
Gislingham
Stoke Ash
Athelington
Sibton
Badwell Ash
Finningham
Wickham Skeith
Thorndon
Worlingworth
Peasenhall
Yoxford
Middleton
Wyverstone
Westhorpe
Bedingfield
Badingham
R. Minsmere
Theberton
Gt Ashfield
Cotton
Thwaite
Rishangles
Tannington
Dennington
Rendham
Kelsale
Mendlesham
Wetheringsett
Monk Soham
FRAMLINGHAM
SAXMUNDHAM
Elmswell
Wetherden
Gipping
DEBENHAM
Earl Soham
LEISTON
Coolpit
Old Newton
Mickfield
Ashfield with Thorp
Gt Glemham
Benhall
Aldringham
kstone
Haughley
Brandeston
Stratford St Andrew
Friston
Thorpeness
ge Shelland
Lit Stonham
R Deben
Hacheston
Snape
Onehouse
STOWMARKET
Stonham Aspal
Monewden
Easton
Lit Glemham
ALDEBURGH
Gt Finborough
Creeting St Mary
Helmingham
Letheringham
Wickham Mkt
Iken
Combs
Gosbeck
Otley
Charsfield
Campsey Ash
Tunstall
Sudbourne
Lit Finborough
Needham Market
Coddenham
Pettistree
Rendlesham
Morieux
Barking
Hemingstone
Bredfield
Ufford
Wantisden Butley
Barham
Burgh
Eyke
ORFORD
tlebaston
Offton
Claydon
Melton
Bromeswell
Bildeston
Akenham
Grundisburgh
Chelsworth
Whitton
Bealings
WOODBRIDGE
Whatfield
Martlesham
Sutton
sey
Aldham
Hintlesham
Waldringfield
Shottisham
HADLEIGH
Brightwell
Hollesley
one
Belstead
Nacton
Bucklesham
Alderton
ford
IPSWICH
Freston
Kirton
Bawdsey
Polstead
Wenham
Capel St Mary
Bentley
Woolverstone
Levington
Falkenham
Higham
Tattingstone
Chelmondiston
Trimley
Stratford St Mary
Brantham
Erwarton
Shotley
Walton
R Stour
East Bergholt
Stutton
Harkstead
FELIXSTOWE
ssington

R. Waveney
R. Dove
R. Aide
R Gipping
R Orwell
R Brett
R Stour

THE
SUFFOLK
LANDSCAPE

Entrance to the former Hardwick House, immediately south of Bury St Edmunds, now the site of the West Suffolk Hospital. The ironwork crest, a lion Proper supporting a decorative column, proclaimed the Cullum family who from the 18th to the early 20th centuries lived here and at adjacent Hawstead. Sir John Cullum's History and Antiquities of Hawstead, *1784, anticipated Gilbert White's* Natural History and Antiquities of Selborne, *1789, which so much delighted John Constable in 1821.*

THE
SUFFOLK
LANDSCAPE

Norman Scarfe

Phillimore

First published in 1972 by
HODDER AND STOUGHTON LTD
as a volume in 'The Making of the English Landscape' series
Second impression 1975; Revised edition 1987

2002

This new edition published by
PHILLIMORE & CO. LTD,
Shopwyke Manor Barn, Chichester, West Sussex

ISBN 1 86077 205 6

Printed and bound in Great Britain by
THE BATH PRESS
Bath, Avon

CONTENTS

To
PAUL FINCHAM

'L'accent du pays où l'on est né demeure dans l'esprit et
dans le coeur, comme dans le langage.' –
François de La Rochefoucauld, 1613-1680.
Réflexions morales.

LIST OF
ILLUSTRATIONS

Frontispiece: Hardwick House gateway

Acknowledgements

The author is grateful to the following for permission to use their black and white photographs: The late Edwin Smith for the frontispiece; The Norwich Castle Museum & Art Gallery: 1 (photograph by Hallam Ashley); The Committee for Aerial Photographs, Cambridge: 3, 14, 16, 18, 19, 23, 24, 29, 30, 42, 50, 73 (photographs by J.K. St Joseph, Cambridge University Collection: copyright reserved); S.C. Porter: 4; The late Angus McBean: 5, 17, 37, 47, 63, 64, 65; The Trustees, The National Gallery, London: 6, 76; Hallam Ashley: 7, 26; G.F. Cordy: 12, 21; Mrs J. Philps: 33; Aerofilms, Ltd: 41, 44; Moyses Hall Museum, Bury St Edmunds: 46; The late F.A. Girling: 59; *Country Life*: 75; Ivan J. Underwood: 79; Ford Jenkins: 83; Peter M. Warren: 55.

The maps (illustrations 8, 9, 15, 39, 57 and 68) are the copyright of Suffolk County Council, whose permission to reproduce them is gratefully acknowledged.

The author is responsible for Illustrations 25, 32, 52, 74, 78. He is also very grateful to Stephen Podd for the maps on pages 142-3.

The colour photographs were all taken by the author over several years, with the exceptions of XXIV (Kim Wilkie); XXV (Simon Robey). The Gainsborough in Colour Illustration XIV is in a private collection. Colour Illustration XVI (Gainsborough) and XXXII (Constable) are published by permission of the Ipswich Borough Council. Colour illustration XXV is reproduced by permission of The National Trust.

Introduction

LOOKING AT THE LANDSCAPE

In one of the many illuminating books in which Edwin Smith and his wife, Olive Cook, opened the eyes of a generation, she wrote (of *English Cottages and Farmhouses*, 1954): 'They are themselves the most moving and vivid expressions of the variety which is still the most astonishing quality of the English landscape'. Alas, Edwin Smith was terminally ill while I was writing the original edition of this book in 1971: Angus McBean, the celebrated theatrical photographer, instantly came to the rescue, abandoned his artificial lighting and went into action in fields like those near his home near Bedingfield. His illustrations 5 and 37 remain among the truest pictures of the heart of Suffolk.

Edwin Smith's remarkable photograph of autumnal sunlight through the wrought-iron entrance to Hardwick, on the edge of Bury St Edmunds, caught the scene and the very atmosphere of Ouida's childhood-walks with her father, an illusive and mysterious agent in Louis Napoleon's France: and just in time. Soon afterwards, Hardwick became the site of the new West Suffolk Hospital (*frontispiece*).

Landscape has its own life as well as the one photographers, painters and writers give it. The landscape itself changes, sometimes imperceptibly, sometimes more abruptly with the advent of powerful machinery. If we don't live in Suffolk, and sometimes if we do, we may come to look at it first through the eyes of painters: Constable and Gainsborough along the Stour valley, Wilson Steer and Harry Becker along the coast and in the old farm fields. Constable made those meadows beyond 'The Haywain', and the farmlands beyond 'Golding Constable's Kitchen Garden', familiar all over the world. At 56, he was getting off the Ipswich coach at the stop near East Bergholt and couldn't help exclaiming at the beauty of the valley ahead: one of the strangers travelling with him said: 'Yes Sir – this is *Constable's* country'. 'I told him who I was lest he should spoil it.' When the painter is as faithful as Constable, the landscape truly becomes his; and succeeding generations are reluctant to let it change.

Higher up the Stour valley, near Sudbury, Gainsborough had already found Cornard Wood. He began painting it when he was 13; perhaps completely repainting it, and making it his own, when he was about 21. (The picture's other name is 'Gainsborough's Forest'.) Unlike the Stour at Flatford, Cornard Wood itself is no longer to be seen: its woodland is now mainly orchard. Ellis Waterhouse believed that 'all the resources of composition Gainsborough had learnt from the still unfashionable Dutch naturalist painters are combined in this almost classic work'. The painter's own account is different: 'There is little idea of composition in the picture: the touch and closeness to nature in the study of the parts minutiae are equal to any of my later productions.' It has been asserted on high authority that he was not directly inspired by nature in the way John Constable was: yet Constable claimed to have learnt so much from him. To believe Gainsborough's own testimony, one has only to think of the wonderful landscape setting of 'Mr and Mrs Robert Andrews' in the sloping cornfields above Sudbury, or of Constable's most moving tribute to him: 'The stillness of noon, the depths of twilight, and the views and pearls of the morning, are all to be found on the canvases of this most benevolent and kind-hearted man.'

The Stour divides Suffolk from Essex, and the arable fields of Suffolk's central clays stretch across from the Stour in the south-west to Beccles and Bungay and Lowestoft in the north-east, where the Waveney supplies the meandering county boundary. Suffolk's western boundary is a purely political one, representing the western edge of an estate that had been the dowry of King Cnut's wife Emma, an amalgam of 8½ Hundreds, a local government administrative unit. It was given to Bury abbey by Edward the Confessor. The eastern edge is of course the sea-shore: I lived for years on it, at Shingle Street, on the solid shingle beach by the mouth of the Alde river, which flows here on a strange course south from Aldeburgh. After arriving at Aldeburgh from inland, instead of entering the sea, the river is deflected southwards by an incipient 'ness' (nose) of shingle: only after 11 more miles and after slipping past Orford castle and quay, does it manage to force its way out to the sea across a treacherous bar at Shingle Street.

Suffolk's shore has steadily given way to the sea south of Lowestoft, and, more notoriously south of Southwold, where Dunwich stood boldly on a 40ft high cliff scarcely sturdier than sand. In the seventh century, Dunwich was the seat of the first bishops of East Anglia: in King John's time, it was a gated town with at least eight parish churches, various religious houses, and markets every weekday. Now, all that is left is a handful of houses, part of a landward medieval suburb and a notable little museum.

The shingle beach still provides a rough-and-ready shield to the 11 miles of Orford Ness, and so shelters, under the National Trust, remarkable reminders of 1935 radar experiments and other remains of once-secret defence-works that helped crucially in the winning of the 1939-45 war. It also shelters the physical evidence of its own piecemeal creation as a shingle spit. Moulded by the sea, it is not the complete pushover people who are used to rocky shores might imagine. A bank of shingle has a stubborn consistency discouraging to the walker. Alan Bennett, impressed by a brief walk at Shingle Street said: 'I think Shingle-Walking could be an Olympic event'. It is certainly a wild-life event, with sea-pea and bladder campion underfoot, and skylarks still cheerfully ascend from that beach.

About the time of the First World War, Harry Becker painted and etched unforgettably every feature of the farmlife he saw in the Darsham-Wenhaston neighbourhood, towards the top end of the A12: hedging, mowing by scythe, cutting chaff, and the great climax of bringing home the harvest. It was the world captured in H.W. Freeman's notable novel *Joseph and his Brethren* (1928, and often reprinted). It was captured by more sociological means in George Ewart Evans's *The Horse in the Furrow* (1960), also by Ronald Blythe in *Akenfield* (1969). My grandfather was a windmiller and small farmer, and I saw the end of it for myself, when horses and horsemen were being reluctantly paid off, to make way for tractors and combine harvesters, for those who could afford them. The story of farming in south-west Suffolk, between the wars, was told, from his own experiences, in Adrian Bell's well known trilogy, *Corduroy*, *Silver Ley*, and *The Cherry Tree*, with many of Harry Becker's paintings chosen by Bell to illustrate the 1940s editions.

We begin this revised look at the Suffolk landscape in Becker country, and with an introduction to Suffolk's 'vanished' landscape.

For example, anyone who has merely glimpsed it on its spur beside the A12 Trunk Road, near Southwold, and on the way to Lowestoft, is unlikely ever to forget that image of Blythburgh church. Its elaborate stonework – forty yards of traceried aisle and glittering clerestory – seems too sophisticated and noble to be standing among a scatter of cottages and above the meadows of the Blyth river at the point where it becomes a bedraggled estuary, its man-made banks abandoned and swamped. The contrast between the magnificence of the masonry, the (attractively primitive) neglect of the estuary, the insignificance of the village and the relentless rush-past of motor traffic, is striking enough to start the most complacent traveller wondering. How is anyone to guess at the story?

Imagine Blythburgh in 1066: an extensive royal manor with woods and farms, a flourishing fishing port, a market, and a rich minster-church hallowed by the shrine of a seventh-century patriot king whose daughter founded Ely cathedral. Blythburgh's market place was laid out at the east end of the parish church, and an age-old highway divided it from the market place, running in those days all along the south edge of the churchyard, round and along its east edge, turning eastwards again, into the line preserved in the present little lane. In that quiet lane, a house called The Priory marks the chapel and gateway to a (long ruined) priory of Augustinian canons, probably on the site of the Anglo-Saxon royal minster. The river flowed away eastwards past Walberswick, then south to debouch at Dunwich, supplying a harbour for that powerful rival – in the 12th and 13th centuries – to the major European port of Ipswich. It was the choking of Dunwich harbour and the move of the rivermouth north to Walberswick and Southwold that brought their later medieval prosperity, and Blythburgh's, and the magnificence of the churches that still bemuse us today. But the trade and the fishing industry declined from Henry VIII's disruptive reign, and except for two of the churches the three little medieval towns dwindled and vanished almost as effectively as if they had been drowned like Dunwich. An Act of 1756 helped to make the Blyth more navigable for barges to Halesworth. In about 1780, Blythburgh's decayed market place was violently intersected by a new turnpike road, the present A12. In 1797, on the brink of the Napoleonic wars, Blythburgh's principal farm, Westwood Lodge, with its marshes, sheepwalks, and sheepfolded arable, earned Arthur Young's tribute as 'without exception the finest farm in the county'; but the sheep, too, have vanished from these light lands, replaced by beet. In turn, pigs are replacing the beet.

The Ipswich-Lowestoft railway reached Halesworth in 1859; and, twenty years later, during the worst local harvest on record, a narrow gauge (3ft) branch line was opened (in a deluge and an almost submerged landscape), winding that day just like an eel along the river below Blythburgh church and on to Blackshore and Southwold. With its 'airy and spacious' carriages, and its remembered erratic and leisurely conduct, it lasted just fifty years before being closed by the more convenient motor car. Another landscape had vanished, replaced by a gradual congestion of motors, but also a new form of leisure. If anything has changed for the better[1] in the 30 years since the first edition of this book, it is the way the Suffolk Trust for Nature Conservation, the Suffolk Preservation Society, and the County Planning Department have come together to establish a network of well signed and mapped footpaths and bridlepaths and well camouflaged car parks.

---

[1] Changes for the worse: readers may be appalled to learn that some 23,000 miles of hedgerow in Suffolk in 1950 had been reduced, in the interests of 'maximising' arable crops, to some 8,000 miles by 1985. This is the rock-bottom minimum to allow what any naturalist would reckon an adequate wildlife habitat. It's a relief to be able to record a modest improvement in 2002. The current *English Nature Research Report*, no.366, 'Estimating the length of hedgerow in Suffolk', p.19, gives its estimate as 8,625 miles (13,800km) with a margin of 1,300 miles either way.

One can now walk from Blythburgh along the earthworks of the vanished railway and explore this relatively recent archaeology.

Nowadays, as we walk, and bird watch, and botanise, and mark the speed with which nature obliterates the ingenious works of men, we may resolve to do everything in our power to prevent nature from invading and dilapidating ever again the parish church of the Trinity at Blythburgh. In 1761, the jackdaws evidently got in among the wooden wings of the angels in the roof and were shot at, with results only less calamitous than when the obsessed puritan Dowsing, on a spring day in 1644, came and ordered the destruction of two hundred Christian glass images in the windows.

The images I set out to capture here in 1972 were these historic sequences, the changes in the face of Suffolk. It was not easy. I had written Shell Guides to both Suffolk and Essex and knew the landscapes as they appeared then. The biggest obstacle to understanding the development of Suffolk through the ages was easily stated. Domesday Book shows it to be already fairly set in its ways in 1086, with over four hundred of its five hundred medieval churches already established, and many of its farms and manors and markets (like Blythburgh's) already located and explorable. But one needed to know how all that came about, in the centuries before 1086. What was there to read? A few very illuminating wills and charters (C.R. Hart, *The Early Charters of Eastern England,* Leicester, 1966, pp.53-78), Bede's wonderful *Ecclesiastical History of the English People,* and the *Anglo Saxon Chronicle.* Domesday Book itself is unfailingly instructive. For the rest, as he considers the formative early centuries of Suffolk, the historian has to team up with, or become, the archaeologist. This historian has been happy indeed in coinciding with a group of expert and dedicated archaeologists banded together under Stanley West, and later Keith Wade, as the Suffolk Archaeological Unit in the County Planning Department. (He is not ashamed, as a nagging committee member of the former East Suffolk's enlightened planning department, to have helped promote one of the first county units in England.) Even so, he will be found here resorting to fairly desperate experiments with, for instance, arguably early church dedications, to try to introduce some means of early dating.

Since 1972, the county unit's revelations have become steadily more impressive, which is the more remarkable since it is still powerfully governed by both the academic and the financial requirements of 'rescuing' known sites ahead of the ubiquitous bulldozers in our rapidly changing region. At West Row, Mildenhall, Edward Martin has uncovered the first known Bronze-Age house in Suffolk. At West Stow, Stanley West had just, in 1972, completed his excavation of the famous pagan Germanic village, partly contemporary with a British settlement that had certainly at one time been Christian, at *Camborito,* just across the (Icknield) way; see illustration 22. Some of the huts of West Stow have been carefully reconstructed, and attract increasing numbers of visitors, if not prospective buyers. I suppose the most impressive demonstration of the degree to which the archaeologists have transformed our view of the landscape is to compare Jude Plouviez' map of Roman Suffolk now (illustration 8), with its predecessor in 1972.

I began my book on *Suffolk in the Middle Ages* with a chapter on the value of place names to archaeology, and I concentrated on names ending with *feld* (now field, as in Ashfield) because it means a wide open space and because such names coincide almost exclusively in Suffolk with the fertile heavy clays. Such land ceases to be *feld*, wide open, without continual clearance of encroaching woodland; and that seemed a pointer to the takeover of *feld* places in good working order by English from British farmers. I still think it was a useful exercise for the archaeologists to have in mind, but I went into it hoping to offer them an indicator to scarce Romano-British farm sites. By the time I published, they had shown that such sites were all too plentiful!

One of the most spectacular and rewarding of the unit's studies over the years is Bob Carr's, on a former islet in the flood plain of the Little Ouse at Brandon. Traces of 20 timbered buildings have emerged from the years *c.*650-890, the very years of the establishment of Christianity. As I was writing, the site of a wooden church was being uncovered, no smaller than many surviving medieval churches, but conceivably going back to the 650s with Bishop Cedd's famous church of St Peter at Bradwell juxta Mare in Essex, the nave of which still stands. At Brandon, the cemetery, too, has come to light and finds include a small plaque carved with the emblem of John the Evangelist, patron of writers, with stylus at the ready. More years of work should determine whether this is a monastic or a lordly site, or both. Similarly striking interpretations of Anglo-Saxon Ipswich, one of the earliest post-Roman trading towns of Europe, have come from Keith Wade, exciting the interest of European archaeologists much as the expanded new port down at Felixstowe is interesting traders from across the seas.

The neighbouring estuary of the Deben boasts tumuli (pl.16) and sensational ship burials from just before the coming of Christianity. In 2002 this extraordinary site at Sutton Hoo has come under the care of the National Trust. They were surprised by the enormous numbers of people, not only from England, who have come to see Dr Steven Plunkett's brilliant reconstruction and presentation. It is not fanciful to think of it as an English version of Tutankhamen's tomb. It illuminates Suffolk and again Europe, in the first half of the seventh century when East Anglia was ruled by the most powerful king on this island.

Since 1972, views of Suffolk's landscape have been changed not only by archaeology but by historians and books. Two of the most remarkable are Oliver Rackham's *Trees and Woodland in the British Landscape* (1976: four years earlier, it would have transformed much of this book!), and *The History of the Countryside* (1986). His gift for relating his great knowledge of trees and vegetation not only to the landscape but to the relevant medieval records is phenomenal. I admired his courage in suggesting that the intrusion of medieval greens and meadows into the weird, presumably earlier, linear pattern of the South Elmham/Ilketshall fields may mean the survival of a very extensive prehistoric landscape (1986, pp. 156-58). Since he wrote, as we shall see, Tom Williamson has taken these ideas much further. I wish Rackham hadn't swallowed the doctrine that 'moats were status symbols' *(loc.cit.,* p.362). In some instances, they probably were. But the hundreds of working farmers who surrounded their houses all over the central clay belt of Suffolk (not just in *West* Suffolk as he implies) were thinking first of draining the damp away from their wattle and daub house walls in this sponge-like, but heavy, moisture-holding clay; and incidentally of supplying a fish store and some first line defence against marauders in times that were often more lawless than ours. Another of the books affecting our views of Suffolk's landscape, at all periods, is a masterly brief *History of Suffolk* by David Dymond and Peter Northeast. Their, and Dr. John Ridgard's, running of successful local history classes over the past decades has brought about a real revolution in our contemporary understanding of Suffolk's history and its landscape. Many of us are hugely in their debt. We also owe very much to our membership, and its fellowship, of the Suffolk Institute of Archaeology and History, which has lately enjoyed 25 of the best years of its life under the exemplary presidency of Dr John Blatchly.

No less than when prefacing my first edition, I must record continuous thanks to the archivists and their staffs at Ipswich, Bury and Chancery Lane, and to the librarians and theirs at Ipswich, the British Library, and Amsterdam University. I gratefully recall Professor W.A. van Es's hospitality at Amersfoort and his exposition of ancient settlements on the Rhine and in modern Friesland. I am deeply grateful to the late Rupert Bruce-Mitford for letting me work at Sutton Hoo in 1966 and for his generous readiness to talk about the Wuffingas at all times. He and John Hurst both gave kind and expert advice on Ipswich origins.

The most widely useful and instructive book to appear since I was writing the introduction to this one is *An Historical Atlas of Suffolk* (1988), edited by David Dymond and Edward Martin (their third splendid edition 1999). Modesty must not inhibit me in commending with delight *East Anglia's History: Studies in Honour of Norman Scarfe*, edited by Christopher Harper-Bill, Carole Rawcliffe and Richard Wilson, full of the knowledge and love of East Anglia with a large and proper bias towards Suffolk: from John Blatchly's initial Appreciation to Sir Michael Howard's Coda on the Caen Controversy which affected the story of the 1st Battalion of the Suffolk Regiment in that battle. I turn these 358 pages, so handsomely produced by the Boydell Press with the Centre of East Anglian Studies, and wonder at my good fortune. I am profoundly grateful to my late friend and colleague William Hoskins for giving me the chance to contribute to the series to which this book belonged when it first appeared. My final thanks are to my agent, John Welch, and to Noel Osborne, of Phillimore, for asking me to undertake this new edition and to Andrew Illes of that firm for his care and expertise.

Norman Scarfe
15 May 2002
Woodbridge, Suffolk

One

THE LAND OF THE SOUTH FOLK

The picture of the land in which I fain would pass my life, in which my only requirements are that I may ... see the ruins of a gothic fortress in the grass, and find hidden among the cornfields ... an old church, monumental, rustic, and yellow like a mill stone.

Marcel Proust, *A la Recherche du Temps Perdu*

The Faces of the Landscape

Like some well preserved elderly persons, Suffolk says nothing precise about its age when one first scans its face. Years later, many of its features remain bafflingly timeless, however rudely one may have reduced the range of possibilities. Winding through oak-buttressed lanes to Helmingham from Woodbridge and then on to Debenham and Eye on the way to Norwich, how does one see that this was surveyed as a turnpike road, and is not a mere sequence of un-urgent by ways established through the woodlands by Anglo-Saxon, or even Romano-British, farmers and their stock? Looking at Tudor surveys that show the marsh dykes of Bawdsey and Hollesley, between the Deben and Alde estuaries, dug already in the form they retain today, how can we judge whether they were not already centuries old, related perhaps even to Romano-British enterprise from the site David Mann farms at Buckanay? Trying to visualise Norman Suffolk and considering that some of the Domesday scribes may have been Normans, one is constantly astonished at the way almost all the 500 parish names, as well as dozens of smaller settlements, are spelt in Domesday Book very much as they are spelt and pronounced now. But can we relate Domesday Book's descriptions of these places to the present landscape? Can we then relate the Domesday features back to the landscape of the English settlers? In the archaeological world of objects divorced from written records, can we ever feel confident that at Burgh (near Woodbridge), say where the medieval church stands in an Iron-Age and Roman enclosure,

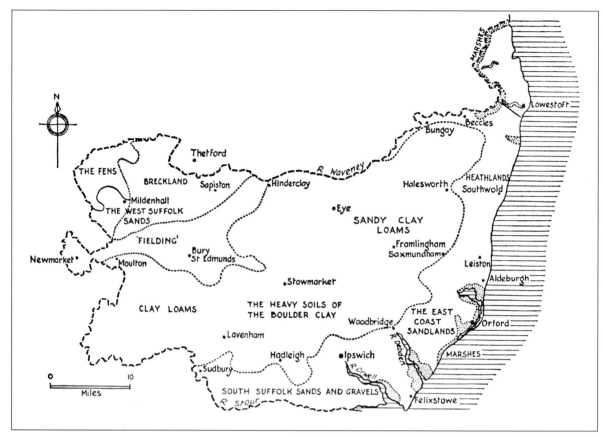

1   *The main soils of Suffolk. Based, by kind permission of P.J.O. Trist, on* A Survey of the Agriculture of Suffolk *(1971), p.65.*

or that at Waldringfield beside the Deben, where at least one pagan Anglo-Saxon was cremated on the site afterwards occupied by the medieval churchyard, we are at a scene of anything like continuous habitation (or mortification) through Roman to Anglo-Saxon times or from early Anglo-Saxon to medieval and modern times?

Such are the kinds of dating problem. At this stage in the archaeological exploration of Suffolk, many more questions occur to us than can be convincingly answered. A justification for writing this history now is that the mere opening up of some of the leading questions may provide other students of the environment with programmes of prolonged and rewarding research. This rather primitive stage of our knowledge, together with the broad differences in the type of Suffolk scenery, suggests that particularising will have more value than generalising, at least to begin with.

2 Newmarket lies in a dip, surrounded by famous chalk-down turf. This view west from the Warren Hill training-ground was drawn probably by Tillemans, c.1720-30. The Heath racecourse and Devil's Dyke lie in the background at the left edge, beyond the post-windmill that stood near the London entrance. A coach, right middle-distance, marks the ancient road to Thetford and Bury. The foreground is used by similar groups of horses at exercise today.

These different faces of Suffolk are easily envisaged (illustration 1). First one must know that, right across the middle of Suffolk, occupying two thirds of the whole area of the county, field beyond field is made of deep soil, mostly a wonderfully heavy clay, called Boulder Clay, though it is distinguished not by boulders, but by having picked up a lot of chalk and flint while it was being tipped and bulldozed here by some long forgotten glacier. This is still called High Suffolk. But its height is mostly round about 100-200 feet above sea level, and hardly rises above 400 feet. It sometimes gives an impression of height, when you have climbed up on to a plateau of it, at Badingham, for instance, when you have followed the Alde valley up from Rendham or the Minsmere stream up from Peasenhall; or at Rumburgh when you clamber up from the Blyth valley at Wissett; or at Kersey or Bildeston above the Brett. West of Lavenham the undulation is more pronounced and the clay plateaux less extensive. The most sensible name for this kind of scenery is Central Suffolk, if it needs a name. Its beauties are subtle, and difficult to define. They depend much on an awareness of the water courses, which from field ditches to rivers give the whole clay belt a fundamental pattern and meaning (illustrations 5 and 37).

3 *Looking south over 'the Fielding' from a plane above Coney Weston, near Thetford. Peddars Way (see pp.43-46) is traced by crop marks and hedges. 'Enclosure' of over 1,600 acres was enabled in Coney Weston and Barningham by Private Acts in 1777 and 1799. Contrast with illustration 15.*

On either side of the clays, to east and west, there are lighter soils. Between Bury and Newmarket 'the Fielding' extends like a rolling, chalky sea swell. It was called the Fielding because it still lay in 'open fields' long after the rest of Suffolk's farmlands had been 'enclosed' (illustrations 2 and 3). At its western edge, near Newmarket, it became grassy chalk downland of the kind we more readily associate with the Gog Magog Hills over in Cambridgeshire, and with Berkshire and Wiltshire. East of Newmarket, the dry grey-white soil of the hill beneath which Moulton church lies is not firm enough to have taken the hopeful carving of a fertility figure, and this may explain the 'Sheila–na gig' sculpture on one of the stones in the church itself.[1] Chalk underlies the whole of Suffolk: near the top, as here and in colour illustration I; but it lies much lower, e.g. under the coastal strip. Flint develops within the chalk bed and so is fairly ubiquitous in East Anglia.

[1] Dr Margaret Murray, *Journal of the Royal Anthropological Institute*, Vol.LXIV, p.93; cf. the prominent carving high up on the south wall of Whittlesford church, near Cambridge.

4 *Breckland: blown sand with sand-sedge at Wangford, near Brandon. Breckland is now much covered by the dense coniferous woodland of the Forestry Commissioners.*

North of the Fielding and west of the central clays and commingling at the edges, the very light soils and sands of the Breckland lie between Bury and Thetford (illustration 4). Here, on a Sapiston farm not far from the arable clays, Robert Bloomfield worked as a boy. Later, making ladies' shoes in London, he turned his rural boyhood recollections into bestselling nostalgic verse: *The Farmer's Boy* (1800). It is the most truly Suffolk poem (though Crabbe is the ablest Suffolk poet: he revealed his powers in *The Borough* (1810), whose most famous inhabitant is Peter Grimes).

> The plough moves heavily, and strong the soil,
> And clogging harrows with augmented toil
> Dive deep: and clinging, mixes with the mould
> A fat'ning treasure from the nightly fold.

5 *High Suffolk: Boulder Clay field on Red House Farm, Debenham. Oak in Field-bank, elm-screen on left deleted by elm-disease; willows and meadows of a feeder of the stripling Deben beyond.*

These four poetically ungrammatical lines summarise the light land corn husbandry, the fields nourished by cattle dung (now a highly chemical affair). And here he remembers Sunday at a nearby isolated church, probably Ixworth Thorpe's, now in good care, whose tower has since been reduced:

> And rampant nettles lift the spiry head,
> Whilst from the hollows of the tower on high
> The grey cap'd Daws in saucy legions fly.
> Round these lone walls assembling neighbours meet,
> And tread departed friends beneath their feet.

Off at daybreak to scare crows from the further fields, he made his way to the Breckland proper:

> His sandy way deep worn by hasty showers
> O'er arch'd with oaks that form'd fantastic bow'rs ...
> But groves no farther fenced his devious way;
> A wide extended heath before him lay,
> Where on the grass the stagnant shower had run,
> And shone a mirror to the rising sun.

West of Breckland stretch the distances of the fenland, once the salt inland sea, an extension of the Wash, with extraordinary islands like Stuntney and Ely and so on. Freckenham and Mildenhall marked Suffolk's western shoreline.

Over in East Suffolk, the edge of the clay is marked fairly accurately by the A12, the main London Lowestoft road. In the Shotley peninsula, loamy soils and steep sunny little valleys are framed by broad waterways, the estuaries of the Stour and the Orwell. North of Ipswich, heathland of bracken and ling, bell-heather and birches lies east of the A12, laced with some pockets of clay, notably at Kelsale and Leiston. The heaths or 'Sandlings' as they are called here, are easily whipped into 'blows' or sandstorms when winds coincide with a dry spell before a farmer gets his seed well rooted. Dust storms are a common spectacle in spring and summer. Beyond the heaths lie more estuaries and marshlands, Orford and Aldeburgh and Crabbe's landscape:

> Lo! where the heath, with withering brake grown o'er,
> Lends the light turf that warms the neighbouring poor ...
> There poppies, nodding, mock the hope of toil;
> There the blue bugloss paints the sterile soil.

Cutting 'the light turf' in the Middle Ages created some small 'Broads', as at Covehithe and Fritton (illustration 7): see the 1837 1-inch OS map, and on Bryant's 1826 map of Suffolk, where the Minsmere river reaches the sea.

6 *Gainsborough's picture of the edge of the Suffolk 'Woodlands' painted at Sudbury in 1748 when he was 21, but 'begun before I left school'.*

Intermittent low sandy cliffs stoop to narrow shingly beaches. 'What a sounding board is that harsh tilted shore for the boom and rasp of cold reverberating sea,' wrote Christopher Morley, about Shingle Street, in 1944, in his Suffolk-American novel, *Thorofare*. 'It needs flashes of sun to brighten bits of amber … pink carnelian … the tender corals of that Puritan shore.'

Those are the essential differences of soil underlying the various faces of Suffolk. As we just saw in connection with the Broads, men have done more than apply the cosmetics, they have done much basic moulding.

For years at Shingle Street, my window overlooked marshes that were claimed from the salt water for the summer grazing of sheep and cattle by building miles of earth banks called 'walls'. Waller is not an uncommon name round here, which is in itself an indication that walling was being done in the

7 *Fritton Lake, near Lowestoft. A 'Broad' made by 'turbary' (peat-cutting), probably in the early 14th century (see p.144). Accessible for fishing and picnics at Fritton Old Hall.*

early Middle Ages. The mute and (very occasional) Bewick's swans, the shelduck, Canada geese and so on, that settle on the marsh in winter in place of the farm stock, would have had a welcome very different from our academic and aesthetic one in times of medieval husbandry. Long before the Middle Ages, the coastal heaths and the Breckland were being made, quite unintentionally, by those first settlers who cut down the aboriginal woods in order to grow crops, and then saw their largely waterless light soils blown away by the winds. As recently as the 1740s, when Gainsborough knew it and painted his first picture of the edge of it, that clay-capped middle of Suffolk was still called 'the Woodlands', and his picture is known as 'Cornard Wood', or 'Gainsborough's Forest' (illustration 6). The woods are now nearly all cornfields or sugar beet fields, and we are exercised how to keep them hedged and with even occasional trees in the hedgerow banks. Despite the harsh economic demands of the huge new farm machines for huge new fields, many moderate sized fields still remain, studded with enough hedgerow oaks and ash trees to suggest visibly the thick woodland from which they were first hewn. The clearest impression of thick forest cover now is given by large areas of Breckland and the coastal 'Sandlings', where private landowners and (since 1935) the Forestry Commissioners have created great coniferous woods, often artfully edged with beech and birch, divided now by majestic rides, and maturing to give a fine effect from a distance.

How old are Suffolk's enclosed fields? Oliver Rackham, with an unrivalled knowledge of Suffolk's woodland history, included it in his category of 'ancient countryside, *bocage*, lonely moats in the clay fields, immense mileages of minor roads, intricate footpaths'; and he boldly reckoned that half the hedged and stone-walled landscape of England dates from periods between the Bronze Age and the 17th century (*Trees and Woodland*, 1976, p17). In 35 deplorable years, 1950-1985, farmers stripped Suffolk's ploughlands of two-thirds of their hedgerows, leaving only some major fragments of that 'ancient countryside'. They even ploughed out the great ditched bridleway that had marked off the Hundred of Hartismere from that of Bosmere since the tenth century, or earlier (it featured as Pl.17 in the earlier editions of this book). Here it is replaced by my photograph of the Hundred boundary between Bosmere and Thredling, taken in April 2002, with the ash-keys hanging from one of the rich hedgerows which go back certainly before 970, when King Edgar gave the soke over 'the Thredling of Winston' as part of his great gift to Ely of 'the Liberty of St Etheldreda'. The 'Liberty' meant freedom from the interference of the King's sheriff; a considerable freedom. It explains why this Anglo-Saxon way appears in the Helmingham records, Stephen Podd tells me, as 'Franches way', meaning Franchise way. And see the Franchise Bank on p.155.

At last we can demonstrate with some assurance that many of the clay fields of Suffolk were probably being cleared and made not only long before the 18th century (which seems to be when so much of Midland England was being remodelled and enclosed), but even well before the coming of the Old English settlers. In our main clay belt, it is very hard to find any reference to 'open-fields' of the sort Midland villagers created in rich clays. (I give a few samples in the section on 'The fields' in Ch 4 below.) Dr David Dymond's map of enclosure and reclamation (*Historical Atlas*, map 46) shows an eccentric handful of pointers to open-fields on the rhinoceros horn of Lothingland Hundred, north of Lowestoft. Otherwise they seem to have been confined to the peripheral light lands of the north-west corner of Suffolk: Breckland and the Fielding. A survey of Walsham-le-Willows in 1577 reveals the existence of open-fields and the way they were being broken up.

Whenever the earliest fields were being carved out of the dense woodland on the boulder clay, those first pioneers would be quick to understand that the heavy clay, once rid of its timber, would need draining to grow crops, or indeed pasture. This involved digging round the fields great moat-like ditches, which led into the streams that slowly carved into our gentle valleys. In this way, the artificial creation of bank and ditch and drain and stream have come to look to us like the 'natural' lie of the land. The key to the occupation of the broad central two-thirds of Suffolk was the development of the beast-drawn plough with an iron coulter. Until this was first brought in by the Belgae, towards the end of the Iron Age and in the early Roman years, the main incentive to fell the woods and drain and settle on the clay was missing. It is no accident that 'coulter' is at the bottom of the word 'culture' and that cultivation is a Roman idea from the same time. The cultivation of the landscape with the plough is the first big step towards Suffolk's civilisation. (Just occasionally it seems to have been the last.) But whenever in Celtic and Roman times the creation of these small farms took place, they soon seem to have spread into all parts of the county. Judith Plouviez has records of over one thousand of them, and she says 'the true number may have been as many as 4000' (*Atlas*, map 16, pp.42-3). Those co-axial field systems crossed by the Pye Road in map 19 (*op. cit.* pp.48-9) are almost certainly pre-Roman.

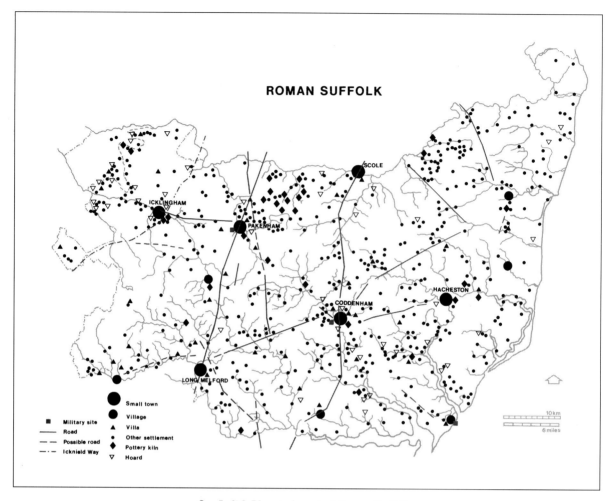

8 *Judith Plouviez's map of Roman Suffolk.*

The banking of fields goes with their ditching. The clay needed draining, the crops needed shelter from the east winds, so a bank was formed alongside the ditch with its spoil as it was dug. (The banks have often been dispersed now, spread into the fields.) But these field boundaries that form a vast network across the Suffolk landscape, are not the only notable boundary features of the scenery. Just as their ditches are connected with the river system, so their banks are often connected up with, and built into, the ancient boundaries of the 500 or so parishes. Walking the parish boundaries, between Charsfield and Hoo in East Suffolk, for instance, or Hartest and Boxted in the west, one is immediately aware that quite ancient bounds between the parishes are following the ditch and hedge boundaries of fields that were already enclosed when limits of the parish were established. (A glance at the 2½ inch O.S. sheets for Suffolk immediately reveals dozens of similar examples of parish bounds following the angular bounds of quite small fields.)

Here in the central clay woodlands, hundreds of the houses were moated like the fields, and framed with timber from the woods. We now begin to see from their structure that a few of these farmhouses, like Woodlands at Brundish, go back to the 13th century: a few more, like Edgar's Farmhouse (from Combs, and now in the Museum of East Anglian Life at Stowmarket) go back to the 14th century. Many of their names go back to the 11th century, and often much earlier. By the later Middle Ages, their steep pitched thatched roofs were being tiled, their old mud walls plastered and colour washed, or bricked. (A Drinkstone man left the residue of his goods for the tiling of his parish church in 1519, which gives an idea of the dating of the general spread of roof tiling.) By the time of the Tudors and Stuarts, great brick chimney stacks with displays of moulded chimneys were adding to the characteristic landmarks. The roomier aisled barns and outbuildings, designed to take the loaded, traditionally blue painted wagons through their doors, sometimes loom like towerless churches alongside the houses. Many such groups continue in our landscape, but increasing numbers are being overshadowed by great grey factory farm sheds. Our own age, as in so many ways, is putting a disquieting emphasis on cheapness and utility above all those considerations of permanence and visual delight that earlier farming generations were not ashamed to indulge.

For all the rustic beauty and historical attraction of those ancient fields and halls, one other feature of the man made landscape focuses most of our attention and captures most of our imagination: the flint-grey parish church, often solitary, away from the farmsteads, surrounded only by the fields. It provides the essential bearings in the detailed settlement pattern, the nub of the local story.

There are just over 500 medieval churches standing in Suffolk; and, as we shall see, there were once about fifty more. Half a thousand represents a high concentration, for in all England there are reckoned to be round about 8,500 surviving medieval churches. Yet Suffolk scarcely seems congested with them. Her landscape is wide enough, and folded enough to hold them unobtrusively; and some of them are quite small. From the top of Wickham Market's tower one is said to see nearly fifty other towers, and from the top of Bradfield St George's, sixty, though not all in Suffolk. (I have tried them only in summer, with the trees all in leaf, and only two other towers visible from each, or three with fieldglasses! I could see that both claims might be more justified on a very clear winter's day.) Neither of those towers reaches above eighty feet, but that is enough height to give a view down into the folds of the valleys, which provide perhaps the chief natural pleasure in all our scenery. When you are down in the winding valley bottom of, for instance Badingham parish, you find that even Badingham's church is invisible, mounted though it is near the top of a spur. On the other hand Wilby and Worlingworth, on the nearby level clay tableland, have bell-towers tall enough to be seen as well as heard from the far corners of their parishes. Next door, Stradbroke's loftier tower can be seen for miles around, its west doorway still bearing the armorial leopard's head of King Edward IV's (and Richard III's) brother-in-law, John de la Pole, whose castle stands beside the flat Green at adjacent Wingfield.

Especially in the claylands, there are few paths and roads in Suffolk from which you cannot spot at least one church tower. There are not many spires, probably on account of those North Sea winds; though Wickham Market's 80-foot tower holds aloft her breathtaking 57-feet of lead-covered oak, where its nearness to the sea provides sailors with a landmark. Hadleigh's beautiful spire is sheltered by being down in the Brett valley; its tip, like Boxford's nearby, just manages to signal a welcome across the higher fields around. There were once a few more spires, but they fell in famous storms like that which celebrated Oliver Cromwell's death, and the one in 1703 which Defoe described. It is said that Lavenham's tower was intended to hold a spire. It is 141 feet high, an extraordinary combination of square strength with grace. That is one of the noblest *campaniles* in England. Some of Suffolk's towers rank with Somerset's in splendour: the best are Stoke-by-Nayland, which so often arrested Constable's gaze; Eye, Laxfield and Walberswick. There are several close competitors, especially on the coast, for reasons that we shall examine; at Kessingland and Covehithe, for instance. At Southwold and Blythburgh, churches of peculiar dignity dominate their different kinds of coastal landscape; the one in a little cliff top town, the other at the head of an estuary, above marsh and heath and vanished market place and quay. Their venerable richness is echoed in the medieval clothing towns all along the Brett and Stour valleys and over in Bury St Edmunds.

These hundreds of ancient churches make a fundamental contribution to the character and the pattern of the Suffolk landscape. Even among streets full of the (modernised) medieval houses and inns, and the shops of the old craftsmen – blacksmith, harness-maker, butcher, cooper and so on – in Clare, or Nayland, or Debenham, no other single building gives so much to the scene: and this is truer still out in the scattered farming parishes, which are the great majority. When the former East Suffolk County Council made a grant towards the maintenance of the famous detached bell tower of St Michael, in Beccles, it was recognising the 'townscape' value of the building to the community, and established for itself an important precedent. 'Combray at a distance,' wrote Proust (of Illiers), 'was no more than a church epitomising the town, representing it, speaking of it and for it to the horizon.'

What 'East Suffolk' and 'West Suffolk' were, we examine in a moment. Political men have shaped the land as decisively as economic men; the object of central and local government is to control, and the shaping of boundaries is as fundamental to an understanding of the landscape as the siting of castles or administrative centres. The contribution of men moved by religion, in building churches, and afterwards nonconformist chapels, is also fundamental to our understanding of the human landscape. Apart from the land itself, and its so far very unsystematically explored archaeological contents, no other single group of objects tells us so much about the early settlement of Suffolk as its churches. For this reason we look very closely in a later chapter at what Domesday Book has to say about them. Four out of every five of the Suffolk churches we look at today stand on sites where a church stood in 1066. Often it can be shown how the pattern of the village settlement has changed since 1066. But the position of the church, in its sanctified yard, has very rarely changed. How long they stood there before 1066 is a more difficult question, one we can begin merely to glance at in that chapter. In terms of the basic pattern of settlements in Suffolk, those 418 churches[2] provide the pegs from which most of the rest must hang.

Domesday Book recorded about 418 churches in Suffolk in 1086, by far the greatest total of any English county. Only 274 churches were recorded in Norfolk, a mere 17 in Essex. There may have been discrepancies in the criteria of the Domesday scribes, but that also seems to cover omissions from the Suffolk record! Whatever their omissions, what they show for Suffolk is very remarkable: in 1086 there were already four churches in Suffolk to every five or so medieval churches surviving here today. (See *Historical Atlas*, 1999, p.52, for more details.)

---

[2] Nineteen of the Domesday church-sites are lost: I hope soon to publish my catalogues of the Domesday churches in the *Proceedings of the Suffolk Institute of Archaeology* (abbreviated in later footnotes as P.S.I.).

DOMESDAY CHURCHES

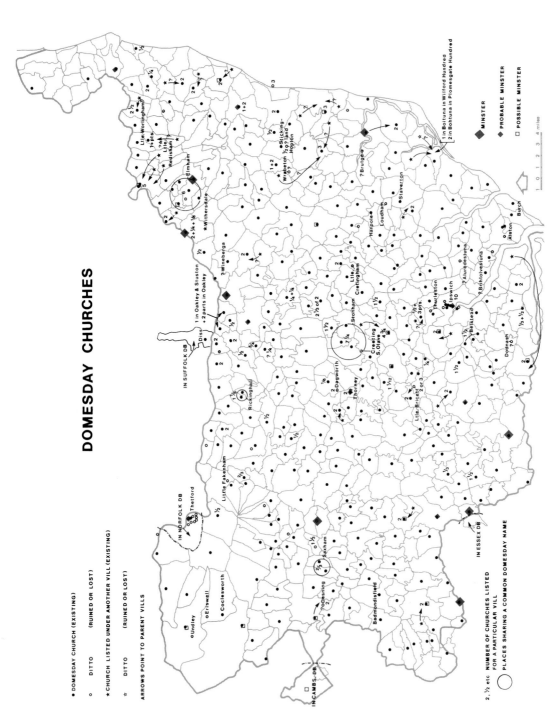

- ● DOMESDAY CHURCH (EXISTING)
- ○ DITTO   (RUINED OR LOST)
- ∗ CHURCH LISTED UNDER ANOTHER VILL (EXISTING)
- ☆ DITTO   (RUINED OR LOST)
- ↗ ARROWS POINT TO PARENT VILLS

2, ½ etc   NUMBER OF CHURCHES LISTED
FOR A PARTICULAR VILL

○ PLACES SHARING A COMMON DOMESDAY NAME

1 in Boituna in Wilford Hundred
2 in Bohuna in Plomesgate Hundred

- ◆ MINSTER
- ◆ PROBABLE MINSTER
- ☐ POSSIBLE MINSTER

0 1 2 3 4 miles

IN SUFFOLK DB
IN NORFOLK DB
IN CAMBS. DB
IN ESSEX DB

1 in Oakley & Stuston
= 2 parts in Oakley

9   *A picture of a truly cultivated landscape. For Suffolk's great record of about 418 churches in 1086, see previous page.*

The rest, as we now see, is an infinitely varied composition, of farms and villages and market towns. But however urban the community, in Suffolk the fields are never far off, indeed they are rarely out of view. However increasingly town-moulded all the upbringing of Suffolk people may be, the fields spread round us throughout our lives. We cannot ride through them without being conscious, if only out of the corners of our eyes, of their daily response to the seasons, their extraordinary fertility, and their endless diversity of shape and pattern, particularly where they retain their old 'natural' enclosures, their framework of ditches, banks and well timbered hedgerows. As we drive along the lanes, these tree frames seem to revolve slowly, on either side of us, the oaks in the foreground hedges moving at different speeds from those on the far sides of the fields, clockwise on our left, anti–clockwise on our right, like slow roundabouts at an old fair or like some long-remembered ritual courtship dance.

It will help if we take a look at the political structure before we set about envisaging the origins of the whole landscape; the far-off founders of the villages, Englishmen and Frisians, a few Irish perhaps (known, then, as Scots, as we may perhaps see in Shotley and Shottisham), and before them the Roman mercenaries, and before them the Iceni, and before them men of the Bronze Age and right back to the Stone Age, whose existence was first suspected in a brickpit at Hoxne in Suffolk, by John Frere of Finningham in the 1790s and whose stone tools remain all round us in the valleys and heathlands, so that it is still no uncommon thing to go for a walk and return with a fine flint hand axe, but whose life here one glimpses only fleetingly as at the end of a dream.

Boundaries: The Two Counties of Suffolk

Suffolk men have had to depend for the perpetuation of their boundaries on the few obvious natural features – rivers and streams, or prominent, long-living oak trees – and on existing man-made features such as earlier metalled roads, field-ditches and hedgerows. The rest they have created for themselves, usually from earth banks. Marshes, heaths and claylands alike are crossed by almost bewildering numbers of old boundary banks and ditches, marking the limits of estates, parishes and local administrative units such as the Hundred (see illustrations 10, 31, 32 and 61).

The political pattern is a shade easier to make out than that of the basic settlements. Its main outlines go back, unchanged, at least nine centuries. It

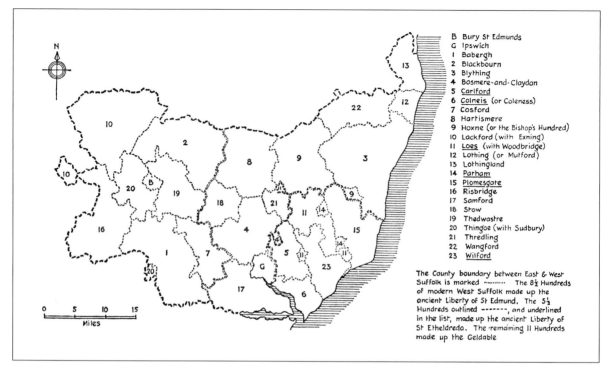

B Bury St Edmunds
G Ipswich
1 Babergh
2 Blackbourn
3 Blything
4 Bosmere-and-Claydon
5 Carlford
6 Colneis (or Coleness)
7 Cosford
8 Hartismere
9 Hoxne (or the Bishop's Hundred)
10 Lackford (with Exning)
11 Loes (with Woodbridge)
12 Lothing (or Mutford)
13 Lothingland
14 Parham
15 Plomesgate
16 Risbridge
17 Samford
18 Stow
19 Thedwastre
20 Thingoe (with Sudbury)
21 Thredling
22 Wangford
23 Wilford

The County boundary between East & West Suffolk is marked ·········· The 8½ Hundreds of modern West Suffolk made up the ancient Liberty of St Edmund. The 5½ Hundreds outlined -------, and underlined in the list, made up the ancient Liberty of St Etheldreda. The remaining 11 Hundreds made up the Geldable

10 *The Hundreds and Liberties. Based on the Domesday map in* Victoria County History, Suffolk, *Vol.I, facing p.357, and Bryant's map of Suffolk, 1826. Small changes between 1086 and 1826 are noted in V.C.H., Vol.I, p.358, and D.P. Dymond (ed.),* Hodskinson's Map of Suffolk, 1783, Suffolk Records Society, 1972.

must be admitted that these territorial boundaries have stood the test of time. In the absence of great economic changes, such as certainly suggest a reshaping of some Midlands boundaries, that is a persuasive argument for leaving them alone. Yet both the Radcliffe-Maud Royal Commission and the White Paper of February 1971 on Local Government Reorganisation proposed extensive tampering with Suffolk's boundaries. Happily, the White Paper of 4 November 1971 announced second thoughts, and, so far as Suffolk was concerned, abandoned the idea of scrapping, over wide areas of the two counties, nine centuries of territorial allegiance. But now, all the changes it proposed have since been publicly renounced by Whitehall, under pressure from local opinion. Only one small boundary change (though entirely reprehensible) was ordained in 1972, and half-heartedly realised in 1974: the transfer to Norfolk, as suburban living-space for Yarmouth, of the five parishes of Hopton, Bradwell, Belton, Burgh Castle and Fritton, against the expressed wishes of the large majority of the inhabitants. Suffolk's proud east-facing rhino-horn sustained a slight crumpling from Whitehall. Nevertheless, one major and formidable change went forward: the unification of East and West Suffolk.

There is no evidence that 'Suffolk' has ever before been a single administrative unit. The evidence of the landscape is entirely against any such idea. Before the Danes arrived and slew King Edmund over eleven centuries ago, in November 869, there was a single kingdom of East Anglia, consisting chiefly of the present 'Norfolk' and 'Suffolk'. Under the Danes, it was known as the Eastern Danelaw: see Hart, *Danelaw*, 1992, p.8 and map. For a time it had two bishops (of Dunwich and Elmham), and occasionally a pair of rulers, but it was one kingdom, with a land-frontier of defence works facing south west in a great series related to the Icknield Way.[3] The Devil's Dyke, still a daunting combination of bank and ditch, its bank still between 12 and 18 feet high, and the ditch going as deep as 17 feet with a width of 65 feet, projects its great hump and scar for seven and a half miles across the exposed outcropping chalk lands between Reach, down on the brink of the Fens in the west, and Stetchworth in the east (still just in Cambridgeshire). This Dyke continued as the boundary of the East Anglian diocese right through the Middle Ages.

The Devil's Dyke is only the most effective of a series of parallel defence-works set across at right-angles to the Icknield Way, the chief prehistoric and historic land route from the Midlands and South into East Anglia. At Reach one arm entered the swampy fen, at Stetchworth the other entered the dense clay 'woodlands', presumably thought to be impediment enough to an army of English or of British in those days.

The Dyke does not provide the county boundary of Suffolk, but the *line* of it does continue south-eastwards, in the form of field-banks and green-ways, and here it is indirectly related to the south-west boundary of Anglo-Saxon West Suffolk. Those green-ways and field-banks and ditches, perhaps the vestiges of a rough early political boundary-line, deviating more and more from the straight line of the Devil's Dyke, now form the eastern boundaries of a group of Suffolk parishes (the Bradleys, Thurlows, two of the Wrattings, Kedington and Withersfield[4]) whose western boundaries form the southern end of the western boundary of the former West Suffolk. This part of the historic county

---

[3] Cambridge Antiq Soc. *Communications*, Vol.XXXI, XXXII and XXXV (1935), cf. R. Rainbird Clarke, *East Anglia* (1960), p.136.

[4] Precisely those parishes which, for a short time in 1971-2, were threatened with transference from Suffolk to Cambridgeshire.

boundary was fixed, at the time when Suffolk's whole political shape was fixed, by the limits of what, in 1044, became the 'Liberty of St Edmund'. Already before 1044, this same territorial unit had been administered for Queen Emma, Edward the Confessor's mother. Already it was measured as '8½ Hundreds' (a measure discussed at pp.82-8 below: Illustration 10 shows the Hundreds as they had survived in 1826) and administered as a unit of almost precisely the same dimensions as those of the County of West Suffolk in 1972, on the brink of submergence into the new, unwieldy, perhaps stronger, 'Suffolk'. There are good reasons for thinking that that West Suffolk unit of administration may go right back beyond the 11th century to the seventh, as a 'miniature shire' of the Rutland kind.[5] Down at Withersfield and Wixoe, its boundary turns east to follow the lines of the *Via Devana* and the Stour. With Essex, it meanders along the Stour as far as Stoke-by-Nayland. There it meets East Suffolk, turns north and meanders even more across country, around the bounds of ancient estates, until it reaches a point close to the soggy watershed of the Little Ouse and the Waveney. At that almost level watershed, the Little Ouse emerges and moves slowly west to the Fens, accompanied by these ancient West Suffolk bounds. From springs close by, in that same glacial valley-line, the Waveney runs east, taking with it the East Suffolk boundary. And in the south, East Suffolk in 1972 follows on, from Stoke-by-Nayland, along the Stour till at Brantham that much painted stream becomes an estuary and meets the sea.

The land boundaries of the County of West Suffolk, that in 1974 became redundant along its eastern frontier, will continue to provide some of the earliest physical features surviving in Suffolk (illustration 10); yet they are only just beginning to attract the attention of professional archaeologists. There are especially interesting sections where they form the present boundary with 'East Suffolk': at its junction with the Finningham to Walsham-le-Willows road, for instance. Here David Dymond and Oliver Rackham found that the hedge-boundary in its course south to Botany Farm (appropriately enough) contains ten species of shrub, useful complementary evidence of the ten centuries of existence of this line as the boundary of St Edmund's Liberty.

East Suffolk has no such ancient unity as West Suffolk: indeed it had no official existence until 1888. Until the formation of the two County Councils in that year, there were two administrative areas to the east of St Edmund's Liberty. One grouped about the Alde and Deben estuaries, was another Liberty, that of St Etheldreda; smaller than St Edmund's, only 5½ Hundreds, but

[5] R.H.C. Davis (ed.), *The Kalendar of Abbot Samson*, Camden Society (1954), pp.xliv-xlv.

11 *Woodbridge Market Hill, at about the beginning of the last century. The magistrates till very recently sat in the Shire Hall, built c.1700 over the Elizabethan market cross in succession to the former Shire Hall of St Audry's Liberty at Wickham Market.*

forming a compact unit, with a headquarters first at Sudbourne,[6] then at Wickham Market, then at Melton and Woodbridge. This explains the presence of that old red-brick 'Shire Hall' over the former market cross on Woodbridge Market Hill: its highly oriental 'Dutch' gables (of *c.*1700, but so far eluding attempts to find its actual date from records) crown one of the most distinctive urban buildings in the county (illustration 11). Its predecessor at Wickham Market, a good timber-framed building with corner posts, was dismantled and reconstructed on a moated site in Letheringham at a time that 'some now living' remembered in 1735: John Kirby, who recorded this, says it became Letheringham Old Hall, and this is possible. But it seems, from the surviving

---

[6] Helen Cam, *Liberties and Communities in Medieval England* (1944), p.185.

structures, rather more likely that it became Letheringham Lodge, which has the oak corner-posts characteristic of a town house, one of them extraordinarily well carved for a farmhouse, or even a park lodge.

This Liberty was probably another 'miniature shire', an early, if not original, endowment of her monastery at Ely by Etheldreda, a daughter of one of the East Anglian kings at the time when Bede describes them as having a *vicus regius*, a royal hall at Rendlesham, near Woodbridge, and when one of her relatives was being commemorated in the burial of that fabulous ship on the heath above the estuary at Sutton Hoo in the same neighbourhood. Etheldreda herself, whose name has naturally contracted to Audry, was born in the year 630 at Exning, which became the parent of Newmarket and was fairly clearly another of the royal 'seats', on the west side of the woodland. (It is just possible that her mother was there while the Devil's Dyke was building; though it may have been already two centuries old.) One of the most perceptive themes in the late Rainbird Clarke's *East Anglia* is the way he saw the shaping power of that thick clay woodland belt lying from north to south across the middle of Suffolk, in terms of both politics and settlement. The Liberty of St Audry's was restored to Ely after the Danish invasions, during the tenth-century 'Reformation', at the suggestion of Wolstan of Dalham. Over on the Newmarket side, that idyllic dale village, Dalham, is most appropriately dignified by a house built, in Queen Anne's reign, by a bishop of Ely: a tall house, from the top of which Ely was visible on a clear day. Its 20th-century owner removed that agreeable prospect-storey.

Subtract St Audry's Hundreds and St Edmund's, and all that were left under the direct jurisdiction of the king's sheriff in 'Suffolk' were 11 Hundreds, bounded by West Suffolk and the Waveney, the sea and the Stour. This is the area known in the Middle Ages as 'the Geldable', precisely because it was the only area subject to the sheriff's taxation or 'geld'. (When the Geldable paid tax to the royal exchequer, the people of the Liberties paid tax to their saint.) We see why Norfolk and Suffolk shared a sheriff down to the time of Elizabeth I: there was little enough of Suffolk for him to be involved in. As we notice in the fourth chapter, this restricted area of the Geldable was also the one where the biggest baronial castles were sited, with the exception of that of the De Clares, at Clare, on the outer boundary. In view of this very ancient division of southern East Anglia into three, it is perhaps not surprising that Suffolk, 'the land of the South Folk', is a word that barely appears in (or at least has survived in only one document from) the Anglo-Saxon period – a will of *c.*1044.

It was next recorded in Domesday Book. It used to be thought to have made its appearance in a charter of 895, but this charter is now reckoned 'a complete fabrication'.[7] (Norfolk's name occurs first in that same will,[8] as David Dymond observes.) Domesday Book does make it clear that the East Anglian bishops had regarded their seat at Hoxne as that of their 'bishopric of Suffolk' (illustration 40). This reflects the earlier time when there had been two bishops, one at Dunwich and one at Elmham, which may, for a time, have been South Elmham in Suffolk, before one of those early prelates adventured up to North Elmham.

This administrative history explains the shape and environment of our lives today. West Suffolk found itself (from 1888 to 1974, at least) with a true centre, at Bury, with a radial network of roads serving that shire efficiently. This is not something to be blithely ignored by reformers of local government in the interests of political, or merely statistical, considerations. Furthermore, all through the Middle Ages, down to the 13th century, Bury and St Edmund's abbey prospered by forcibly discouraging markets elsewhere in the Liberty, except on the perimeter, as at Haverhill or Sudbury or Clare, where they had powerful owners to contend with. From the middle of the 13th century, markets were granted closer to Bury, at Lavenham and Melford for instance (see illustration 48): but it is unlikely that Bury's own trade suffered much from their competition. Grants at Barrow and Felsham, nearer still, seem to have come to nothing. Ixworth got its market going in the later 14th century.

East Suffolk has never developed a satisfactory centre. Ipswich is its modern capital *despite* its administrative inconveniences; it has grown as the county town by outstripping the others in trade, and as a port. The proposals of November 1971 to add Harwich and Colchester to the new administrative county would have made more use of Ipswich's geographical position. We return to such themes. Now that we know the external boundaries and the three physical divisions of Suffolk, with relatively light lands on either side of the clay woodland, and the three administrative divisions which seem to have been established at a remarkable early stage, we can try to see what the landscape looked like at the very start.

The Dawn in Suffolk
'The woods decay, the woods decay and fall,' wrote Tennyson. Most of Suffolk's aboriginal woods were hewn down and cleared over centuries to make either

[7] Hart, *Early Charters of Eastern England* (1966), pp.70, 53.
[8] Ibid., p.85.

12 *Staverton Thicks. A relic of the primeval Suffolk oakwoods among the coastal heathlands.*

fields, houses and ships or just fuel for fires; but some have managed to survive for timber or coppicing. An account of some of this cultivated and very healthy woodland on the central Suffolk clays comes at the end of the fourth chapter. A third possibility was for it to be 'emparked', to provide cover and pasture for deer, as well as pasture for other beasts. A highly professional botanical and historical study of a surviving belt of ancient and apparently prehistoric woodland[9] has lately been made on the light lands 'the Sandlings', at Staverton, a manor recorded in Domesday Book and lying in the parishes of Eyke and Wantisden, between Woodbridge and Orford.[10] Mr Peterken's findings are of very wide interest. It has long been postulated by botanical amateurs that Staverton Park (illustration 12 and 13, based on his Fig.1 and Plate 2), being a park from the early Middle Ages (at least from the 13th century), was likely

[9] The mixed-oak forest began to 'colonise' sometime during the Mesolithic period, about 5000 B.C., which was roughly when Britain became an island.

[10] G.F. Peterken: 'Development of Vegetation in Staverton Park, Suffolk', *Field Studies* (1969), pp.1-39. This is a monumental monograph. I was grateful to the late Mr Peterken for sending me a proof copy, and so readily agreeing to my quoting from it. See also Miss E.D.R. Burrell's admirable London University M.Sc. thesis, 'An Historical Geography of the Sandlings of Suffolk, 1600-1850' (1960).

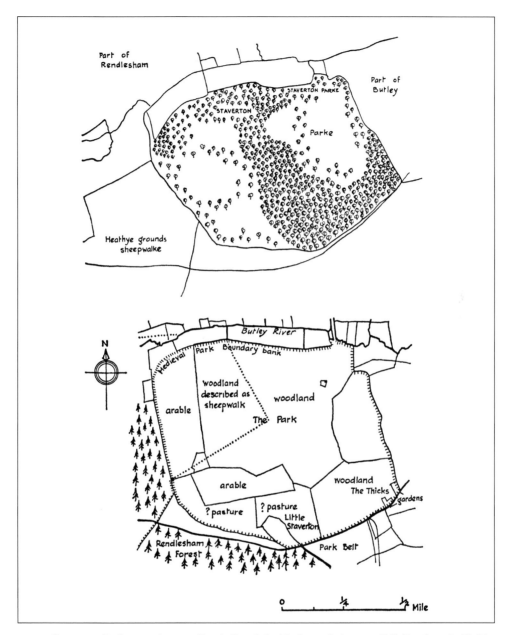

13 *Staverton Park: a native woodland. Based, by kind permission, on G.F. Peterken, in* Field Studies, *1969.*

The upper map is redrawn from John Norden's survey of Staverton Park in 1600-1, now in the County Record Office. He mapped the bounds of the park fairly accurately as they remain, with bank and outer ditch. The distribution of trees was probably meant to be part of his 'trew description'.

Within the park bounds, the main area of woodland today, especially The Thicks, is shown as woodland on the 1846 Tithe Map (lower map).

to have been enclosed at least partly from existing woodland rather than from wholly cleared land; and that the ancient oaks surviving here in that part known as 'The Thicks' are therefore probably natural descendants from the primeval woodland on the same site. The place-names themselves suggest the prominence of woodland at the time of naming: Eyke is a Scandinavian word for oak, and Staverton an Old English word for 'farm enclosed by stakes' (or even, perhaps, 'farm where stakes are made'). But this is a highly professional study of botanical matters, nor had any historian attempted such an immensely careful study as Mr Peterken's of the maps and manuscript records of this park right through the historic period down to the present.

From ring counts he showed a wide range in the age of the pollard oaks, and that some trees were well over 400 years old. From a manorial extent in the Public Record Office he showed the park woodland being let out for grazing in 1362, a quite usual use of medieval parkland. The delightful *Chronicle of Butley Priory*, edited by A.G. Dickens, revealed the park as mature woodland in September 1528 when Henry VIII's sister Mary and her husband the Duke of Suffolk went fox-hunting through it and ate their dinner in high spirits *sub Quercubus* – under the oaks. It is very unlikely that this park has been cleared in historic times. In Peterken's words: 'The evidence, such as it is, suggests that the oaks in Staverton Park have originated naturally over a long period and that the existing trees are the product of natural regeneration between the sixteenth century or earlier and the early nineteenth century.'

There are two convincing ecological arguments. A podsol, a recognisable condition at a certain level of the soil, would have developed here if the site of the Park had ever been heathland. This has not happened. Furthermore, here are 'Atlantic' species of lichen flora that are usually present only when there has been continuous woodland cover. In the most 'natural' part of the park, the Thicks, 'dead and fallen timber lies where it falls, and a balance is developing between death and decay on the one hand, and regeneration and growth on the other'. In the rest of the Park, the oaks are famous for their grotesque and moribund appearance, with hollowed out heartwood and great birches sprouting from their tops. Here regeneration is prevented, apparently, by wood-pigeons devouring all the acorns. But now holly thrives, and one holly-tree is thought to be the tallest in Britain, 22.5 metres, or 73 feet 9 inches: taller than many Suffolk church-towers. From the naturalists' point of view, 'Staverton Park is one of the few places in which the natural decline of a native woodland and its subsequent development can be studied.'

Here, in looking at the historic landscape, one gets a rare sense of the prehistoric landscape. The forest would have been denser on the heavy central clays, less formidable again in the Breckland over towards the Fens. Charles Doughty, himself brought up at Theberton beside the heaths of Westleton and Dunwich, wrote a vast, robust poem, *The Dawn in Britain*, 6 vols., 1906:

> This Isle lay empty, a land of cloud and frost
> And forest of wild beasts; till creeping time
> Brought man's kin forth ...
> To them were holes, delved underground, for bowers:
> Trees were and streams and hills and stars, their gods.

The people who started to fill and shape at least parts of Suffolk's landscape were the New Stone Age Men, or 'early Agriculturalists'. Our knowledge of them gradually grows, and their period covers about 23 centuries: 4500 to 2200 BC. There is fleeting evidence from many places in Suffolk that men ('hunter-fishers') were living here some 4,500 years before that, but they made no lasting mark on their environment. Many of the New Stone Age people remained nomad herdsmen. But some of them began the felling of the trees and the process of erosion that ultimately produced our heaths. A handful of their axes have even been found in the clay woodland as far into the middle as Mendlesham. But at present this hardly seems to add up to their settled presence away from the river valleys and light lands. Their ambition was to raise a few cattle and some rudimentary crops,[11] as well as hunting the deer and boar in the woods. Mixed farming had made its beginning here, and that, at least, has gone on continuously ever since.

Their remains show them quite densely settled in the north-west, the Mildenhall corner. One characteristic form of the pottery they made is now called Mildenhall Ware from its profusion: it includes rather thick bowls that are shapely as well as serviceable. Several thousands of their implements have been found in a single little valley in Icklingham. It is perfectly feasible that land-hunger was already present in that corner of the Breckland, and led to the first appreciable burning of trees, extracting of stumps. People were also living on the first low slopes above the flood-plain of the Stour on its north bank between Sudbury and Higham; along the Gipping valley; and all over the eastern light lands, particularly between the Blyth and the Waveney and between the Orwell and the Deben. Already one sees the effective division

---

[11]   At Hurst Fen, Mildenhall, they cultivated emmer and barley, 'and may have kept oxen and swine as well as sheep or goat': J.G.D. Clark, *Proc. Prehist. Soc.*, N.S. 26 (1960).

between East and West Suffolk imposed by the clay woodland. From their remains, more than two 'cultures' have been detected by the archaeologists, but an essential difference was perhaps that people came to the Breckland along the Icknield Way, from southern England, and ultimately from northern France. The east side was, naturally enough, being colonised by people who had coasted from the Low Countries and Denmark and Germany to the Channel, then round the Thames estuary and past the Essex estuaries and marshes.

It is curious that not one of their long barrows is known in Suffolk: the nearest is on Broome Heath, Ditchingham, just across the Waveney from Bungay. (At Worlington, men of the 'late and secondary' Neolithic Age constructed a round barrow, later modified for another burial-rite during the Bronze Age: another of their round barrows was at West Stow.) Their funeral mounds and ceremonies have left clearer marks on the landscape than their everyday life. The same is true of their successors of the Bronze Age into whom they merged. Their mounds are solemn enough monuments: their contents moved, in *Urne Burial*, one of the noblest of all reflections on mortality. (Sir Thomas Browne, its author, was himself a settler in Norfolk.) Yet for centuries East Anglian farmers have been vigorously ploughing and bulldozing these mounds out of existence. 'Time which antiquates Antiquities, and hath an art to make dust of all things, hath yet spared these minor Monuments …'

A celebrated Bronze-Age barrow group on the heath at Brightwell and Martlesham, just east of Ipswich, is now reduced to about thirty three, and dwindling fast. Yet how far the process had gone in earlier centuries is only recently exposed in aerial photographs, most notably in those of Dr J.K. St Joseph, of Cambridge University. The large ring-ditches, visible from the air though not from the ground, suggest that we now need to apply to the surviving mounds a multiplier of at least five in trying to imagine this early necropolitan landscape. A more singular revelation of aerial photography has been that the circular, ritual 'henge' monuments were not confined to the stone-belt of England, but were built of wood in East Anglia. One at Arminghall, just south of Norwich, was excavated in 1935. A ring-bank, 120 feet in diameter (perhaps used by the 'congregation') surrounded a circular timbered 'sanctuary'. Another was revealed to the south of Kings Wood at Stratford St Mary in south-east Suffolk, but has never been excavated, and few people have even heard of it. Another impressive revelation of Dr

14 *Prehistoric ring-ditches or barrows, tracks or boundaries, revealed by aerial photography above the Deben at Shottisham. A detailed map, 1631, by omission suggests that these mounds were already ploughed flat. It shows 'Alborowe waie', a track leading half a mile direct from this field towards a surviving earthwork.*

St Joseph's is what appears to be a cursus, a ceremonial 'way', almost a mile long, near Bury St Edmunds, running parallel to the river Lark just above the flood-plain on its left (west) bank.[12] It crosses the parish of Fornham All Saints, whose church may have been sited with reference to some remote memory, or tradition of it. It stops short of a field in Hengrave which aerial photographs show to be full of marks of (presumably) prehistoric occupation—ring-ditches and more complex furrows.

As one worked through the shelf loads of boxes full of aerial photographs taken over the 1950s and '60s by Dr St Joseph one tried to imagine what the prehistoric landscape was like when the forest stood inviolate over most of Suffolk, but with its edges singed by these first centuries of farmers,

[12] J.K. St Joseph, *Antiquity*, Vol. XXXVIII, No.152 (1964), p.290; ibid. (1965), p.61.

applying their torches, then wielding their heaviest axes, and when each of those very large circular ditches, revealed now only as crop-marks, contained a great mound. Some of the mounds must have been enormous before they were reduced by the successive ages of ploughing.

All these mysterious monuments, invisible except from the air, and reduced on the ground to a point somewhere near extinction by deep ploughing, convey only vague messages until several of them can be excavated: large round ditches often imply barrows, but at Mucking in Essex, for instance, proved to encircle a fortified Iron-Age house. Nevertheless, from these photographs one or two general conclusions can be drawn about the shape of the Prehistoric landscape. In the Suffolk coverage of Dr St Joseph alone, round ditches were to be seen, singly or in clusters, in no fewer than 28 parishes. These are grouped very strikingly. The most prominent group lies all along the Stour valley, from Stoke-by-Clare to Melford, Acton, Stoke-by-Nayland and Stratford St Mary, with a related group in the Brett valley, the Stour's tributary, at Layham and Hadleigh. In the Gipping valley, they are to be seen at Barking, Creeting, Little Blakenham and Bramford. Then, beside the Stour, Orwell and Deben estuaries, they lie in Stutton, Erwarton, Shotley, Bucklesham and Trimley, with perhaps the most spectacular group of all not far from the church on its rise at Shottisham (illustration 14). Round the edge of the Breckland they lie at Moulton, Kentford, Hengrave and Ixworth, as well as Brandon. That leaves a couple of strays – at Wenhaston, near Blythburgh, and right up beside the Waveney at Belton.

Plainly, the almost complete absence of evidence from the Waveney is nearly as telling as the concentration of so much along the Stour. One must beware of negative evidence. It has often in the past been suggested that the reason for such a scarcity of prehistoric sites along the Waveney valley may be partly that the professional archaeologists have been based on the Victorian museum-centres of Ipswich and Norwich: the Waveney lay in a 'no-man's-land' between them. But now these impressions produced after at least a century of random fieldwork are strengthened by twenty years of aerial photography. Dr St Joseph told me, in 1971, that he had certainly scrutinised the Waveney valley: indeed that is clear from his evidence of old field-systems and moated sites in the area. He is careful to add that naturally more flying-time tends to be spent over 'rewarding' areas than over blank ones. His evidence, taken together with Rainbird Clarke's distribution map of round barrows and late Bronze-Age urn-fields,[13] must be accepted as showing that the broad Suffolk clay-belt, unlike most of Norfolk, remained virtually uninhabited till the end of the Bronze Age. This is conclusively borne out by Edward Martin's maps of Bronze-Age Suffolk in the three editions of the *Historical Atlas of Suffolk*.

Looking in detail at some of the photographs, one guesses that many of the clustered round-ditch sites like that near Smallbridge Hall on the Bures/Stoke-by-Nayland boundary, will prove to be Bronze-Age barrows – complexes of burial mounds such as those that survive still as tumuli in Brightwell and Martlesham on the coastal heath. (But one cannot feel much certainty: Smallbridge, for instance, may yet prove to be a defended site.) What is specially interesting about some of the pictures is that they show the mounds as part of a complicated pattern. This may one day be shown to be a later settlement pattern superimposed on a Bronze-Age burial site. For, so far, though we have considerable evidence of their burials, we have little idea of their homes and more usual activities. What would be remarkably interesting would be to find that a burial-mound and associated farm-site were both of the Bronze Age. Their farms and fields were not necessarily close to their burial mounds, and might well be found a mile apart.

To move from the frustrating zones of speculation to what is known of one of these ring-ditches, let us take a look at Grimstone End, in Pakenham, near Ixworth.[14] Here, at the junction of the Black Bourn and its tributary, known as Pakenham Fen, a single round ditch (as usual just above the flood-plain) was revealed in one of St Joseph's air photographs. Excavation in 1953 revealed the base of an early Bronze-Age barrow, with an urn like a small flower-pot beside a heap of cremated bones at the heart of the barrow. Then, eight Romano-British cremations were found on the inner lip of the ditch. Even more remarkable, in terms of the intermittent settlement in this one particular spot, the ditch proved to have been occupied by early Anglo-Saxon arrivals: there were loomweights (no fewer than 62 loomweights lay on the floor: they had been fired rather badly), and a spindle-whorl, combs, bracelets, etc. Dr Stanley West's interpretation is that a hut stood here with a working loom.

All this from a site indicated by a simple ring-mark on an air photograph. The place itself has obvious attractions for rural settlers of every age down to our own. Beside the winding stream (blue on a sunny day, rather than

[13] *East Anglia*, p.79.
[14] *P.S.I.*, Vol.XXVI (1954), pp.189-207; Vol.XXVIII (1959), p.166; Vol.XXIX (1961), p.100.

the black implied by its name), sheep graze within view of a watermill in a place where one was recorded in Domesday Book, and a tower windmill preserved in good working order. As for the present small hamlet of Grimstone End, its position is one of the most archaeologically exciting in Suffolk, amid what appears to be a large area of Romano-British settlement, with clear remains of a Roman fort to the north, controlling the Peddars Way, and with an excavated Roman villa just across on the east side of Mickle Mere.

Another of the ancient sites revealed by St Joseph is a pair of ring-ditches, with other markings that adjoin and presumably underlie Alton Hall in Stutton. Alton is thought to represent the large Domesday manor and settlement, Alsildeston, and its beautiful farmhouse, watermill and farm were marked and awaiting sacrifice to the water-god of Ipswich. A reservoir was to submerge the house, water mill and most of the farm. Happily, the mill and its house were removed and rebuilt as part of the Museum of East Anglian Life at Stowmarket.

From all this, it is clear enough that the heaths and the valley-gravel terraces just above the flood-plain provided dwelling and burial-sites attractive to early settlers in Suffolk right through from the earliest times. Questions remain: were these sites occupied at all continuously, and how far and how soon did settlers venture away from the valley-gravels and the heaths into the clay woodlands?

One motive for trying to move off from the Breckland, coastal heath and river-terraces was probably a gradually growing population and steadily sharpened competition for the available grazing land. Already in the middle of the Bronze Age (B.C.1400-B.C.900), weapons seem to take on a new significance, as though these settlers were armed for war as well as for the chase. A rapier-like bayonet has been dredged from the Orwell. Two spear-heads were found in Shotley, two in Felixstowe. Others come from Nacton, Akenham and Coddenham (where a wooden shaft survives as well). Socketed bronze axe-heads are the famous attributes of these people, and how much they were produced in response to the need to fell trees for more farmland we cannot know. Two 'founders' hoards' (hoards of old axes assembled by the local travelling bronze-founder to melt down and remould) recovered from Butley, with a lump of raw metal, included a dozen or more small spear-heads. Another of these hoards, from Levington, contained just a jumble of axe-heads, formidable enough in 'the wrong hands'.

If this analysis is right, and the clay woodlands proved impracticable before the advent of the iron plough-coulter, with the result that the Bronze-Age inhabitants at the edges of the woodlands resorted to fighting one another for the land, they soon had need also to fight raiders from overseas. In the sixth century B.C., raiders from Belgium were using sword-scabbards that have been recovered from Lakenheath. They were followed across, about 500 B.C., by farmers forced to migrate from the Low Countries. These men knew the use of iron. They made possible the great transformation of the Suffolk woodlands into fields. It was a very slow business. The old name of 'the Woodlands' for Central Suffolk survived into the 19th century. Nevertheless, from the beginning of the Iron Age, two thirds of the Suffolk landscape faced the possibility of total change.

Romans and Natives

The Iron Age lasted about six centuries, and culminated in the Roman Conquest. The archaeological finds, spread over so long a period, do not yet build up into a very coherent picture. Much remains speculative. Admittedly we know of a number of scattered settlements, and villas, and kilns, four or five forts, and some roads. The late R. Rainbird Clarke, who did so much to establish the pattern of Iron-Age finds in East Anglia, seems to have shrunk slightly from the conclusions of his own distribution-maps, which made overwhelmingly clear the significant area of concentration of the Iceni (one would like to spell them Ickeni: they were certainly pronounced thus,[15] but the Roman alphabet lacked a 'k', with the result that this famous tribe often suffer the pronunciation 'Ice eeni'). Their tribal 'heart-lands' were apparently limited to the north-west corner of Suffolk, around Ixworth in the Blackbourn valley, and Icklingham along the Lark valley; across into south-west Norfolk, and then strung out to the north and south along the line of the Icknield Way. In the Norwich area there was a scatter of burials and two coin-hoards – nothing of much consequence. The distribution maps point to this proud tribe, the famous disturbers of Nero's legions, as based in a fairly compact area to the west of the clay woodland, and especially perhaps in the Cavenham-Thetford neighbourhood. Clarke allowed two isolated burials, at Snailwell (Cambs.) and Elveden, containing what seemed to be 'Belgic' pottery, to suggest that by A.D.43 the Iceni had retreated before the Belgae to the north

---

[15] See Caesar's reference to them, p.37 below. He would have spelt them with an 's' if they were 'Ice-eeni'.

15 *The Roman Pye Road (modern A140) cutting through an organised, co-axial landscape around Yaxley. Based on Tithe Award and early 19th-century estate maps: a – a represents the suggested line of Grimm's Ditch, a possible Roman linear earthwork (after Scarfe, 1986). These are revolutionary ideas about the antiquity of our landscape.*

Norfolk coast.[16] It sounds not quite like them, to be so frightened of the Belgae, for they showed no terror in the face of the superior Romans. The Romans established Venta Icenorum at Caistor-by-Norwich less because that was the main Icenian settlement than because it made a good military base from which to take them in the rear if ever they turned nasty again.

---

[16] Recent work shows that pottery of 'Belgic' type persisted after the Roman Conquest, and so would not relate to tribal movements.

As we see later, the Trinovantes, the Iron-Age people living to the south of the Iceni, occupied the Stour valley below Sudbury, and the Sandlings, the light lands around Suffolk's estuaries: spreading up the Deben to Hacheston and Burgh, and the Gipping to Darmsden. This must be the time when those interesting areas of 'co-axial landscape' were being created around the South Elmhams, and Yaxley, for instance: see Tom Williamson's map here, p.34: they presumably represent the pioneering activities of both the Iceni and the Trinovantes in the clearing and the colonising of the heavy clay woodlands. It is curious that these areas of Iron-Age colonisation now bear Anglo-Saxon names, almost without exception. One supposes that the Celtic, Iron-Age names were meaningless to the occupying Anglo-Saxons, whose place-names have survived so accurately into our time (see N. Scarfe, *Suffolk in the Middle Ages*, 1986, 'Place-names and Settlements in the Landscape', pp.1-29: also *Land of the Iceni*, Davies and Williamson, Ch.3, 'Suffolk in the Iron-Age' by Edward Martin).

There is not very much yet in the distribution-map of Iron-Age 'cultures' to suggest any great advance into the woodland. Once again, there are the most extraordinarily tantalising air pictures of complex small enclosures, with round ditches that might represent huts, and trenches that enclose all sorts of wedge-shapes: conceivably small Iron-Age or Old-English field and stock yards? There is a particularly vivid series in Mr Mortier's Barn Field above the marsh-line at Cedar Court, Alderton. It is just on the edge of the old 'mainland' across the water from Buckanay when that was, judging by its name, a 'beech-island'. (Buckanay Farm now stands on a distinct rise in a well drained marsh.) Romano-British pottery has been found at Buckanay. Similar complexes appear in an almost identical piece of old shoreline at Valley Farm, Sudbourne. Another remarkable complex appears at Cauldwell Hall, Hollesley, where a 'cold spring' still wells up in a sedgy patch beside a beautiful ruined farmhouse, and trickles across the marsh to enter the River Ore. This must have been the site of a small Iron-Age or Old-English harbour-settlement: perhaps both? What a lot about the early shore landscape could be learnt from a systematic excavation here. Such work, properly done, costs money. The return is incalculably valuable in helping people to understand more fully and imaginatively their environment, as recreation and for its own sake.

Such sites are particularly promising, because they are detached, away from the main areas of later settlement. One of the most interesting discoveries in Suffolk was made during the laying of drains in 1958 at the backs of the houses along the whole length of the south west side of Long Melford's celebrated long main street. The late Mr Norman Smedley, then of Ipswich Museum, moved into action at once and showed that the Belgic and Roman settlement of Long Melford occupied virtually the whole of that long stretch.[17] Of course the whole site can never be fully examined, underlying as it does dozens of inhabited houses and back gardens. Nevertheless, here the shape of this early settlement along an ancient main road strongly *suggests* the possibility of continuous settlement through to Old English times, and so to the present day. The Green and church may have been the focus of the main Old English settlement here, but the thoroughfare village is a characteristic type of Suffolk village, and Roman Long Melford must be regarded as one of the prototypes. From the finds excavated in the line of a sewer, the settlement seems to have been in decline after the second century A.D. This might well have been the case, but equally the findings may mean no more than that there was a shift away from, or decline in, one part of the inhabited area, and that traces of third-, fourth- and fifth-century settlement are concealed beneath the main area of the existing medieval dwellings: the 'scatter' of finds so far is so narrowly confined to the sewer-trench that we should avoid dismissing the possibility of complete Romano-British English continuity merely because of a lack of late Romano-British finds in one comparatively narrow line of trenching. But nor can we positively span the gap – either archaeologically or historically – between the long Roman village and the long medieval one. It would help greatly if we could get a clue as to the antiquity of the mill-site at the ford that gives its name to the village. The likelihood is that it is a very early English name, like so many of the ford-names, perhaps especially those where Roman roads crossed. This south-north road (Margary's 33a) that goes through the mill ford crossed an east-west road (Margary's 34a) that ran from the Midlands on to Coddenham and the coast, and is traceable on Melford Green as a distinct terrace not far south of the church. Could we but find a hint when that noble Green at Melford was set aside for grazing, we should know a great deal more about the shaping of Suffolk villages, for the Greens are an ancient and characteristic element in the communal life of East Anglian 'vills'. Melford's, with its spectacular church at the top end, manor house of the abbots and their successors (given them not long before the Norman Conquest) along one side, and manorial conduit in the middle, is visually the most striking and widely known of them all. It may be a deliberate extension,

---

[17] Norman Smedley, 'Roman Long Melford', *P.S.I.*, Vol.XXVIII (1960), pp.272-89, with an excellent map.

of the late Old English period, to an existing early linear settlement in which the English first occupied lands of the villa and village to the south of the Mill-ford. Mere speculation again.

Before trying to delineate the Romano-British landscape waiting for the English when they came, we first take a closer look at the degree of settlement by the Britons themselves, to use their Roman name: the English, when they arrived, called them 'Wealh' – the word has now become 'Welsh' as so many of them withdrew to 'Wales' – the archaeologists find it helpful to think of them as people of the Iron Age, from their distinctive technical advance.

For some years, archaeologists have seen three successive main 'waves' of Iron-Age people. For the first time, we can study actual settlements, large ring-shaped houses, of a kind uncovered at West Harling across the border near Thetford. An important settlement of the period in Suffolk has been revealed at Darmsden, in the Gipping valley.[18] Here, though no house-site was found, very large storage-pits seem to be associated with some sort of settlement that persisted from *c.*400 B.C. right through to the first century A.D. – a period of prodigious change. However, this site says nothing new about any advance into the clay woodland. Nor does a later site (*c.*300-150 B.C.) at Rickinghall, where the buildings were rectangular. The one completely studied Iron-Age settlement is at West Stow, underlying the early Anglo-Saxon village.

The story of farmers and colonisers was overlaid, until the Roman peace was imposed, by tribal politics. The newcomers brought chariots and mobile warfare, and presumably therefore began to improve the rudimentary road-system of cattle-paths. Nothing yet seems to be known of their roads. One branch of them took over the farming areas on the west of the clay woodland: these became the Iceni. Indeed Caesar, in the first century B.C., referred to them as the Cenimagni – presumably the 'Great Iceni'. What about the old settlers in the Stour valley and the coastal heaths? They were taken over by a separate tribe, partly Belgic, with a headquarters called *Camulodunum*, on the slopes below the later (Roman) town at Colchester. This tribe, the Trinovantes, occupied the light coastal lands, giving expression to some sort of cultural unity in north-east Essex and the eastern edge of Suffolk that had been developing since the Bronze Age. The Trinovantes seem to have extended their territory northwards beyond the Blyth river and a little way into the clay woodland, for in 1855 a most illuminating find was made at Westhall, on a two-acre site in Mill-post field. Rainbird Clarke interpreted it as the richly

---

[18] *P.S.I.*, vol.XXV (1951), pp.210-11; Barry Cunliffe, *Antiquaries Journal*, vol.XLVIII (1968), pp.175-91.

16   *Clare Camp, formerly Erbury, and presumably an Iron-Age fort. We are looking south towards the church, market place and castle of the great Norman 'honour'. The superficial markings are recent and unexplained. See p.39.*

caparisoned contents of a chieftain's harness-room – the terret-rings and harness-mounts of the pair-in-hand that drew his chariot.

The final expression of Iron-Age culture was that of the Belgae. They too were formidable chariot-borne warriors and farmers. They certainly had broad-blade ploughshares and iron coulters stout enough to turn even the Suffolk woodland clays. They cannot yet be seen to have advanced the settlement-line very far.

They presumably arrived in East Suffolk about the year A.D. 1, when they defeated the Trinovantes and finally took over *Camulodunum*. The great Iceni tried to hold them to the south of their West Suffolk territories. If they retreated before the Belgae, as Rainbird Clarke believed, I think it must have been temporarily, and that they soon took advantage of the peace-keeping Romans to return to their old tribal settlements round Ixworth and Cavenham. Though they may be four centuries later, one would like to be able to date 'the Black Ditches' at Cavenham to this episode and suggest that they enabled the Iceni to keep the Belgae at bay: there seems to be no firm dating evidence for the Black Ditches at present. The Trinovantes in the east certainly caved in under the Belgae. This presumably explains that hulking rectangular Belgic emplacement at Burgh-by-Woodbridge, which to this day deflects all traffic, and another Belgic settlement right up at Chediston, a step further inland along the shallow slopes of the Blyth valley from Westhall. They were established, too, at Coddenham among the long-settled terraces of the Gipping valley. They presumably controlled the whole length of the Stour valley. For the magnificent fort known as Erbury (or sometimes Houndswall) on the north side of Clare, protected by great double walls of earth (J.K. St Joseph, PQ32: Plate II), was seen by Rainbird Clarke as possibly an outpost constructed by the Iceni in a desperate effort to stop them from pushing any further west into the more open Icenian landscape. Whether any of the surviving series of those vast linear earthwork defences which shape and orient so much of that landscape were made as early as those momentous times must await the results of more archaeological work. At present they are thought to be the very late constructions of the Romanised Iceni, in the fifth century, to try to stop the overspill of Anglo-Saxon colonists from the south; or, alternatively, defences erected in the sixth century by these English settlers to exclude powerfully counter-attacking bands of Britons based in the Chilterns.

The map of Roman Suffolk, like that of Iron-Age Suffolk, leaves no doubt about the relative importance of the open country about Ixworth, and of its inhabitants the Iceni. They made their mark on the Roman Empire about the year A.D.61. Under their exasperated queen, Boudicca, they and their neighbours the Trinovantes from East Suffolk and Essex swept into Colchester, smashed the temple of the Emperor-god Claudius and the small Roman garrison, and then reduced London and Verulamium to a layer of ashes that may still be seen. Although the first Roman reprisals were terrible, moderation prevailed under Classicianus, and the Iceni's name and tribal leadership survived in the new cantonal capital at Caistor, three miles south of Norwich. *Venta Icenorum* was at first hardly more dignified than a series of huts laid out beside a grid of streets, but from it were controlled, it is thought, the old Icenian settlements in Norfolk and Suffolk. Trinovantian East Suffolk is believed to have had its local administration in either Colchester or

Coddenham (*Combretonium*). It is significant that, immediately after Boudicca's revolt, the Romans erected forts at both Pakenham (covering Ixworth on Peddar's Way) and (probably) Coddenham: both were riverside sites at important road-junctions. (It is not absolutely certain that the 'fort' at Coddenham was not a temple.)

Apart from the Colchester-Norwich road, and the Icknield Way and its branch from Kentford to Bury (or rather Ixworth) in the west, only brief stretches of the Roman road-system are still in use in Suffolk. In Essex, it seems possible that their road-system covered the landscape more thoroughly than the Victorian railways (with perhaps 423 miles as against 375).[19] Four hundred miles is perhaps not a rash over-estimate of the mileage that they laid down in Suffolk of their more truly 'permanent' way. (The various roads now in use in Suffolk run to eight or nine times that length.) Absolute straightness they rarely achieved: what one finds is slight corrections and shifts of alignment at relatively high points. What distinguishes their roads from those of their predecessors and successors is their essential directness, providing the fastest and most efficient communication between military and civil centres. This was especially necessary in the first brief period of conquest and surveillance, and again from the third century when the 'Saxon Shore' had to be manned against raiders. But during the two centuries of peace, the more parochial needs of villa and village presumably resulted in more small and not necessarily straight roads than we shall ever identify or suspect. The major network itself forks off into several secondary developments. And there may have been centuriation.

The exact course of most of these roads must be to a certain extent hypothetical. In East Suffolk it is practically impossible to trace a Roman road-bed where it runs beneath a modern road: both are made of the same local gravels. Only to the west of the county can the roads sometimes be identified by a bed of rammed chalk and large flints. That need not deter us from looking for other evidence. But it is clear that we shall never know the true extent of Roman communications in coastal Suffolk.

So often, the Roman design has been largely distorted by the Old English settlements and the tracks that linked them. The two most striking exceptions are perhaps the north Suffolk part of the A140 to Caistor-by-Norwich and the Kentford-Bury road, A14. A glance at Ogilby's road maps of 1675 shows that their course was the same before the turnpikes as it is today. A third exception,

---

[19] Miller Christy, *Trans. Essex Arch. Soc.*, vol.XVII, Pt. iv (1925).

though a less important road and one Ogilby did not travel, is 'Stone Street', between Ilketshall St John and Halesworth. Why these particular roads should have survived without suffering diversions is not at all clear. The woodland on either side of the A140 between Stonham and Diss was colonised very late (by Suffolk standards): some of it as late as the 12th century, by which time the value of the road as a highway would be recognised and established. The oak woods themselves would have surely obliterated it if it had not been kept in some steady use? Ogilby indicates that in 1675 the stretch from Little Stonham to Thwaite was still thickly wooded. 'Stone Street' has not only preserved its pristine straightness, it has contrived to make the hedges and lanes of the whole surrounding landscape conform rigidly with it. Students of centuriation would do well to examine this landscape carefully. The A14 from Kentford to Bury ran through lighter more open land: the value of fields and the needs of field drainage were less likely to prevail over the needs of communication. This road may well have been in continuous use as a highway, connecting the Ixworth area, and later the shrine of St Edmund at Bury and the medieval capital of West Suffolk, via the Icknield Way to the south and to the Cambridge crossing to the Midlands.

Already we begin to detect the leading threads amid the tangle of modern Suffolk roads: the prehistoric Icknield Way and the stretches the Romans paved – or at least cleared and gravelled – and that we sometimes use and sometimes are made aware of in a flash by place names that embody the Old English word for a paved road, like Stradishall and Stratton Hall and – most vividly of all, though not Old English – Silver Street Farm, down at Withersfield.

It is impressive that so much should survive so long across the fertile Suffolk fields; the implication may be that they never dropped wholly out of use, for the structure and metalling of these roads is poor compared with those of most other parts of Britain, and they would have been quickly reclaimed by vegetation. In his standard book, *Roman Roads in Britain*, Ivan D. Margary wrote of the East Anglian network: 'Except upon Peddars Way north of Ixworth the eastern main road … and perhaps a few other sections, it is rare to find much evidence of an *agger* [a rampart on which many of the main roads were raised and thereby drained], and when the road has gone derelict all traces of it seem to vanish entirely.' Certainly some stretches have vanished utterly, but others are still marked by a single great length of hedge, as a buoy marks a wreck. The region's lack of building-stone is reflected in all this. The particular sections of road that have been examined consist of little more than a bed of gravel 18 inches thick: yet those studies were made in roads running through Central Suffolk, the sticky clay woodland, where drainage and a good foundation would have been more use than under the roads that cross the light lands. The reason why the Romans now appear not to have continued their lateral roads eastwards over the coastal heaths to Dunwich, for instance, and Aldeburgh, where their people were certainly established, may be simply that the heaths seemed not to call for road-construction in the usual highly durable form. If so, there was never any specially useful structure to try to preserve. In short, the present simple tracks straight across the heaths to Dunwich may represent the remains of Roman roads.

Where measurable sections survive, the widths vary considerably. The main London-Colchester road that was quickly extended north to Coddenham (*Combretonium*) and Caistor-by-Norwich measured 23 feet wide at Coddenham, just north of the crossing of the River Gipping at Sharnford (Old English for 'dirty ford', a reference to the local mud). In the settlement area of *Combretonium* it was increased to the exceptional width of 32 feet. Just to the north of *Combretonium*, it becomes part of the busy A140, the main Ipswich-Norwich road, and is still only wide enough for single-lane two-way motor traffic. Just to the north of the Stonham 'Magpie' Inn, the line of the old low *agger* can be seen to the east of the present road. At Scole (*Villa Faustini*), where it crosses into Norfolk, the original road measures 21 feet. The transverse road running from near Coddenham out to Hacheston and perhaps beyond, was as much as 25 feet wide at Otley Bottom (where, in one of the gaps in a series of straight alignments, ploughing has not obliterated but merely reduced the thickness of the gravel). The road from Bildeston (and presumably Colchester) that joins Peddars Way at Ixworth seems to have been only 15 feet wide. But it does have a flint bed beneath the gravel surface. At a high point south of Rattlesden (264 feet) it forms Mitchery (formerly Misery) Lane, and its great drainage-ditch survives like a length of moat all along its east side: that along its west side is now reduced, but here one gets an immediate idea of the formidable amount of digging and uprooting that went into the making of even a subsidiary Roman road through the woodlands.

These roads marked out permanently in the landscape Suffolk's age-long division into two. Two main traffic-hubs or arteries, Ixworth and

Coddenham, perpetuated the main tribal division (Iceni and Trinovantes) and the underlying geographical division imposed by that dense central woodland. Massive, towering oaks may have been partly responsible for the unusual number of deviations and realignments in the perhaps hurriedly constructed road to *Venta Icenorum*. Its termini were London and Caistor-by-Norwich, and so it provided Norfolk with a capital but Suffolk with only a thoroughfare and one major road-junction (or series of offset junctions). Villas were established not far from it, at Capel St Mary (early), at Whitton, Stonham and Eye. Roman remains on both sides of the road at Stoke Ash, just where the old White Horse now stands, were accepted by Rainbird Clarke as those of a posting-station, without, alas, any leaning that way from the finds. Lateral roads, too, soon extended east and south-west from *Combretonium*. That 25-foot road to Hacheston may have been early, for the great interest of the Hacheston settlement is that it lasted right through from Claudius to the fourth century. (Now it is nothing but a series of open cornfields lying all round the Framlingham-Orford road at its crossing of the A12 just north of Rackham's Mill at Wickham Market.) The other easterly roads may have been developed in the second century. The most easterly, leading to Burgh Castle (and perhaps a ferry to Caister-on-Sea), is inferred merely from the coincidence of straight road-lengths with parish boundaries. That a road led to the now-drowned Saxon Shore fort at Walton-Felixstowe (formerly also known as Burgh) can hardly be doubted. The old parish name of Stratton and again the coincidence of parish bounds with straight stretches of ancient road has led us to dot in a probable route on the map (ill.8). An (apparently) early road ran south-west from *Combretonium* to join the so called *Via Devana* down at Wixoe. One glimpses it as a wood-boundary and double overgrown hedge approaching the Cambridgeshire border west of Haverhill, as a slight bump in Melford Green, as a lane near Bassett's Farm, Acton, and again as a hedge at Hill Farm, Brent Eleigh. In Chelsworth it seems to have vanished totally. But at least it was still visible enough in the late tenth century to provide part of the boundary of an Anglo-Saxon estate we shall be discussing later. This road may have been designed to service the frontier between Rome and the Iceni before Boudicca's rebellion.

Like the east, the west side of Suffolk was overlaid by a main highway (it is known as Peddars Way) running up from Chelmsford and straight through Ixworth in the tribal area of the Iceni. It still provides the main

17 *Icknield Way, looking south from Cavenham towards Kentford and Newmarket. This great prehistoric track runs from the Wash down through Buckinghamshire and Berkshire to Dorset. It was improved by the Romans and more recently landscaped here into a monumental avenue of beeches. As the main road in and out of East Anglia, it is now replaced by the A11. See also colour plate III.*

18 *A Roman 'corridor villa' revealed in crop-marks at Lidgate in 1971 and hitherto entirely unsuspected. The corridor is on the south side. A buttressed granary stands detached to the south of the villa. Notice the double ditches of man-made farm roads on the north side (bottom) of the picture.*

street in the two ancient thoroughfare villages of Long Melford and Ixworth. Just north of Melford, it was joined by a link road from Colchester. Mr Ivan Margary drew attention to the exceptionally solid structure of Peddars Way to the north of Ixworth, and this is borne out in another of Dr St Joseph's remarkable air photographs (AIR 53: illustration 3). Where the *agger* was used as one of Barningham's parish boundaries it would be interesting to count the species in the tree-studded hedgerow. If a new species establishes itself every century, as Dr Max Hooper successfully maintains, then there could be anything between ten and twenty species in that hedge. The structure is a sign of the road's importance to the Romans. They obviously wanted a supplement to the Icknield Way, providing their transport with a fast route to the Wash direct from London, Chelmsford and (perhaps later) Colchester.

Over this stout *agger*, Peddars Way led across West Norfolk and down into the marsh at Holme-next-the-Sea, where a ferry presumably crossed to the Lincolnshire coast. By taking the (apparently older) right fork at Stanton Chair (the Old English *cerr* or *cyrr* means 'turn'), the Roman traveller went on to Attleborough. To the south of Ixworth a series of lesser roads converged on the neighbourhood. One of these, not hitherto recorded, marks the boundary between Rougham and Hessett. Another, Dr S.E. West has followed from Deadman's Lane on the Woolpit-Drinkstone boundary, past Little Haugh Hall (in *Stanton Street*, Norton), with its tumulus, and on to the extraordinary Roman settlement at Grimstone End. Then there is the beautifully engineered A14 which from Kentford to the Fornham-Westley roundabout is followed in long straight stretches by a series of parish bounds which thereafter follow it, as a fine hedge, to the golf course. Just outside the site of the medieval North Gate of Bury St Edmunds it passes Fornham Priory as Hollow Road and approaches Ixworth through Barton. David Dymond has noticed that in early manuscript maps of Fornham and Barton it is called 'Peddars Way'. Mr Margary says that this 'may well be' a road linking the Icknield Way to the main Roman Peddars Way, 'though this is not proved'. But is there any alternative explanation?

Mr Margary shows how the Icknield Way itself, one of the most famous prehistoric trackways of Britain, was 'straightened and Romanised' on its wide course through (the later) Newmarket High Street and Kentford and then north through Cavenham and Lackford at the very heart of the Iceni's territory. Edward Thomas explored it before the motor car had imposed its own peculiar transformation of all our ancient roads, and his book, *The Icknield Way*, preserves part of the road's lost character. North of Kentford, the road remains delightful, with an enchanting medieval improvement at Cavenham, a packhorse bridge, whose old brick arches are now grass-grown, and north of Lackford it nowadays leads once more through uninhabited woodland (illustration 17).

Whether anything of the Roman farming landscape survived into Anglo-Saxon times we shall discuss in a later chapter. A most interesting row of four great burial-mounds south-east of Bury, near the junction of Rougham, Rushbrooke and Bradfield, suggests that the nearby building was a very important villa: but whether the important people buried there were Icenian aristocrats or immigrants from East Belgium 'is uncertain', as Rainbird Clarke concluded. The great villa at Stanton Chair was excavated in 1925 but the

19 *Burgh Castle. The view west over the Waveney, with no trace in this picture of the seventh-century 'monastery' of St Fursey within the fort, nor of the Norman castle in the south-west corner; nor of the early Anglo-Saxon or Frisian cemetery in the field east of the fort.*

findings were never fully published: it is thought to have been the headquarters of the farm-manager of a big estate. A splendid 'corridor' villa has been detected at Lidgate for the first time in 1971, and should prove to be remarkably undisturbed (illustration 18). But apart from the roads, and from a very large-scale industrial pottery at Wattisfield, the chief Roman feature surviving in the Suffolk landscape is Burgh Castle, *Gariannonum* (illustration 19). (Technically, Burgh Castle was transferred to Norfolk in the absurd boundary changes of 1974: Suffolk and Norfolk archaeologists find it hard to take such juggling with antiquity seriously.) It was built at the end of the third century, to protect a garrison and presumably a flotilla, whose operational role was to keep marauding Picts and Saxons away from the gaping estuary that occupied the present mouths of the Yare and Bute and led straight in to *Venta*, the cantonal

20 *Burgh Castle, south wall (estuary here running south/north). Flint laced with red brick: local vernacular building materials since the late-Roman period in defence against the Anglo-Saxon invaders. (Looking west across the wide Waveney estuary to distant marsh drainage wind-pump.)*

capital. It is one of the most evocative of all the features of the East Anglian landscape. One approaches on foot over flat fields from the north and east. The entire length of the east wall, 640 feet, is intact to its full height, approximately fifteen feet. The proportions are so horizontal as almost to achieve the effect of merging the regular courses of flintwork, laced lightly with brick, into the regular furrows of the great surrounding fields. It would be difficult to approach the narrow main gate, the Porta Praetoria, set in the middle of this east side, without that feeling of intimidation induced by so many of the colossal monuments of Imperial Rome: the theatre at Orange, the arena at Nîmes, the Colosseum itself. It is a real relief to find the south wall toppling romantically, the west wall gone, apparently quarried away, and an unforgettable view of the Waveney marshes and water and wind pumps. What one does not see is an Anglo-Saxon cemetery beneath the field to the east, which provides a leading clue to the next significant phase in the shaping of the land.

Two

THE ENGLISH SETTLEMENT

Though I have considered Mr Whitaker's remarks ... I do not perceive the absurdity of supposing that the Frisians, &c., were mingled with the Anglo-Saxons.

Edward Gibbon, *The Decline and Fall of the Roman Empire*

The Forerunners

In 1774, John Ives published his valuable *Remarks upon Gariannonum of the Romans*, not only noting the 'great numbers of Roman urns' found spread across the broad field to the east of the inscrutable walls of Burgh Castle, but adding that they 'are made of coarse blue clay brought from the neighbouring village of Bradwell', and including, for good measure, sketches of two of these 'Roman urns'. The sketches tell more: the urns were Anglo-Saxon, and of fifth-century types. They were found, Ives said, with 'several fair pieces of Constantine'.

The presence of Constantine's coins among early Anglo-Saxon pots does not make this historic field an Anglo-Saxon cemetery of his day, right at the beginning of the fourth century. But it vividly recalls the testimony of Gibbon's 'accurate and faithful guide', the fourth-century historian Ammianus, which indeed is now generally accepted: that German tribesmen were settling in eastern Britain from perhaps the middle of the fourth century, originally as allied defence forces, known as *foederati* or *limitanei*, and charged with the repulse from Roman Britain of their prowling and intrusive fellow barbarians.

These very early military settlers have for some time been authoritatively located by finds of a type of pottery that looks 'hybrid', wheel-thrown the Roman way but with 'Anglo-Saxon' decoration.[1] Experts now think that one class of these pots had a different, earlier Roman origin nothing to do with

---

[1] J.N.L. Myres, in *Dark Age Britain*, ed. D.B. Harden (1956), pp.16-39.

21 *The remains, in 1786, of the Roman fort at Walton-Felixstowe that had guarded the estuaries of Deben and Orwell. The Deben mouth lies between the fort and the crag-cliffs of Bawdsey in the right background. The same building materials as in illustration 20.*

foederati; but recent work in Essex shows a striking coastal distribution of hybrid pottery, from Mucking (by Tilbury) through Canvey Island, Wakering, Wickford and Bradwell to Colchester.[2] In any case, Anglo-Saxon *foederati* are also locatable by distinctive metalwork strap-ends and 'belt-furniture' and extremely early non-hybrid Anglo-Saxon ware exactly comparable with the pottery of their homelands, from Schleswig-Holstein westwards across the mouth of the Elbe to those strange artificial mounded settlements in Frisia, known as *terpen*. The extraordinary multiplication of people and settlements along that seaboard in the fourth century, combined with steady lowering of the land and encroachment by the sea, led to the great invasion of Britain by these illiterate pagans in the fifth and sixth centuries. It may not be a mere coincidence that in East Anglia the earliest settlements seem to be related to the *foederati*.

[2] *Antiquaries Journal*, Vol.L (1970), pp.262-6.

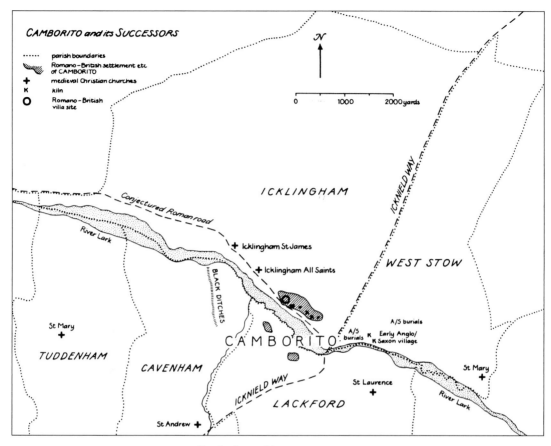

CAMBORITO and its SUCCESSORS

```
······    parish boundaries
         Romano-British settlement etc
         of CAMBORITO
+        medieval Christian churches
K        kiln
O        Romano-British
         villa site
```

N

```
0        1000      2000 yards
```

ICKLINGHAM

ICKNIELD WAY

Conjectured Roman road

River Lark

+ Icklingham St James

+ Icklingham All Saints

WEST STOW

BLACK DITCHES

A/S burials

A/S burials

C A M B O R I T O

St Mary
+

TUDDENHAM

CAVENHAM

A/S
burials

K Early Anglo/
K Saxon village

St Mary
+

River Lark

ICKNIELD WAY

St Laurence
+

LACKFORD

St Andrew +

22 *Camborito and its successors.*

Where in Suffolk we should reasonably expect to find remains of settlement by *foederati*, or their descendants, is near those forts at the mouths of the two main estuary-systems that offered seaborne marauders the most inviting shelter to be found along these shores: Burgh Castle (controlling the Yare water approach to *Venta Icenorum*), and the submerged fort at Walton-Felixstowe (controlling Stour, Orwell and Deben estuaries, and also called 'Burgh' all through the Anglo-Saxon period). Where such early pottery remains have certainly been found in E. Anglia, is in a great cemetery outside the walled town of *Venta*. They were described by J.N.L. Myres as 'Anglo-Frisian', and go back in date before the year 400. A similar cemetery lies across the river from *Venta*, at Markshall. So somewhere alongside the (perhaps Christian) Romano-British community at Caistor-by-Norwich at least two Anglo-Saxon pagan communities had been settled, on terms of mutual toleration with the British. In late fifth-century Suffolk there was no town like *Venta* calling for protection by *foederati*;[3] but, as we saw in the last chapter, there were the populous Ixworth and Coddenham neighbourhoods, antecedents of Bury and Ipswich respectively, in the way Caistor was the forebear of Norwich. Here we might one day come across the evidence of Romano-British and early Anglo-Saxon juxtaposition as remarkable as that which has lately been uncovered in West Stow Heath, a mile or so up the little river Lark from a Roman villa and presumably Romano-British settlement at Icklingham (illustration 22).

Flowing north-west from Bury through the Breckland, the Lark has turned almost due west at Lackford, before it reaches Mildenhall. The Icknield Way crosses it at Lackford, and half a mile east of that ancient ford, on a low knoll above the north bank of the river, in light sandy soils colonised by birch trees, a virtually complete Anglo-Saxon village has emerged: truly a home-from-home for any settler who remembered the *heide*, the heath and moorland of Holland and Hanover and Holstein. Known as Leech Moor on the 1836 Ordnance Survey map, it is now known as West Stow Heath. From 1965, in eight successive summers, Dr S.E. West examined, for the Department of the Environment, this seven-acre site, where the Anglo-Saxon remains are unobstructed by those of any later settlement.

Anglo-Saxons were settled here at least by the year 400, and were here for about 250 years. They had early boundary-ditches along the north side, but seem to have been largely islanded: the north side is boggy. No fewer than 70 hut-sites were examined, varying in size, but almost all oriented east-west. There seems to have been a grouping for six families, each associated with a slightly larger 'hall-like' structure, but nothing like the great long-huts of the continental villages of this period.

Eight or nine of the huts, all fifth-century ones, were built with three posts at each end. Several had only one at each end, but the structures show good knowledge of carpentry. The bases of the huts were dug down into the soil, but there is much evidence of plank flooring, in some cases forming a two-foot-deep kind of 'cellar'. This should not suggest romantic ideas about their hut-planning. It seems that *all* their refuse was kept there. As this included some thousands of discarded meat bones, a useful study can be made of their 'animal economy'. It already looks as if this was largely based on sheep,

---

[3] It is very likely that Dunwich was a Romano-British port, but the sea has washed all the evidence away, except the approaching roads.

in the age-long tradition of the Breckland. But there were also plenty of oxen, and pigs. Four large hollow areas, Dr West thinks, were temporary animal pens.

Squalid though these earliest English were, they had two huts for the weaving of clothes and over 120 bone combs were recovered, extremely well made, and more than half of them double-sided, perhaps for wool-carding. And they made pots for themselves. In short, the village was largely self supporting, and capable of more sophisticated building than might have been supposed.

From the point of view of the contemporary settlement of both Romano-British and Anglo-Saxon in this neighbourhood, as at Caistor-by-Norwich, great interest lies in all the late Romano-British pottery, coins and other objects found among these huts. Of over 250 coins, nearly all are of the second half of the fourth century. These things *could* represent loot from an Icklingham villa that had already been abandoned. But, for Dr West, the number of late Roman pots at West Stow suggests 'a more reliable source than a deserted Roman site'.[4]

It is mortifying that we know next to nothing of the Romano-Britons, descendants of the Iceni and Trinovantes, in the fourth century, whether at Icklingham, just downstream from West Stow Heath, or anywhere else in Suffolk. We return to Icklingham in a moment. Let us try to follow the descendants of those Anglo-Saxon villagers into the Middle Ages. The fifth-century settlement seems to have extended slowly over the knoll until the middle of the seventh century. Then abruptly, but not violently, it came to an end.

Why was the site abandoned? The weaving-sheds, on the north slope, were burnt, but there is no other sign of calamity. This suggests that they moved deliberately; presumably to a more convenient place to live. They would have gone upstream or downstream, keeping fairly close to the better grazing and corn lands watered by the river. The chances are that they settled themselves about a mile upstream on the present (medieval) village-site. It does not seem in any way unlikely that in the middle of the seventh century the families occupying those three or four groups of unsavoury huts, each linked to a small oblong 'hall', became, or begat, the prospectors and founding-fathers of 'Stow', which by *c.*1200 was being called 'Westowe' to distinguish it from another Stow nine miles due east, which has itself been distinguished as Stowlangtoft.

---

[4] *Medieval Archaeology*, Vol.XIII (1969), p.18.

The little village of West Stow is remarkably well documented from Domesday Book onwards, for it had (probably fairly recently) been acquired by St Edmund's abbey. As usual, the archaeology is lacking once the villagers had moved to a site that has been continuously occupied ever since. Nevertheless, there are still some archaeological conclusions and possibilities. Christians preferred inhumation after death; 'to submit', as Sir Thomas Browne observed, 'unto the principle of putrefaction, and conclude in a moist relentment.'

In the first half of the seventh century, Christianity came to Suffolk. Dr West has suggested that a possible reason at least contributing to the move from the primitive village (which lies at the south-west corner of the parish) may have been the establishment of the Christian holy place, with cross and inhumation burial-ground, in a favourable corner where two tributaries enter the Lark, right at the south-*east* end of the parish. Two of the possible meanings of the Anglo-Saxon word *stow* are 'holy place' and 'place of assembly', and here the first seems the likelier. A peculiarity of the Domesday description of this Stow is that its church, with '12 acres of free land in alms', is reckoned as 'lying in another Hundred'. We shall look later at the Anglo-Saxon arrangement and rearrangement of Hundreds. There seems to be no chance that the adjoining Hundred, called Thingoe, once extended physically to include this sacred corner of Stow. More probably, the Christian Stow had been founded from the neighbouring ancient church of St Lawrence, at Lackford village in Thingoe, and continued to be reckoned in that Hundred. For at Lackford, too, a famous primitive pagan Anglo-Saxon cemetery lies about a mile westwards and downstream of the medieval village; and it was at Lackford in Thingoe Hundred, according to Domesday Book, that 21 'freemen' of Stow did their 'socage' services for their land – that service which they owed to the Hundred, and which was originally owed to the East Anglian King.

How complex the lives of the descendants of the 21 West Stow Domesday freemen became officially, by the time of Abbot Samson of Bury (1182-1211), may be read (but not entirely understood) in his *Kalendar*.[5] However, a charter of the same abbot shows him and the convent letting to Gervase, the son of a moneyer, for 60 shillings a year, the two water mills at Stow whose rent was devoted to providing parchment and ink for the abbey's *scriptorium*. A tax return of 1283 shows a third water-mill at Westowe being held for the service

---

[5] Ed. R.H.C. Davis, pp.40-1.

of '*i paris cyrotecarum*'[6] – one pair of gloves – not, as was once thought (from *cyratus*, waxed), one Paris candle. This return shows that by 1283 not only were there three water-mills turning on the West Stow bank of the Lark, for the smooth running of Bury abbey, but also that the Master of St Saviour's Hospital, founded by Abbot Samson outside the north gate of Bury, had appropriated a fishery which was regarded as rightfully the common property of the West Stow 'township' and 'which extended from the westernmost watermill of Stow to the bridge at Lackford'. This shows that at least by 1283 and quite likely since the seventh century, the *vill* (or township) and parish of Stow was regarded as extending as far west as Lackford bridge and the Icknield Way. In short, that parish may already have achieved its final shape, its shape today. Another 'encroachment' by the Master of St Saviour's Hospital was upon 120 acres of West Stow Heath, again regarded as the 'common property of the township' and conceivably including that sandy knoll occupied centuries earlier by its presumed earliest forefathers.

If those three mill-sites could be identified and excavated, our picture of the medieval landscape of Stow would be amplified in a way that would help to illuminate most of our ancient valley-villages. Dr West's excavation of the primitive village has shown that it was actually being ploughed over during the 12th and 13th centuries, probably by the very forward Hospital Master in an attempt to increase the hospital's revenues. Dr West has also shown that, quite dramatically, round about that time in the late 13th century, the wind took over, as it still does with our light soils when their natural tree-cover or scrub or ling is stripped from them. Sandstorms, of the kind vividly described at Santon Downham in the 17th and 19th centuries, turned this site into a sand-dune. From at least an archaeologist's point of view this was a most satisfactory turn of events: it's an ill wind … Sand is almost as excellent a preservative as the lava that saved, for us, the house-furnishings of Herculaneum. Here at Stow one could see the actual plough-furrows of the 13th century, and the ridge and furrow shape of the field.

We return to those Anglo-Saxon pioneers in Romano-British Suffolk, and their successors. There is small doubt about the presence in the Roman settlement-site at Icklingham of Romano-British contemporaries of the earliest English at West Stow. Incidentally, the Romano-British lead cistern from Icklingham, bearing the Christian monogram, and now in the British Museum,[7]

---

[6] E. Powell, *A Suffolk Hundred in 1283* (1910), p.64.
[7] *Guide to Antiquities of Roman Britain*, B.M. (1951), p.69, fig.30; *Antiquaries Journal*, Vol.XXII, p.219; *Journal of Roman Studies*, Vol.XXIII, p.80.

is labelled by the Museum 'probably a Christian font of the fourth century'. Even more remarkable, a second, almost identical, font emerged from that same Icklingham field in October 1971. So here, between fourth-century Icklingham and seventh-century West Stow, we may be within measuring distance of the gap between official Roman Christianity and that of the missions to seventh-century East Anglia. It is to our purpose to note that, early in the seventh century, when the orthodox St Felix, from Burgundy via Canterbury, was established at *Domnoc*, probably Dunwich, by the East Anglian king, those kings (known as Wuffingas, descendants of Wuffa) were careful to include among their ancestors Caesar: a possible indication that they numbered Romano-British among their subjects. Furthermore, at the same moment an Irish visionary, St Fursey, to bring the Celtic view of Christianity to Suffolk, chose to establish himself within the very walls of *Gariannonum*. Apart from the strategic importance of the place, may not his choice of Burgh Castle mean that there were sub-Roman Christians, however subservient, surviving in or very near this place, where one would have expected Romano-British and *foederati to* have been co-existing from the fourth century?

How subordinate they were (if we may assume their existence), is to be deduced from the way the name *Gariannonum* was now replaced by that of *Cnobheresburg*, which is believed to mean the *burh*, or fort, or, as Bede put it, *Urbs*, the town, of Cnobhere, or perhaps Cnofhere, otherwise unknown. True, 'Yare' still preserves a part of *Gariannonum*, but there is no doubt that the language of the dominant folk took on very little from the British.

Place-names

The conclusion is not that the British had entirely gone from here; nor that we should stop looking out for possible name-transfers in areas where we now suppose the British co-existed with *foederati*. Such topographical coincidences as Ickeni-Ixworth-Icklingham, *Combretonium* – Coddenham, *Camborito* – Cavenham are seldom seriously explored by place-name linguists.

Mr S.E. Rigold has lately argued that St Felix's *Domnoc* was the Roman fort at Walton-Felixstowe, now submerged. Certainly no Anglo-Saxon place-name approximating to that now survives in the Felixstowe area, and indeed the linguistic comparison of the Celtic *Domnoc* (based on *dubno*, meaning 'deep') with Dunwich is one reason for anticipating other signs of early Anglo-Saxon settlement there. The 11th-century spelling *Duneuuic* and the 12th-century spelling *Dunuuoc* (*Liber Eliensis*) seem to identify *Domnoc* with Dunwich finally.

(The sea has probably removed any signs of early settlement – as also, to a great extent, at Felixstowe and for that matter Aldeburgh, whose Anglo-Saxon name, meaning 'Old Fort', indicates some pre-English fortification there, too.)

But at Felixstowe, may not the name 'Burgh' itself be taken as a primary name, indicating very early English settlement? 'Old Felixstowe', with its medieval church of SS. Peter and Paul, was called simply *Burch* in Domesday Book. 'Felixstowe' is a comparatively late development. Part of *Burch* was known as Fylthestowe in the 14th century, which means 'place, or holy place, or meeting-place, where hay grows'. There was a meeting-place of the Hundred of Coleness at the south end of the adjacent parish of Walton, which also had an ancient church dedicated to St Felix. This church was given in the time of William the Conqueror to Rochester Priory, which established a subordinate little priory of St Felix at Walton. Its site a few hundred yards north of Walton parish church has been briefly excavated in 1971. It is not impossible that an early Anglo-Saxon church of St Felix was overlaid by medieval and post Reformation buildings. At all events, Fylthestowe began to be called Felixstowe about the time of the Dissolution, a natural 'rationalisation' at the time when St Felix's little priory disappeared. Whether he himself originated that church must await more prolonged examination of the site. But there is not much doubt that this was one of the scenes of primary settlement, by *foederati* or their descendants. Whether the name Walton is interpreted as *tun* (farmstead) of the *Wealh* (Welshmen, i.e. Romano-British) or *tun* 'near the wall' (i.e. Roman fort), it is likely on the place-name score to have been an early settlement. It is sometimes argued by the linguists that *ham*, a 'homestead' or a hamlet or village indicates early settlement, but by 'early' they seem to be content to mean 'pre-Conquest', not 'fifth-century as distinct from sixth'. Similarly, *tun* has for long been regarded as implying a secondary settlement. Yet the clear deduction from A.H. Smith's analysis of *tun*[8] is simply that if *tun* is a name that was applied early to a settlement then it meant 'a farmstead'; if applied later then it meant 'a village', the embryo of all *towns*, which explains that modern word. There is no reason why Walton should not be regarded as one of the earliest settlements in Suffolk.

Since J. McN. Dodgson[9] suggested that *-inga* place-names, such as Framlingham, Badingham, etc., may not, after all, derive from the earliest

---

[8] *Place-Name Elements*, Vol.II (1970), pp.188-98.
[9] *Medieval Archaeology*, Vol.X (1966), pp.1-29.

period of settlement, we may all feel freer to work from actual settlements to names, instead of assuming that certain words automatically imply early or late dates. We shall perhaps be spared any more maps of Suffolk fairly evenly and meaninglessly spattered with crosses marking *-ings, -hams,* and the like, until we can be sure what chronological significance such categories have. The map on p.7 of his article finally demonstrates the pointlessness of such arguments at this stage in our knowledge of English settlements. Names and actual pagan burials tell quite conflicting stories.

I set out various views and conclusions on the name Icklingham in the 'Place-names and Settlements' chapter of my book *Suffolk in the Middle Ages.* I included the British name *Camborito* in the discussion, since that precisely describes 'the crooked ford' by which the Icknield Way crossed the Lark (see illustration 22), and so *might* be reflected in *Canavaham,* now Cavenham. In a recent study of the English Wickhams as an early name, the great majority of them fairly closely related to Roman remains, Wickhambrook in Suffolk was regarded as one of the few exceptions.[10] It need not have been. We now take a look at an important group of names noticed in 1936 by J.N.L. Myres,[11] but not much noticed since. Discussing the marshlands of the north German coast and Frisia, he mentions the great artificial mounds, or *terpen,* 'many of them still covered by villages bearing names strongly reminiscent of eastern England'. Looking through the long lists of Roman finds in W.A. van Es's paper 'Friesland in Roman Times', in *Berichten van de Rijksdienst voor het Oudheidkundig Bodemonderzoek* (1965/6), one sees that finds have been made in villages called Barrum, Blÿa, Hyum, Jislum and Nÿland (among many others). Without thoroughly checking all their early spellings, I suppose these may correspond exactly to the Suffolk place-names of Barham, Blyth, Higham (2), Gisleham and Nayland, since *um* derives from *heim,* which in Anglo Saxon is *-ham,* and Blÿ is the modern Dutch for blithe, a reference in old Suffolk to that river's cheerful flow. Also, in Friesland Roman finds were made at Engelum, which (as 'farm of the Angle') corresponds notably to the Suffolk Saxham ('farm of the Saxons'), and Flempton ('farm of the Flemings') and Freston ('farm of the Frisians', see above, p.50) and Fressingfield (and conceivably Friston, too, though that name had not appeared in the time of Domesday Book, despite Ekwall's note in his *Dictionary of English Place-names*: the settlement at Friston in that time was called Bohton, a name no more in

[10] *Med. Arch.,* Vol.XI (1967), pp.87-104. cf. ill. 8 above.
[11] *Roman Britain and* the *English Settlements* (1945 edn.), pp.340-1.

use). In Norfolk, too, Docking presents a notable parallel with Dokkum in Friesland and Fincham with Finkum (*fink* is Dutch for finch). One may add Shotley and Shottisham, names of Suffolk coastal villages, and meaning respectively 'clearing' and 'farm' of the 'Scots', who in those days came from Ireland. It may be remarked that each place of these 'Scots' is associated with extensive vanished earthworks revealed by Dr St Joseph's air-photographs.

The implications of those identical Frisian place-names are these: either families from Frisia settled here directly, and gave their Suffolk homes the names of their old home-villages, or 'Anglo-Saxons' settled both in Frisia and Suffolk, giving the places identical Anglo-Saxon names. The second explanation seems to fit better. The late F. Tischler, Director of the Lower Rhine Museum, at Duisburg, wrote of Angles and Saxons in their continental homelands,[12] that from the middle of the fourth century onwards, 'I am inclined to use the term 'Anglo-Saxon' in order to indicate that one can no longer talk of a homogeneous tribal unity … I must emphasise, however, that in my view native elements of the population in each case survived with all their peculiarities.' It was in this way that the settlers of Saxham could think of themselves as distinctively 'Saxon'. It is natural, and perhaps conclusive, that in East Anglia there is no strict counterpart of Friesland's Engelum, for an Angleham or an Angleton in East Anglia would presumably have been as meaningless as a Saxham in Essex or Sussex. (We come later to George Homans' powerful arguments in favour of basically 'Frisian' settlement in East Anglia, based on similarities of the early social systems of East Anglia and Friesland, by which he means the seven medieval *Seelande* forming the coastal strip from Scheldt to Weser.) In these points of ethnic differentiation, the linguists have more to go on, at present, than the field archaeologists. They can confirm a predominantly Anglian, or Old English, settlement in East Anglia, where archaeologists without place names might, like Tischler, be reduced to a more generalised Anglo-Saxon story. And we cannot forget those co-axial field- and lane-patterns underlying the Pye Road in illustration 15.

The Main Settlement of the East Angles
The forerunners, *foederati* or their descendants, were at West Stow all through the fifth and sixth centuries. What was going on around them? We have only archaeological finds and place names to work from during these two centuries of transformation, when the Angles, or Old English, arrived and formed the

[12] *Med. Arch.,* Vol.III (1959), p.4. Like Proust's M. Brichot, 'I must add that toponymy … is not an exact science.'

main settlements of southern East Anglia, Suffolk. There can be no doubt about the importance of these two centuries in the creation of the Suffolk landscape. By the beginning of the seventh century, Raedwald, grand-son of Wuffa, was not only established as king of the East Angles, his kingdom was strong enough for him to be recognised as 'Bretwalda', with his power extended over the whole of England. Pagan Anglian burials should give us some idea of at least the extent of settlement during the fifth and sixth centuries. But there is confusion about cremation and inhumation, and the archaeologists admit that their evidence is inadequate. It says too little of the living – even of their whereabouts, for cemeteries have rarely been matched by hut-sites. Even at West Stow, where much is known of the living, that has yet to be certainly related to one (or both) of two possible cemeteries.

However, *A Gazetteer of Early Anglo-Saxon Burial-Sites* was assembled by Audrey Meaney in 1964. In her map, East Anglia appears with Lincolnshire as an area mainly of cremation. But this is because of the enormous number of cremations in one or two cemeteries, like Lackford, where there may have been thousands. Of the 68 early sites listed in Suffolk, only 12 contained cremations. Not that cremation necessarily implies an earlier Anglo-Saxon ritual than inhumation. The chief trouble is that 68 sites, many marking single burials, hardly relate satisfactorily to two centuries of death in Suffolk, 200 years that culminate in East Anglia's supremacy over all the English kingdoms.

So far as they go the burial-sites suggest that those early East Angles were as content as the men of the Bronze Age had been with the easy arable lands of the valley-gravels: particularly the Lark and the Waveney, the Gipping, Deben and Alde. Presumably at this stage the English were arriving in such numbers that they dispossessed, by fair means or foul, many, if not all, of the old sub-Roman farmers in areas of dense settlement like the Icklingham-Lackford neighbourhood. From this Breckland area, the tendency would soon be to follow the lesser streams right up into the heavier clays, to fell the trees; contrast words ending in *leah* ('a clearing in the woods', as in Westley) and *field*, which usually implied a larger and older clearing, more of the sort of open country one might expect to find perhaps, where the Romans had already established an arable farm in the woodlands, and left it being at least kept cleared and cropped and grazed by the British (see full study of *-feld* names, *Suffolk in the Middle Ages*, pp.13-26). However, looking at the names that lie eastwards from the Lark valley, and from the Black Bourn which flows through Pakenham and Ixworth, one sees as many *-hams* and *-tons* as *-fields*:

23 *Wickham Skeith. Here a Green was provided near church and hall, and gives some sense of a 'nucleated' village. 'Skeith' is a Scandinavian word for a racecourse, or training-paddock, and one wonders if the green was used for raising and watering race-horses, or war-horses.*

Walsham-le -Willows, Stanton, Wattisfield. Their names alone merely suggest that *all* were relatively early settled. Early burial-sites have been found at Badwell Ash (originally part of a large area cleared in the ashwoods and called Ashfield) and Finningham. Early settlement at Ashfield may imply an eastward colonisation from Ixworth: that at Finningham possibly a westward movement from Wickham Skeith (illustration 23), or a longer northward movement from Finborough, near Stowmarket, as Ekwall thought – 'the ham of the Finborough people'. Finborough (*Fineberga*) took its evocative name from 'a woodpecker's hill', but, alas, it has no known early English burials.

In brief, we cannot hope to draw simple, or even complex, diagrams to show the sequence of the English settlement of Suffolk, whether in the fifth or the sixth centuries or later. We look soon at some very important arrivals in the south-east corner, but for the detailed founding of village-settlements we shall have to wait for a great deal more archaeological evidence. Meanwhile we can, reasonably, indicate a few early settlements from the artefacts and the names and some speculative reconstructions that future students can perhaps put to the test.

For instance, one Suffolk place-name that was allowed by the late Dr O.K. Schramm to refer to the Romano-British was Walpole ('Welsh pool'). The pool was a broad swamp made by that lively tributary of the Blyth river. Its 'Welshness' suggests links with Iron-Age and Romano-British sites at Westhall and Chediston, and, since Walpole is an English word, also with the adjacent English there and at Heveningham, the farm of the otherwise forgotten family of Hefa, or Hefin. Another simple name recalling an early English lakeside settlement is Soham ('farm by the lake'). At the west end of Earl Soham village, south of Soham Lodge, a big reedy bog betrays the site of that original lake, and aerial photography suggests the site of the early English farmstead, and medieval records reveal its communal fishing. (Siam Hall, in Newton, near the little river above Boxford, has a similar attractive derivation and its own possible, but obscure, reference in Domesday Book. It is clearly recorded *c.*1200.) Other reasonably early names, in view of the clear evidence that the earliest of the English settlers preferred valley-gravels and that the surviving Roman roads would have disappeared totally if there had not been some degree of continuous use, are *-ford* names like Melford, the two Stratfords and Lackford.

The Wuffinga Kingdom

One ford-name may be fairly precisely datable to about 550. It is Ufford, a little above the highest point reached by the tides of the Deben estuary. It is presumed to bear the name of the eponymous Wuffa, from whom the East Anglian kings descended. (Domesday Book spells Ufford *Uffeworda* as well as *Ufforda*, which suggests, interestingly, that Wuffa had a 'worth', an enclosure, here as well as at least one ford.) The parish is distinguished by three important fords across the Deben, and lies almost directly across the river from Rendlesham, which Bede named as one of their seats, a *vicus regius*. Bede's brief allusions to the exploits of the Wuffingas, and the spectacular ship-burial commemorating one of them at Sutton Hoo, provide a few more detailed hints about the development of the human landscape in this most formative time.

Bede was specific about the *vicus regius* at Rendlesham, which he spelt out: '*Rendlaesham, id est mansio Rendili*': 'Rendlaesham, that is, the homestead of Rendil'. Bede was writing at the beginning of the eighth century, within a century of the East Anglian events he described, and, though he wrote in the distant north, his informants seem very reliable. We are thus prevented from imaginatively deriving Rendlesham from Raedwald, but it is slightly disturbing, for those of us taking place-name evidence seriously, to reflect what interpretation might be made of that important place-name without Bede's instruction. Domesday Book is the regular stand by for early spelling of most Suffolk place-names. And there, in three almost adjacent entries among the holdings of Robert Malet's mother, are Rennesham, Renlesham and Remlesham. (It appears once in Domesday Book as Rendlesham: Mendlesham is much more erratic, appearing as Melnessam, Meldeham and Mundlesham, all of which might still be phonetic transcripts from Suffolk countrymen today.) Such renderings as Evelincham, for Heveningham, make one sympathise with a possible Norman-French scribe, remembering one's own derisory efforts to say Scheveningen to the satisfaction of the Dutch. Nor is there anything in Domesday Book that would have led us to look at the topography of Rendlesham as Dr Rupert Bruce-Mitford[13] has, for the site of the great wooden hall of the kings whose necropolis, before they adopted Christian burial, was on the heath-edge above the estuary four miles downstream from Rendlesham. At Rendlesham, various possible sites for the impressive building of the kind traced at Yeavering, in Northumberland, include field-names on an 1828 map – Great Woodenhall, Great Hall Wall, Middle Hall Wall, etc. – that seem too good to be true. The occasion of Bede's reference was his description of the baptism here of the King of the East Saxons in the presence of the king of the East Angles, who helped him from the font. This was presumably a libation baptistry, a feature perhaps of churches of the time of the Conversion. One remembers the two tanks from Icklingham.

The dedication of the handsome late-medieval church at Rendlesham becomes additionally moving in the light of Bede's evidence: it is to St Gregory, the Pope who sent the first Roman mission to Canterbury in 597. Some sixty years later, a church in use at Rendlesham might very well have had him for patron. It is remarkable that the dedication seems to have survived the subsequent invasions of heathen Danes and Vikings. When we look at other Suffolk churches dedicated to Gregory we find them associated with

---

[13] *P.S.I.*, Vol.XXIV (1949), pp.228-51.

24 *Some of the famous mounds of Sutton Hoo, above the Deben (which lies beyond the top of the picture). There are possibly seventeen mounds, at least one off the picture to the right. The (covered) trench containing the royal ship is easily made out beside the farm-track.*

demonstrably early English settlements to a convincing degree. The late Alan Carter saw the same connection in Norwich.

The celebrated symbols of the former heathen rites of the Wuffingas survive among the twelve (possibly as many as seventeen) earthen mounds in the bracken of Sutton Heath (illustration 24). Pollen analysis of the soil suggests open conditions in woodland during Bronze-Age occupation, followed by the accumulation of blown plough-soil, before the site came into use as a cemetery during the century before the ship-burial. At that time the landscape presumably looked much as it does in the 21st century. Those mounds have already said more about the Anglo-Saxon world than any other archaeological remains, even Yeavering. They have been invaluable, as well, in spreading (except in one recently neighbouring farming family) a belated understanding and respect for the silent heaps of earth that remain in valley-side fields right across Suffolk. Subject to looting all through the centuries, some of them yet contain messages as marvellous as those entombed in the great pyramids beside the Nile. Associated as it is with the East Anglian kings, Sutton Hoo helps to define the political shape of the Suffolk settlement of the sixth and seventh centuries, much as West Stow helped with the fourth and fifth.

Some time then in the sixth century, the stick-in-the-mud farmers of West Stow and all those settlers in Ashfield, Finningham, and so on, whose complex settlements we failed to reduce to a diagram, were confronted by boatloads of more heroic figures from Sweden via Denmark and Friesland (both of which feature prominently in the *Beowulf* poem). They presumably made the short sea-crossing to Kent, and up to the Suffolk estuaries. If Wehha led them, he presumably came in the 520s. If it was Wuffa, he presumably came *c*.550, and may be thought to have sailed up the Deben and settled straight away in the Ufford-Rendlesham area. It has often seemed to me likely that Uffa's son, Tyttla, who succeeded *c*.577, may have devoted himself to organising the East Angles of remote central Norfolk, for Tittleshall seems to bear his name. (It lies just west of North Elmham, whose origins in relation to Billingford, Peter Wade-Martins[14] has outlined in a masterly way.) By *c*.599, the mighty Raedwald succeeded Tyttla and ruled all Britain. Within one temple, he combined an altar to Christ with another 'for offerings to devils'. His successors in East Anglia, in rather quick and painful succession, particularly Eorpwald, Sigeberht, Ecgric and Anna, saw to the establishment of a more effective Christianity in Suffolk, and ended the practical example of Raedwald. Felix, the first bishop, set up a centre of religious instruction at *Domnoc*; Fursey, or Fursa, the Irish visionary, practised Celtic Christianity at Burgh Castle; and St Botolph founded an orthodox, model monastery, famous throughout England, at *Icanhoe*.[15]

Icanhoe is nowadays agreed to be Iken, where the parish church today partly reconstructs the beautiful desolation of the marshy southern shore of the Alde estuary below Snape that early monasticism required. Signs have been found of this exemplary monastery: an earlier timber building under the present parish church, and a remarkable length of a carved Anglo-Saxon cross-shaft. *Domnoc*, if Dunwich, has been almost entirely devoured by the sea; I doubt if Mr Rigold is right in placing it at Felixstowe; anyway the Roman fort there, which Felix would have used, is also submarine. Only Burgh Castle of those three East Anglian centres of Christianity survives, its site excavated and

---

[14] *Norfolk Archaeology* (1969), pp.358-62.
[15] More thinking about Raedwald, Sutton Hoo, Botolph and Iken will be found in chapters 2 and 3, *Suffolk in the Middle Ages* (1986). Iken is illustrated overleaf.

25   *Iken Church (site of St Botolph's monastery: see p.65), near head of Alde estuary (centre picture). It catches the eye from Snape maltings, part of which is now converted into one of the finest concert halls in Europe for the Aldeburgh Foundation.*

the results are published in *East Anglian Archaeology*. All three are not only in the southern part of East Anglia, the land of the South Folk, but are noticeably coastal; a reflection of the new emphasis on maritime activity associated with the Wuffingas' kingdom. Ship-burials have been uncovered not merely at Sutton Hoo (at least twice), but also at Snape, and at Ashby (between Burgh Castle and Lowestoft). A great merit of Charles Green's book on Sutton Hoo (1963) is that he thoroughly explores the nature of the ship at Ashby Dell: 54 feet long overall, found in 1830, a more primitive build than those at Snape and Sutton, but apparently deliberately buried, and its burial therefore unlikely to be earlier than *c*.600. He also examines the sea-going capabilities of these ships, comes to the persuasive conclusion that they and their fellows were for long-shore rather than ocean-going use, and suggests that a major explanation of the close social and political connections between Kent and East Anglia was that 'Kent was the first, or last, port of call on the voyage to and from the

Baltic'. If he is right, some of those Lark Valley settlers earlier on had rowed all the way round to the Wash from the Channel coast, ignoring the estuaries that the Wuffingas made their own. One wonders why – or had they all come to Lackford on foot up the Icknield Way?

Origins of Villages, Towns and some Early Parishes

Felix, Fursa and Botolph began their great Conversion in an apparently newly oriented Suffolk. This had profound consequences for the story of the landscape, and first for the types of settlement, as we began to see at West Stow. There seems to be nothing specifically tribal, or heroic, about those descendants of *foederati* at West Stow or about their early neighbours, who may have trekked up the Icknield Way to find *lebensraum* and a place to farm. But the settlement of the South Folk in Suffolk east of the woodland is different.

Just south of Lowestoft, a warrior was unearthed from a barrow in a hollow called Bloodmore Hill near the north boundary of Gisleham (one of those identical Friesland names) in 1758. With him was a Visigothic copy of a coin of Justinian I (527-65), which makes him a contemporary and fellow-warrior of the Wuffingas. Further south, until 1974, the Rural District of Blyth related to the large and ancient Hundred of Blything, the people, or tribe based on Blythburgh, whose territory stretched from the Hundred River at Kessingland (now almost a suburb of Lowestoft), south through Southwold, Dunwich and Minsmere to that other Hundred River dividing Thorpeness from Aldeburgh, and dividing 'the people of the Blithe river' from those of the 5½ Hundreds of 'Wicklaw' (illustration 10). Wicklaw was that great chunk of south-east Suffolk, which initially centred on Rendlesham and Sutton Hoo and which constituted the heart of the Wuffinga kingdom, the lands flanking those vital estuaries of the Alde and the Deben and extending to the north bank of the Orwell and to what was soon to become the town of Ipswich.

The recorded presence of very early Christian tombs at Blythburgh, taken with the discovery of a seventh-century whalebone writing-tablet (now in the British Museum), strongly implies a royal minster at Blythburgh, presumably one of those destroyed when the Danes killed Edmund and took over his kingdom in 869. Like Edmund's body the hallowed remains of King Anna and his son at Blythburgh, and of St Botolph at Iken, were somehow preserved through the half-century, 869-917, under the Danish kings of East Anglia. We may guess that, after Guthrum's acceptance of Christianity, a Christian Danish king or one of their English successors revived the church at Blythburgh and sheltered it through the Viking storms. For in Domesday Book the market town of Blythburgh was among the hereditary (as distinct from acquired) possessions of King Edward the Confessor and William the Conqueror. And whereas the average glebe held by a Suffolk church in Domesday was roughly 24 'acres', Blythburgh church held no less than ten times that acreage. Finally, from the statements of Domesday about the *soke*, the ancient royal rights in Blythburgh, we can be reasonably confident that the large medieval Hundred of Blything is one of the pre-Danish administrative units in Suffolk that passed, more or less intact, from its tribal state, in the sixth and seventh centuries, with a *vicus regius* at Blythburgh, right through to the early tenth century when Hundreds were formed in the West Saxon tradition, and on into the Middle Ages.

We return to the hundreds later, with their remarkable boundary bridle-ways, and their enduring effect on rural and agricultural custom. South of Blything lies the very complex group of 5½ Hundreds with which Anna's daughter's foundation at Ely was endowed. During the heroic period of the Conversion, a boat-burial was undertaken at Snape, on the common heath 800 yards east of the church. Its excavation in the 1860s was imperfect, but clearly a 50-foot boat had been hauled up to this part of the heath from the estuary and buried perhaps in the 620s, in a small group of barrows (robbed by two carriages-full of reported 'Londoners' *c.*1820, and now almost entirely destroyed) straddling an ancient, perhaps Roman, road to Aldeburgh, and amid the large urn-cemetery of a well established community. It is assumed that there was an occupant of the boat, and that he was another associate of the Wuffingas, chief of a tribe known perhaps as the Becclingas, 'Beccel's people'. A small estate named Becclinga is recorded here in Domesday Book, and the name survived as one of the chief medieval manors in Snape. (A notable later Beccel became Guthlac's disciple at Crowland *c.*700.) Why was the boat not buried on a promontory down by the estuary? Mr Bruce-Mitford gives the answer: 'So that it might be buried in the pre-existing grave-field, and near the settlement this served.' There must have been a well-established settlement nearby, and it was probably near the present church. It may indeed have been nearer the urn-field and the barrows, and then moved, like those earlier West Stow villagers, to a new settlement near the church when Christianity came. Or it may always have been a rather scattered community, of which we shall trace several in the Domesday record. These were by no

26 *The Deben estuary from the tower of St Mary's, Woodbridge. Sutton is away to the left across the river, Kyson (formerly Kingston) at the right-hand edge of the picture, on the tip of the river's elbow.*

means the only tumuli on Snape Common. A fine tall one, half a mile south of the ship burial, was looted *c.*1828 by a wood-turner who built a turning-mill on top of it. Another is recorded near the church itself. High-water in Anglo-Saxon times may have come up even as high as the 25-foot contour, as one notices when one tries to explain the weird parish-boundaries of adjacent Friston.

In 2002, it is still hard to be precise about the dating of the boat-mounds at Snape and Sutton Hoo. Bruce-Mitford thought the latest coin studies pointed conclusively to a burial nearer 630 than 650 at Sutton Hoo.[16] In general, one would expect such rites to have preceded all but the earliest years of the effective Christian missions of Felix (c.630-647) and Fursa, and Botolph whose monastery was founded probably in 654, the year of Anna's death and Christian burial at Blythburgh. The missionaries' choice of this area in East Anglia must have been related to the royal activities, the consolidation of security. What we now need, if such a thing can be found, is a sixth- to seventh-century settlement-site in the Snape-Woodbridge region, an eastern 'West Stow'. Aerial photographs suggest several possibilities. But at present our slender knowledge is confined to burial-sites (of every degree of eminence). Place-names again help. 'Kingston' (now Kyson), a riverside corner of Woodbridge with a small 'hard' opposite Sutton (illustration 26), is surely an early estate of those kings. Which is a reminder that they were not neglecting the west side of their kingdom, for the earliest spellings of Coney Weston, beside Peddars Way to the north of Ixworth, *Cunegestun* and *Kinigston*, show that it was another Kingston. And this is confirmed: in 12th-century records, Coney Weston was receiving socage services, royal rights, from Barningham, Hepworth, Hopton and Market Weston. It was perhaps, like Blythburgh, a centre of one of those earliest small shires that in the early tenth century became Hundreds.

Exning, which had a Roman aisled hall in the second century, and which founded Newmarket at the end of the 12th, may have been another such place. There Etheldreda was born, perhaps when her father was inspecting his western frontier, the Devil's Dyke, against the onset of those heathen Midlanders whose army somehow reached Blythburgh and slew him. Anna's equally unlucky predecessor Sigeberht, who had initiated Felix's mission, himself established a small monastery at *Bedericesworth c.*630 and hopefully retired into it. (*Bedericesworth* later took the name Bury St Edmunds.) The town was described by Abbo of Fleury (St Benoît-sur-Loire) in the tenth century as having been a *villa regia*, another Kingston, and this may reasonably be thought to have been its status in Sigeberht's time. Here, in the early seventh century, we have the likely origins of the little town; also of the minster church of St Mary. St Mary's, the mother church of Bury, had to move to its present site to make way for the north transept of the great abbey of St Edmund

---

[16] Since this was written, the 2nd edn. of the B.M.'s Sutton Hoo *Handbook*, pp.54-64, has set out the dating evidence reliably and in full. The outside limits are now set between 615 and 640, and the likeliest date is 624 or 625, when Raedwald died.

during its late 11th-century rebuilding. This gives us the clue that the royal *vill* of the seventh to tenth centuries was probably huddled close to its wooden minster along the west bank of the river Lark in what are now the 'abbey gardens'. It probably spread south as far as the river Linnet before the great rebuilding of St Edmund's church and town in Abbot Baldwin's time, 1065-1098 (illustration 45).

There is no evidence as to whether or how the Deben 'Kingston' developed into Woodbridge, nor, apart from its name, that Coney Weston ever became much more than perhaps a large royal manor of the Wuffingas. A *villa regia* seems to have been anything from a royal manor to a major administration centre.[17] But at Blythburgh and at Bury it seems reasonable to see that the Wuffingas were organising their kingdom in ways that are implicit in the extraordinary richness of the grave goods at Sutton and elsewhere. Widespread trade involves places of trade, market places, at first confined to the neighbourhood of the royal halls, possibly, but soon involving burgesses and towns.

Their most impressive new foundation was Ipswich, which we can date fairly precisely. In Roman times the main settlement in this south-east corner of Suffolk was *Combretonium*, beside the Gipping river at Coddenham. They had a villa at 'Castle Hill', at the northern edge of Ipswich's Anglo-Saxon borough-boundary, and probably a road linking *Combretonium* with Felixstowe. There is a significant 'Peddars Way' running north-west to south-east across the southern edge of Christchurch Park on Kirby's 18th-century map: renamed Anglesea Road in the 19th century. But the earliest Anglo-Saxon settlement of any consequence in the area was across on the west bank of the Gipping, some way from the present town-centre, and associated with an important large cemetery just south of Hadleigh Road, after which the cemetery has been named.

Then, during the seventh century, *c.*625-700, Ipswich came into being on its present site. It seems first to be traceable along the line of its main east west thoroughfare, Carr Street-Tavern Street-Cornhill-Westgate Street (illustration 27). For just south of the east end of Carr Street, in Cox Lane, Dr West excavated an area close to the kilns (found in 1928) that produced some very revolutionary pottery, now called, from these kilns, 'Ipswich Ware'. As it is distinctive, it is fortunate that its date of manufacture can be fairly

---

[17] R.H.C. Davis, *Kalendar*, p.xlvi, sees it as 'a centre of economic administration ... at the head of a hundred or a lathe'.

exactly fixed, starting *c.*625, and giving way *c.*850, to what the archaeologists, for obvious reasons, call 'Thetford Ware'. Dr West's exposition of the industrial origin of Ipswich reads:

> Ipswich ware owes its origin to the Rhineland and Frisia. Dorestadt on the Lek Rhine is known to have controlled the trade routes from the Rhine and the Baltic in the eighth and ninth centuries, and it is worth while to note here that Ipswich is on the shortest route from the Rhine mouth. [He seems to think that ships would by now have been able to manage at least this distance. He adds, as 'a reasonable hypothesis' that] Ipswich owes its inception and early development to the establishment of some form of trading station in contact with the continent, almost certainly with a settlement of immigrants bringing with them the new potting techniques.

The leading authority, John G. Hurst, has summarised the date-range of Ipswich Ware in J.N.L. Myres and Barbara Green, *The Anglo-Saxon Cemeteries of Caistor-by-Norwich and Markshall* (Soc. of Antiquaries Research Reports No. 30, 1972). One find in particular, in the Ipswich kiln-area, a sherd stamped with human faces closely identical with faces in both the whetstone and the shield from the Sutton Hoo ship, seems to link the Ipswich industry, from its seventh-century origins, directly with the dynasty. In a letter to the author in June 1972, John Hurst wrote:

> Clearly most of the Ipswich ware finds in the town are eighth and ninth century, but I still think it must have started in Ipswich. There is now no doubt that Ipswich ware started between 625 and 650 ... The main Sutton Hoo bottle has been taken apart and found to be wheelthrown. This must be Ipswich ware. So if the barrow is 625 that clinches it, for the bottle is very rough and must be the start of the tradition. I am publishing this fully in D.M. Wilson's forthcoming book, *Anglo-Saxon Archaeology* (Methuen).

This pegs the east end of that main thoroughfare to the installation of the pottery, in the first half of the seventh century, and implies some connection with the quayside, as does the town's old name, spelt *Gipeswic*; the river-name, Gipping, like all Suffolk rivers except the Waveney, and perhaps the Stour, is a 'back-formation'. There is good 14th-century testimony that it took its true name, Orwell, from a spring of that name in the village of Rattlesden, not far from Bury. But 'Orwell' is now used only of the estuary at the 'corner' (*gip*) of which Ipswich has so long stood.

Now for the west end of that thoroughfare and its most important point, the Cornhill, whose south edge is delightfully flanked by the mid-Victorian Town Hall. It was long overlooked by archaeologists that the Town Hall

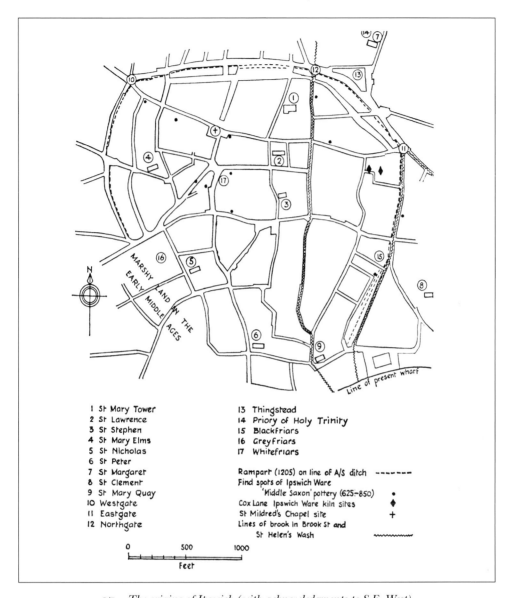

27   *The origins of Ipswich (with acknowledgments to S.E. West).*

occupies the site which the medieval Moot Hall shared with the Church of St Mildred. The whole site, unfortunately, was cleared in 1867 for the present building, so that all we have to work with is St Mildred's dedication. For once, it seems enough. It is a rare dedication, and her church occupied what appears always to have been the Capitoline Hill of Ipswich, the centre of its government. St Mildred herself died in about the year 700, at a moment when the development of Ipswich's pottery industry was well under way. At her death she was abbess of a nunnery at Minster, between Richborough and Reculver, in Kent, whose links with the East Angles we have noticed. The Wuffinga king, now old, was Aldwulf, who as a boy had seen the two altars in Raedwald's temple. His mother, Hereswith, took the veil at the very nunnery in France, at Chelles, where Mildred was educated and where they could easily have been contemporaries. The queen of Kent, Etheldreda's sister, was Aldwulf's first cousin. It is not difficult to believe that any church dedicated to St Mildred in Ipswich was founded for the Wuffingas: they may indeed have had a house where the Town Hall now stands. We can see those stock civilising influences, religion and trade, as their contribution to the development of East Anglia.

How far can we use the dedication of churches as dating evidence? Rendlesham and Ipswich inspire confidence. The vast majority of Suffolk churches have commonplace dedications, to Mary, All Saints, the Trinity, and so on.[18] In the rare cases where the dedication is to a figure connected with the Conversion, or to a local heroic saint like Ethelbert, it is fairly safe to assume a direct connection. Of course, such dedications may date only from Theodred's revival of organised Christianity after the Danish interlude 869-c.890. But that is not a long interlude and, taking all the other evidence into account, they are likely to have been genuine revivals if there had been any actual hiatus.

The few dedications that seem to be linked by St Gregory with the actual Conversion are Rendlesham, Barnham (just outside Thetford), Hemingstone (near Coddenham: it has late Anglo-Saxon work in its nave walls from the time of its first rebuilding in stone), and Sudbury. From the fact that Sudbury's name is sometimes held to mean 'southern burh' in relation to Bury St Edmunds as the northern 'burh', and remembering that *Bedericesworth* took the name Bury only in the early 11th century, it might be argued that Sudbury and its church of St Gregory, whose grey flintwork reclines venerably above the Stour in the ancient green space known as The Croft, were creations of the later Anglo-Saxon age. But Christianity in eighth-century Sudbury is indicated by the *Anglo-Saxon Chronicle*, which records a bishop's death there

---

[18] The Domesday church at Whepstead, a medieval Bury hospital, and chapels in Little Wenham Hall, Stanton, and beside the Ipswich-Bucklesham road shared the remarkable dedication to St Petronilla. Their founders, presumably, either had been on a pilgrimage to Rome or were Frenchmen: see Emile Mâle's wonderful book, *The Early Churches of Rome* (English edition, 1960).

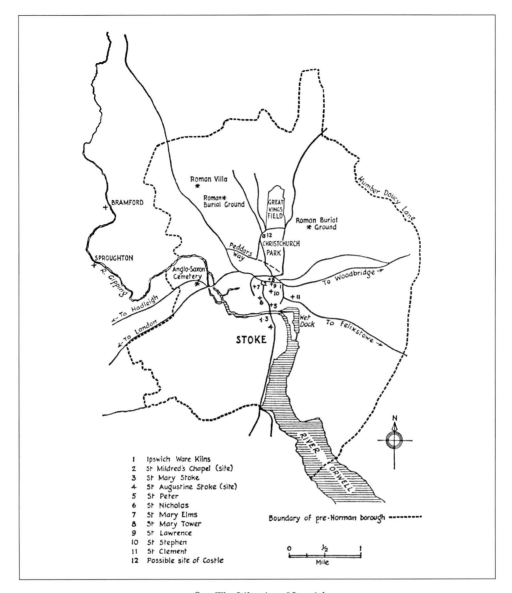

28 *The Liberties of Ipswich.*

in 797. At the end of the tenth century, bequests were made in two wills to St Gregory's church, in terms implying a pre-Danish church.

So the dedications to St Gregory suggest an early scatter of churches right across Suffolk, for the first time drawing no distinction between the clay woodlands of mid-Suffolk and the light lands on either side. This same picture is suggested by the very 'local' dedications to St Ethelbert, the East Anglian king slain at Hereford in 794.[19] And all this implies a largely settled countryside around them. We don't know the dedication of the church excavated on an island in the Little Ouse at Brandon, but a gold plaque was found showing St John the Evangelist; and the 20 rectangular wooden buildings included large halls as well as the church (Bob Carr and A. Tester, *Antiquity* 1988, pp.371-7).

King Aldwulf, involved in the founding of Ipswich, was succeeded by his very civilised son, Aelfwald. Aelfwald's encouragement of East Anglian Christianity may be assumed from his correspondence with the great English missionary, Boniface, who reformed the Frankish Church and was slain in Friesland trying to convert the descendants of those Frisians who had not emigrated. When Aelfwald died, in 749, the Wuffinga house came to an end, and their kingdom was divided between Hunbeanna and Ethelbert (or Albert). The date of this division is itself important in terms of Norfolk and Suffolk. The see had already been divided in Aldwulf's day. A generation later an East Anglian king, Ethelbert, was slain at Hereford, and naturally some Suffolk churches, as well as Hereford cathedral, were dedicated to his memory. One was at Herringswell on the brink of the Fens, west of Cavenham and Lackford, another was at Falkenham in the Deben valley between Woodbridge and Felixstowe, two more were in the thick of the clay woodland, at Hessett, near Stowmarket, and Tannington, near Framlingham: another was at Hoxne. The site, south of Burstall Hall, of a chapel dedicated to him, was recorded in a 15th-century perambulation of the Franchise of Ipswich. The Hoxne dedication does not survive. We know of it through the will of Theodred, the tenth-century bishop who reorganised East Anglian Christianity after the Danish interruption and granted his estates at Horham and Athelington to 'God's community at St Ethelbert's church at Hoxne'. The effective supplanting of this dedication belongs to the story of Norman Hoxne.

[19] Indeed it has had apparently striking confirmation in the discovery, in 1970, close to St Ethelbert's church at Larling in south-west Norfolk, of a bone plaque of *c.800* carved with the 'Wolf and twins' motif which had distinguished that sainted king's own silver pennies: Barbara Green, *Antiquaries Journal*, LI (1971), pp.321-2.

Three

A CONQUEST OF NATURE

That clearing and settlement of the upland forest which continued steadily through the later Saxon centuries, a conquest of nature more significant than the political triumphs of Alfred and Athelstan, can be read in the unconscious record of Domesday Book.

J.N.L. Myres, in *Roman Britain and the English Settlements*

The Impact of Danes and Vikings

There seems to be abundant historical, if not archaeological, evidence that by the end of the eighth century, when Ethelbert was killed, villages and churches, and so presumably parishes, were established and marked out right across the Suffolk landscape. We examine boundaries and other features later on. The place-name evidence points firmly to the conclusion that the names of most of the medieval parishes, and a great many other estates had come into existence not only by the time of Domesday Book, but before the Danish interruption of 869-917. There are barely a handful of Danish parish-names in Suffolk. Three – Lound, Ashby and Barnby – are up on the Norfolk boundary. A fourth, Risby, lies west of Bury. Wilby, sometimes cited, is not Danish, but Anglo-Saxon *Wilebey*: 'ring of willows', and appropriately Willow Farm lies near the church today, with willows leaning out from the ditches of those fields of good heavy clay. A fifth is Eyke, a late settlement in the 'oak' woods of Staverton. Otherwise there are interesting Anglo-Danish compounds, like Grimston, Gunton, Thurston, Kettlebaston and Bildeston, which can only mean that Danes and English mingled in the same settlement, the Dane dominant, perhaps, but reduced to speaking English. In a late 11th-century list of the peasantry of three of the eastern Hundreds of West Suffolk, one in every twelve peasants still bore a racial name traceable to Scandinavia, and often to East Scandinavia where, after all, the Wuffingas had come from.[1] But

[1] D.C. Douglas, *Feudal Documents from Bury St Edmunds* (1932), p.cxx.

so far as the names of *places* are concerned, the proportion is nearer one in a hundred. There are some Thorps and Thorp Halls dotted about, usually outlying hamlets in a parish. They may be Danish but it is a common Frisian name.

Rainbird Clarke showed four villages at Norwich developing, in the late ninth century and the tenth, into an Anglo-Danish town. Thetford, on the Suffolk side of the Little Ouse (and for centuries part of Suffolk), was the creation of the Danes in the late ninth century. Mr B. Davison, who examined a large area in 1964, reported that the site seemed to have been 'laid out afresh on a generous scale' in the tenth century, with large detached buildings, each in its own ditched enclosure, a spacious layout more like some early towns of eastern Europe. Four successive cobbled flint road-surfaces, 22 feet wide, suggested a high standard of 'maintenance' and so did the remarkable (and frustrating) absence of rubbish. One great range of building was over 130 feet long. Thetford is now firmly in Norfolk, but it would be surprising if some features of this kind were not once part of Ipswich. Indeed, Bishop Theodred, in his will dating from the 940s, referring to the house he bought in Ipswich, used the word *hage* ('a hedge, an enclosure') which sounds very like one of Mr Davison's 'large detached buildings' in a ditched or hedged enclosure. And, sure enough, Dr West found just such a ditch, dug to defend a single important property, its bottom strewn with iron caltrops, on the Cox Lane site close to those early industrial pottery kilns. It might be an almost unique *physical* clue that the Danes once occupied Suffolk. Dr West showed that, later on, a Town Ditch was dug, 20 feet wide and five feet deep, on the line later occupied by a great earth rampart. The Ditch encircled the built up area of the old borough and gave it its characteristic rounded shape (illustration 27). This formative outline, still affecting the street- pattern and shopping habits of thousands of people, may be presumed to date from the period of about 991-1010. In 991, the Vikings 'harried' Ipswich, whatever the *Anglo-Saxon Chronicle* meant by that, on their way to the epic Battle of Maldon. In 1010, a large force under Thurkill the Tall landed at Ipswich, after Easter. They may not have done much damage in the town. The *Chronicle* says they went 'straight to where they heard that Ulfcytel was with his levies', that is to Ringmere Heath in the Thetford area. But both episodes would have given the people of Ipswich a nasty enough jolt to get that ditch dug. The earth rampart, which still gives a part of the town its name 'Tower Ramparts', was not built up over the Ditch till the tiresome reign of John, two centuries later.

29 *South Elmham: All Saints, the Church and Church Farm. These round towers are fairly common in the Waveney district: there are 41 of them in Suffolk. Isolated churches do not necessarily imply 'vanished villages'. (See also illustration 30.)*

Both the Battle of Maldon and Ulfcytel's great battle at Ringmere ('Hringmara heath was a bed of death': it may have been fought near Rymer Point on the road from Bury to Thetford) are related in various ways to the story of the landscape. These were resounding classic battles of northern heroism, in which the Anglo-Danish leaders lost the fight against the Vikings, but not their honour.

The family of Byrhtnoth, the leader at Maldon, feature in several surviving wills referring to Suffolk estates; and the bravest and most distinguished of all, Offa, might just possibly be commemorated in the name of Offton, in the Ipswich hinterland. If it be objected that most Suffolk parishes had their

30 *South Elmham: All Saints Green, away from church and hall, and part of a more complex system (see illustration 31). The shape of the Green is comparable with Wickham Skeith's (p.61). The site of a mill-mount is in the bottom triangle. This is conceivably a Bronze-Age landscape (O. Rackham, 1986, pp.156-8).*

names long before this, we have also to explain the very interesting group of parishes immediately to the south-east of Bungay (illustration 31). Four of them bear the name Ilketshall – St Andrew, St John, St Lawrence, St Margaret – and together with All Saints, Mettingham, and St Mary and Holy Trinity, Bungay, formed a district known, at least in the 18th and 19th centuries, as 'The Seven Parishes' (in contrast to the group of parishes lying immediately west, across the Roman Halesworth-Bungay road, which are known as 'The Nine Parishes' of South Elmham, or sometimes simply as 'The Saints').

A famous predecessor of the late Anglo-Saxon earls of East Anglia was Ulfcytel, or Ulfkell Snillingr. *Snillingr* is the Norse for valiant, and after his great battle against Sweyn, in 1004, East Anglia was known in the north as Ulfkell's land. Though his name was not rare, it is permissible, in the circumstances, to see it surviving in Ilketshall, as Ekwall recognised. 'Hall' may be the Old English *halh*, a 'secluded corner', rather than 'hall' meaning a building, for that meaning seems to make its first appearance in Domesday Book and very rarely before. In any case, if his hall was in these parishes, its site may be marked by what is now known as 'The Mount', a large, conical mound of earth, all scrub covered, in Ilketshall St John. But his base is more likely to have been in Bungay. Bungay, whose name seems to mean 'island of the reed-dwellers', occupies the neck of an almost complete loop of the Waveney, a good defensive position. Early defences, deep ditches dug by Angles or Danes, are still visible to the north of the town, in the old railway goods-yard, and to the south of the town in Quaves Lane. Steep slopes to the river provided defences enough on the east and west sides.

The most prominent feature of Bungay, apart from its two churches and its ruined castle, is Outney Common, about 400 acres of rich grazing in the 'outer' loop of the river, which provides it with a natural moat and lovely open views across to sloping fields and woods on the Norfolk side. Outney Common is matched to the south-west of the town by Stow Fen, 88 more acres of common grazing. Both commons are 'extra-parochial', the one managed by common-reeves, the other by fen-reeves. The common-reeves have for centuries been appointed by the owners of 'beast-goings', common-rights attached to different properties within the two medieval town-parishes. Each 'beast-going' counted as pasture for two head of cattle, and being freehold, many have been sold to non-residents over the years. Stow Fen lies north of the medieval site of Stow Park, which, like West Stow, has yielded pagan Anglo-Saxon remains. These extra-parochial commons of Bungay

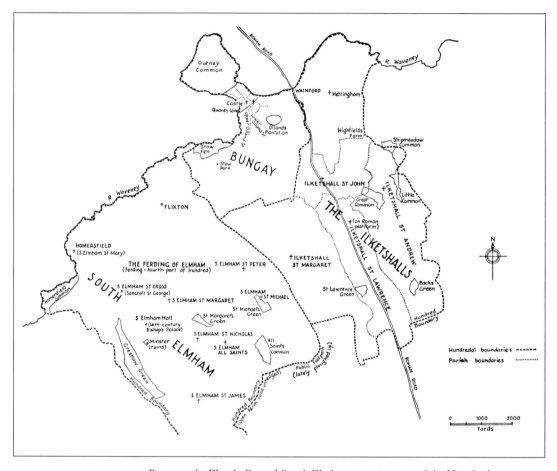

31 *Bungay, the Ilketshalls and South Elmham: components of the Hundred.*

provide the key to the basic structure of much of the landscape of Suffolk. Although, with the commons of Ilketshall, they seem to go back no further than the time of Ulfkell Snillingr, when we go on to look at the adjoining landscape of the East Anglian bishops, we find indications that some of the landmarks are pre-Danish and indeed go back to those formative years of the Conversion. In this process, we shall have a chance to understand the part played by the Hundred in the making of the landscape.

Looking at the map of Bungay, the Ilketshalls and South Elmham, we are looking at two western parts of the 'Hundred of Wangford' as it appeared in Domesday Book and right through to the 19th century. Wangford presumably took its name from 'Wainford', the waggon ford where the Roman road crossed the Waveney slightly east of Bungay, and which one supposes was a natural

I *Blakenham chalk quarries from Blackacre Hill.*

II *Badingham. Decaying barn and sugar-beet harvest on boulder-clay.*

III *Icknield Way in Cavenham, just west of Black Ditches. Medieval pack-horse bridge.*

IV *Thornham Parva's partly Anglo-Saxon church and Grimm's Ditch, a Roman boundary.*

V *Oulton St Michael, originally Flixton St Michael, a very early, very rich, foundation.*

VI *Little Livermere church and mere: M.R. James country.*

VII *Sapiston Ford: Robert Bloomfield country.*

VIII *On the Orwell, Stratton Cliff and Levington Marina from Trimley foreshore.*

IX *Freston Tower: Tudor Ipswich merchant's 'folly' lookout above the Orwell estuary.*

X *Freston Tower: view down the estuary.*

XI *Ipswich from Freston Tower.*

XII   *Cow pasture opposite Wilby Manor House: how Arthur Young would have seen High Suffolk.*

XIII   *Little Glemham boulder-clay cover of the central farmlands of Suffolk.*

XIV   *Hadleigh church and Deanery, by Thomas Gainsborough.*

XV   *Hadleigh Guildhall, facing the south side of the church over the graveyard.*

XVI *Chillesford, at head of Butley Creek. Tower of Coralline Crag, which is seen in pit beside Mill Lane.*

XVII Holywells Park, Ipswich *by Thomas Gainsborough. A windmill on Stoke Hills on the horizon.*

meeting place for the Hundred. These Hundreds, as recorded in Domesday Book, were brought into being in the middle of the tenth century after East Anglia, as part of the Danelaw, had been reconquered by the English (West Saxon) kings. The Domesday-Book Hundreds, like Wangford, were compounded of older estates and units, with even older boundaries. The bounds of South Elmham, one of the components of Wangford, may be seen, in illustration 31, to follow a planned, rectangular lay out related to the line of the Waveney, and discussed later. The rest of the boundary is still marked out by long stretches of footpath and straight field-hedgerow, both of which are suddenly beginning to vanish, after all these centuries, for the greater convenience of the combine-harvester. One might accept this slightly more philosophically if the farming in the neighbourhood were conducted with less general disregard for the appearance of the landscape than has lately been evident in the Rumburgh corner.

The most spectacular of the surviving hundred boundaries in Suffolk divided Bosmere from Hartismere, and in one place was as impressive as any landmark of its kind in England. It wound boldly eastwards across the clay from the main Ipswich Norwich road in the form of a trackway, or lane, drained and defended on either flank by a formidable ditch (lately vanished). The point at which it could be seen is OS. 119628 – slightly less than a mile and a half to the north of the Stonham Magpie Inn (with its well-known sign, framing the whole road), and just a mile to the south of the 1,000-foot mast of the I.T.A.'s television transmitter. (To the west of the main road, the Hundred Lane has lately lost its ditches, and looks like any farmtrack. In 2002, that impressive boundary east of the main road has been bulldozed into oblivion in the ordinary, rich surrounding fields: its picture, in Pl.17 of the first edition of this book, is replaced by one of a less commercially vulnerable section of the lane in Highrow Wood, Helmingham. See illustration 32.)

Another remarkable Hundred Lane runs from Nowhere Farm and 'High Pastures' on the Wyverstone-Wetherden boundary, and runs north towards Allwood Green, formerly Hallow Green, a scene of 'inter-commoning' between parishes and itself still bounded on one side by a great hedge.

We now return to Bungay, Mettingham and the Ilketshalls, and to the adjoining Elmhams, in the west part of Wangford Hundred, along the south bank of the Waveney. Bungay's 'urban area' now occupies only two or three hundred acres; but there is a hint in Domesday Book that urban development may have begun. The total area of Bungay, including its commons, is about

32 *The Hundred Boundary between Bosmere (left) and Thredling at Highrow Wood, Helmingham (OS 197584). The great hedged and ditched bridleway dates back, presumably, to the first half of the tenth century, possibly even as far back as the seventh century. See p.83.*

2,500 acres, its southern boundary related to the line of a stream about a mile and a half to the south of the built-up area. Domesday Book shows the whole of this in the most active state of cultivation, in two main 'manors' of nine carucates and five carucates (roughly 1,000 and 600 'acres' respectively), apart from several smaller estates, and 'manors' as small as 30 'acres', a quarter of a carucate. There were then five churches in Bungay. How little related their endowments were to the size of the estates they belonged to! The church attached to the thousand-'acre' estate had only five 'acres' of its own, while a church attached to a freeman's holding of seven 'acres' had an endowment of eight 'acres'. Not a word was said about pasture, though there was a good deal of woodland for swine, and varying amounts of meadow, with each of these busy ploughlands. Furthermore, several sheep and goats and a few cattle were recorded. For some reason, pasture was not recorded in the Domesday account of Suffolk, or rather was recorded in only one celebrated and significant instance: 'In Colenes Hundred [lying between Ipswich and Felixstowe], there is a certain pasture common to all the men of the Hundred.'

In Bungay, there must have been pasture, on Outney Common and Stow Fen. And, at least on Stow Fen, it is likely to have been common to part of the Hundred. Both were 'extra parochial', which immediately suggests that they were part of the Hundredal organisation. Look now at the four Ilketshalls on the map. Their common pasturing arrangements are mostly concentrated in Ilketshall St Andrew, of which White's 1844 *Directory* records: 'Its houses are scattered round the margins of several *Greens,* lying east of the other Ilketshalls and being, like them, in the Duke of Norfolk's Liberty.' The first part means not that this Ilketshall went in for pasture farming while the others concentrated on cereal growing, but that all of them were planned and laid out as a unit with arrangements for 'inter-commoning'.

Indeed the whole of the 'Seven Parishes', referred to as 'the Duke of Norfolk's Liberty' and descended to him from the Bigod family who built Bungay Castle in the 12th century, was a unit from at least the pasturing point of view. Whether it was a fundamental unit before the Conquest cannot be discerned from Domesday Book, as one of the two chief holders in 1066 was the grasping archbishop Stigand, whose presence may well have been an unseemly interruption. There are other indications that this Liberty was a unit from before the Conquest, and even from before Ulfkell's day, whoever this Ulfkell may have been. The landscape itself says this plainly enough. Ilketshall St Margaret appears to have no pasture at all of its own. White's *Directory* explains: 'A limited number of the tenants of the four parishes of Ilketshall have the privilege of pasturing a certain number of cattle on Stow Fens.' Such elaborate inter-commoning arrangements are unlikely to be later adjustments: it would have been against human nature!

The inference is, then, that when the hundred of Wainford came to be 'marked out' in the tenth century it was made up of a series of existing units, one of which was organised from Bungay, and included what was called Ilketshall though that name and some of its settlements were perhaps acquired only after the formation of the hundred. The ancient parish boundaries of Ilketshall St Lawrence are strikingly laid out with two long sides (almost three miles long) parallel with the Roman road. Though these parish boundaries are no longer marked by ditches or hedges, the entire landscape of field-boundaries here is a vast series of parallelograms aligned on the Roman road. There is not a scrap of evidence to suggest the presence of a Roman villa nearer than Chediston (a parish which is itself something of a parallelogram). Yet it is highly likely that when the East Angles and the Danes started farming the area they found some regular marking-out of the landscape by their forebears, for their own inclinations as farmers were not at all towards the rectangular. Late Iron-Age ploughing and Roman centuriation may underlie all this, for such landmarks survive only through use. Neighbours still speak of South Elmham people as 'the Welsh'.

The other signs are these, for what they may be worth. The church of Ilketshall St Lawrence stands on a rectangular earthwork 'said to be' Roman. The road through the parish is indubitably Roman, as indeed might also be the transverse Waveney valley road. And if the name of the parish immediately to the south-west, Rumburgh, really begins with *hruna,* a fallen tree (A.H. Smith), *burgh* suggests something more impressive, though the area is admittedly now devoid of all earthworks other than the fine moats around the church of the former priory. The most formidable earthwork of the district lies in an area immediately west of the Ilketshalls, within another of the large components of Wainford hundred, known as the Elmhams. It is perhaps the co-axial field systems of this (and other) areas that are most significant.

South Elmham

The Elmham earthwork is a rectangular ramped and ditched enclosure of four acres and, though the recorded finds have been few, it is accepted by the archaeologists as probably Roman. Within sits the ruin of a church of a most unusual plan, known locally, in the Middle Ages and afterwards, as the Minster (illustration 33). More than this, the enclosure itself sits within the whole area of several parishes called Elmham, whose common boundary is a rectangle measuring a little over four miles by three, its north side on the Waveney, its east side parallel to the Roman road a mile or more away.

How does one explain this extraordinary arrangement of the landscape? Its part within the Hundred of Wainford is recorded. It was a *ferding,* that is, one-quarter of the Hundred. (We may guess that Bungay and the Seven Parishes made up another quarter, and that the third division, including the town of Beccles and 11 other parishes, was reckoned at half the Hundred.) As a unit, this *ferding* of Elmham may go back beyond the tenth-century formation of the Hundreds to the seventh century, or even earlier. Mr Derek Charman, who has made a study of the medieval manorial organisation of this and the adjoining half-Hundreds, Mutford and Lothingland, has pointed

33 *South Elmham Minster, see pp.86–90. The gap in the right-hand wall represents the west doorway, leading into the narthex.*

out the singular relationship of Greshaw Green, the major common pasture of this quarter-Hundred, with the site of the minster itself[2] (see illustration 31).

In the Middle Ages, the leet-courts began, like the Hundred courts, as royal, or folk, courts; they gradually became feudal and manorial. One of Charman's most important discoveries is that 'a large part, if not all, of the Commons in both the half-Hundreds appear to have been under the direct control of the leets, and were sometimes specifically described as belonging to the Hundred'. At Mellis, too, near Eye, the vast Green was administered by the court-leet, which in the 19th century was still called the *Hundred* Court. His other very significant conclusion is that he saw 'no example of evidence anywhere in Mutford or Lothingland of any common right of pasture over the open fields after the harvest – which was the normal bane of open field

[2] Mr Charman's studies remain unpublished. Dr John Ridgard has in the press an extremely interesting article on references to South Elmham Minster in the Account Rolls of South Elmham Manor: *P.S.I.*, Vol.XXXVI (1987).

agriculture'. This is a corollary of the organised provision of common pasture, or Greens, or Tyes (as they are called from Stowmarket south across north-west Essex to Hertfordshire). It meant that the freemen and sokemen were free to enclose their lands as soon as they liked, a licence of great consequence for the landscape. For the moment, we notice the commons of Bungay and Elmham, and their possible connection with the creative days of the Wuffingas.

Greshaw Green lies at the gates, as it were, of South Elmham Hall and Minster. What is to be said about the date of this ruin and its meaning in terms of the landscape? I addressed my observations to the Society of Antiquaries in 1963, and they have been admirably summarised by Peter Wade-Martins in the interim reports on his work at North Elmham.[3] They concern the location of the diocese of the East Angles and the possessions of its bishops during the early stages of their extremely effective mission; they thus affect one's views of the origins of Suffolk churches, and their organisation in deaneries (groups of ten) within the Hundred.

St Felix started work in about 630, at *Domnoc*, perhaps Dunwich, where nothing remains of his church. Nor are there any other remains of a seventh century church fabric in East Anglia, but at South Elmham the ruin called the Old Minster is *in plan* unlike any other church building in England except the seventh-century churches of Kent and Essex. (That link at once suggests the activity of the Wuffingas.) With them it has the most striking affinities of size and proportion. It differs from them in having a square west chamber (the same width and build as the nave: it *might* be the base of a tower) with twin doorways leading into the nave. This feature is not paralleled in Kent or Essex, but Sir Eric Fletcher has lately reminded us[4] that 'a seventh-century church in England, not identifiable by literary evidence, is recognised by the absence of normal Saxon characteristics'. Mr A.B. Whittingham, the leading authority on East Anglian church fabrics, thinks the present ruined stone structure of the Old Minster dates from *c.*1050. It incorporates, below its south-east wall, part of a carved stone Anglo-Saxon coffin-lid, which shows it to be a rebuilding in the vicinity of an earlier church; and its plan strongly suggests that it occupies the exact site of a seventh-century building, presumably wooden. But it now seems more likely, from the field-walking of Mike Hardy, that the site of a seventh-century church stood in close proximity to South Elmham Hall.

---

[3] *Norfolk Archaeology* (1969 and 1970). The Report by Norman Smedley and Elizabeth Owles on the excavations of 1963 and 1964 at South Elmham appeared in *P.S.I.*, Vol.XXXII (1971).
[4] 'Early Kentish Churches', *Med. Arch.*, Vol.IX (1965).

The second of Felix's successors, Bertgils Boniface (*c*.652-*c*.670), was bishop at the accession of Aldwulf, whom we associated with the founding of Ipswich and St Mildred's church there. Bede noted that Bertgils was a man of Kent, and, indirectly, that he was closely associated with the bishop of Essex. He is just possibly a builder of a church with this remarkable plan, and set in this very significant (especially if Roman) earthwork, at South Elmham. Fursa's Irish mission had been established in the Roman fort at Burgh, lower down the same river. If the name Dickleburgh means what it says, their message had spread up river (Diccul was one of Fursa's disciples). Might that be a reason for the Roman mission to have set up shop at South Elmham?

Bertgils' successor, *c*.670, was called Bisi, and Bede recorded that when Bisi was still alive but infirm, presumably not before the 680s, two bishops were consecrated in his place. Thereafter, until the Danish Conquest in 869, there were two bishops in East Anglia. In the later years they signed themselves Dumnoc and Elmham, and because bishops are known to have been seated after the tenth century at North Elmham, the modern textbooks of Anglo-Saxon history all assume that North Elmham was the site of the second see from the moment of its creation late in the seventh century. Yet years of accomplished excavation at North Elmham have made it increasingly plain that the earliest phase of that building belongs to the late ninth or early tenth century.[5]

If Bisi's predecessor had already built a church on his estate at South Elmham, it would be a natural one for a second bishop to occupy, still within reasonable reach of the government of the kingdom. That probably continued at Dunwich, though doubtless, like the bishops, the kings moved about a lot. (In Essex, Bishop Cedd's cathedrals outside London were both together in the south-east corner, at Bradwell and Tilbury.) At South Elmham, the second bishop could exploit the successes of the Irish mission in the Waveney valley, which anyway provided a convenient waterway.

It also provided the Danes with an obvious main entrance. They were covetous rather than pointlessly destructive. What is known, as we saw earlier, is that Theodred, the bishop of London, revived Christianity in East Anglia. Another thing his will (written in the 940s) reveals is that many of his own personal estates were in Suffolk, indeed in the Waveney valley. We have noticed

---

[5] In his report, *Norfolk Archaeology* (1971), p.264, Peter Wade-Martins moved towards an interesting idea of the 'symmetrical dwelling site plan' of 'a pre-Danish cathedral community' at North Elmham. It might suggest an earlier move from south to north: a possible date would be 750.

his bequests to St Ethelbert's church at Hoxne. He also left ten pounds to be distributed 'for his soul' at his episcopal estate (*'min bishopriche'*) at Hoxne. And the stock that he had added there to be divided between the Minster (presumably St Ethelbert's) and the poor. Now Theodred seems not to have died before the 950s. But a new 'bishop of Elmham' was consecrated apparently in 942. This may be the moment when North Elmham came into being as the seat of the Elmham bishops: it seems to fit the archaeology. He would not have needed to be at South Elmham with Theodred only four parishes away along the Waveney at Hoxne. When Theodred died there remained and continued only one East Anglian bishop. By the time of Domesday Book, the church on the bishop's great manor at Hoxne was described specifically as 'the seat of the bishopric of Suffolk in the time of king Edward the Confessor'. By 1066 the bishop was Ailmer, Archbishop Stigand's brother. He founded a small priory[6] at Rumburgh in the parish of Wissett, just south of the rectangular boundary of the quarter-Hundred of South Elmham. If Mr Whittingham is right about the date of the stone walls of the Old Minster, it was Ailmer who had them rebuilt, not long before the Normans came.

Domesday Book recorded that the Normans were already busily 'developing' the town of Dunwich, but that, of the two carucates (240 'acres') of farmland of the main manor in 1066, only one carucate remained in 1086: 'the sea made off with the other.' It is possible that any Roman site and associated seventh-century cathedral church had also by then been carried away. This would explain Hoxne's becoming the new southern seat of the East Anglian bishops. It might also explain the care of the late Anglo-Saxon rebuilder to preserve the proportions of the surviving mother-church of the diocese at Elmham. There it took its place among the various minster churches recorded in late Anglo-Saxon, more precisely Anglo-Danish, Suffolk, and notably in the Waveney valley. *Minster is* the Anglo-Saxon form of *monasterium*, and implies the presence of a religious community. Apart from those recorded in contemporary wills, at Stoke-by-Nayland, for instance, there was a group of churches taken over by the Norman FitzGilbert of Clare from his Anglo-Danish predecessor, Wisgar (well, so-called by the French), including Long Melford and St Peter's, Ipswich, that were almost certainly minsters from their extremely rich endowments recorded in Domesday Book.

But in Suffolk the only building that has preserved the name *minster* down to our day is the ruin at South Elmham. It also seems to be the one building

---

[6] Dedicated to (St Michael and) St Felix, his only surviving ancient dedication in Suffolk.

associated with an original deanery, in the sense of a group of ten churches, the parishes contained within that large South Elmham rectangle, three miles by four, the quarter of the Hundred of Wangford. Domesday Book shows that all the 'Almeham' churches were in being by 1066. But, as the map shows, not all the parishes were called Elmham. Here, once more, we are reduced to isolating some extraordinary coincidences and posing them against the linguistic findings of place-name students, if we are to resolve the history of these miles of High Suffolk, and of the East Anglian see, and of the Hundred. They all point to a pre-Danish date for the episcopal connections with the South Elmham *ferding*.

Domesday Book shows the bishop's manors and estates in Norfolk parcelled out fairly evenly over the western half of the country; one estate in each of 11 Hundreds. (In east Norfolk the acquisitions are late, by Stigand, and have no bearing on the argument.) In Suffolk there is a different picture. First there are the bishop's two personal estates, one at Hoxne derived from Theodred, the other at Homersfield. Homersfield occupies the north-west side of the Elmham rectangle. Then Domesday Book records that the bishop has 'sake and soke', the royal rights, over the '*ferting of* Almeham', the whole rectangular quarter-Hundred, and goes on to list the 35 estates of the 'Bishops Fee', the feudal possessions of the bishopric, as distinct from the bishop himself. Their distribution is remarkable. They are almost entirely related to the Norfolk-Suffolk boundary, the Waveney valley. There is a group of 14 small estates in Hartismere, another of the Waveney valley Hundreds. The most notable of all is the tight cluster within the Elmham rectangle, where the whole area is marked out into some 15 estates, mostly called Elmham but some in Homersfield, and others in a place called Flixton. Finally, there are two erratics. One of them need not detain us, but the other, very notable, a whole carucate of arable, a half-share in a water-mill, and so on, was in another place called Flixton, 15 miles away down the Waveney, in Lothingland half-Hundred. Furthermore, it was held of the bishopric by St Michael's church there, which suggests another minster church, for a carucate is at least five times the holding of the average village-church, or estate-church, in Domesday Suffolk.

So the main bundle of the bishopric's estates in Suffolk lay in the quarter-Hundred of South Elmham whose rectangular outline and close connection with the Hundredal organisation suggests a very early shaping. Those estates within the group not lying in a place called Elmham, lay in Homersfield or

Flixton. Homersfield is spelt *Humbresfeld* in Domesday Book, which Ekwall translates as 'Hunbeorht's *feld*', or open-space. The name of the last East Anglian bishop recorded before the Danish interruption, or, rather, of one of the last pair of *joint* bishops before that unsettling experience, was Hunberht. It does not seem impossible that in some way the place-name, since it is embedded in this episcopal bundle of estates, refers to Bishop Hunberht. It seems equally likely that the name Flixton refers to the first bishop, Felix, especially in view of that isolated Lothingland possession of the bishopric, also called Flixton. Given the relatively small number of the episcopal estates in relation to the scores, indeed hundreds, of Suffolk settlement-names in Domesday Book, can it be seriously held to be a mere coincidence that two of them happened to be in widely separate places of that name? Only if it can equally be thought a coincidence that two of the major episcopal estates in pre-Conquest East Anglia with two ruins that have reasonable claims to be the seats of the Anglo-Saxon bishops find themselves in otherwise unconnected landscapes called Elmham. (Elmham is a rare enough name.) It is not unreasonable to think that the new East Anglian bishop appointed in Theodred's day wished to perpetuate in Norfolk the old name of the former northern seat in Suffolk, much as early Norfolk settlers took Castle Rising's name to Wood Rising, or Field Dalling's to Wood Dalling: and very much as more recent pioneers have taken names from the East Anglian landscape to the New World.

The most obvious connection between the two Flixtons, since their land was among the scattered possessions of the bishopric, is that these estates came to the office by ancient title, that of having been possessions of the first bishop himself, Felix, long before the Danish intrusion. No document survives to prove this, but there is logic. Felix began under the aegis of the Wuffingas in the coastal heathlands east of the Woodland, and perhaps to the west in Exning and Barnham St Gregory and the Breckland. But meanwhile Fursa's visionary message was spreading from Burgh Castle, in Lothingland. The visions included perhaps the first well-attested glimpse of the Hell that found only slightly more sophisticated expression in such supernatural landscapes as that painted eight centuries later on the wooden tympanum in Wenhaston church. We know on the authority of the *Liber Eliensis* that Felix founded a church at Reedham, an aptly-named Norfolk parish immediately across the broad estuary from Burgh Castle. We may fairly guess that, in the process of keeping in touch with St Fursa's mission, the bishop became associated by name with the Flixton-in-Lothingland which, after the Danish and Viking

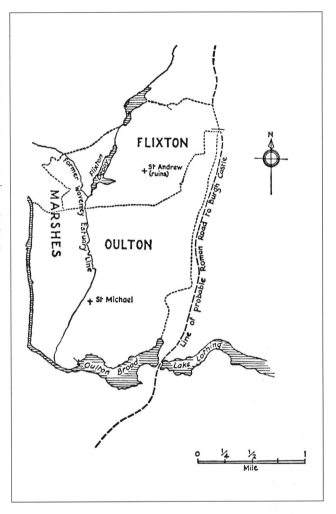

34 *Flixton-in-Lothingland, and Oulton's origins. The short eastern stretch of Flixton's boundary (with Corton), coinciding with the A.117, is called Stangate in an early 17th-century estate survey. In this area of Danish settlement, 'gate' meant 'street', so here was a length of 'stone street' – arguably Roman. It looks as if this was once all Flixton, the successor to a small Roman estate. See bottom of page and over.*

incursions, was among the more distinguished possessions of his late Anglo-Saxon and Norman successors.

His church at Reedham was destroyed by the Danes. So, probably, was the church we suppose he built at Flixton. All that survives now in the reduced parish is the ruin of a church dedicated to St Andrew whose roof blew off in the famous tempest of 1703. The surviving herringbone-work in Roman tiles running through the flint rubble of the south wall suggests a Norman structure almost identical with that of the post-Viking church at Reedham. The tiles themselves suggest the remains of a Roman building reasonably close at hand.

It is unlikely that St Andrew's was the original church of Flixton. Illustration 34 shows the area covered by Flixton at the time of Domesday

Book. St Michael's in what is now Oulton was the mother church: holding that large estate of the bishopric, it was one of the ten best-endowed churches in Suffolk in 1066. The name *Aletun*, the estate of someone called Ala, appeared about a century after Domesday Book, and later became Oulton. Who this prosperous Ala was need not concern us here, but he managed to get hold of the greater part of the ancient Flixton. St Michael's with its central brick tower (basically Norman) and simple Norman doorways, is clearly a post-Viking building (and like Reedham church in many ways). It may well be a rebuilding of an earlier church founded by Felix. For it occupies a superb site on a low ridge above the marshes, where it would have been at the edge of the waters of the Waveney estuary in his day, looking west to Burgh St Peter. St Felix came to England as one of the second generation of Pope Gregory's mission. It was Gregory who caught a glimpse of the Archangel Michael sheathing his sword over Hadrian's mausoleum, the castle of St Angelo, beside the Tiber. It is not too fanciful to see in St Michael's church above the Waveney an allusion to Gregory's famous vision.

To summarise, I think that the whole *ferding* of South Elmham (including Flixton-by-Bungay) and also the estate at Flixton-in-Lothingland (now in Oulton) which together constituted the main body of the bishop's Suffolk estates in Domesday Book, were among Bishop Felix's original endowment by the Wuffingas. So much detail about the quarter-Hundred of Elmham and the bishopric's possessions in the half-Hundred of Lothingland seemed worth exploring to see some actual churches rising among the farms, and also to discuss some of the ways in which the Hundred contributed to the landscape, not only at the time of its formation in the tenth century, but perhaps as early as the seventh in the case of the *ferting* of Elmham. Elmham also supplies useful material for comparing linguistic explanations of place-names with a study of the settlements themselves. Knowing nothing of the distribution of the estates of early East Anglian bishops, compilers of place-name dictionaries naturally translate Flixton as 'farm of Flick'. This is reasonable, for Flick is a good Suffolk surname today, though I cannot trace it back before the 1524 Subsidy list. Nor can one be sure that it is not derived from Felix, for an East Anglian saying Felixstowe invariably clips it down to Flickstoo.

In the hundred of Wangford, driving over the expanse of (the former) Greshaw Green, one sees more clearly than perhaps anywhere else in East Suffolk the Hundred's part in, for instance, the arrangement of common pasturing in a society composed largely of freemen and sokemen. It does not follow that all the Greens in Suffolk were affairs of the Wuffingas, or go back even to the tenth century. Many seem to have been purely local affairs of the manor. But there is much more work to be done on such questions. Before we take a more general view of Domesday Suffolk, we must glance quickly at the very few surviving descriptions of Suffolk estates before 1066.

Late Anglo-Saxon Wills and Estates

So far, the Anglo-Saxon and Anglo-Danish outlines of Suffolk, at West Stow and Ipswich, Bungay and Elmham, and in the Hundreds, have been found by digging, and by historical inference, rather than by contemporary specification. Yet five detailed 'perambulations' survive, describing in Old English the boundaries of large estates as they were walked, or ridden, in the tenth century. They bring pre-Norman Suffolk a degree more clearly into focus.

The earliest is the old royal township of Bury, over which St Edmund's first collegiate church was given the royal rights by the king in 945. The boundaries recited at that early date coincide precisely with those of modem Bury, except in the west, where bits of Westley and Fornham have lately been brought in and subjected to wholesale suburban housing. We need not rehearse them here, as the whole perambulation is worked out clearly in *The Early Charters of Eastern England* (1966, pp.54-8) by C. R. Hart, who rightly declines to reject the charter's authenticity on the grounds that the early surveyor was hazy about the points of the compass: Dr Hart is himself affected, and turns west instead of east in *Hamarlund*, 'the grove with the smith', at the point where the public bridle way (signposted to 'Tollgate Lane') and Beeton's footpath reach the line of the Kentford-Ixworth Roman road. The lapse is forgivable in the excitement of this guided walk through the landscape of Anglo-Danish Bury.

The bounds of Stoke (illustration 28), which is the 'Southwark' of Ipswich, were described in 970. Stoke counted as 'ten hides', that is, as a tenth of a Hundred (hides), and was one of the many lavish endowments of Etheldreda's monastery at Ely. The Hadleigh Road cemetery of those first pagan English in the Ipswich neighbourhood, when the Wuffingas were founding their kingdom, lies just within the bounds of Stoke. As at Bury, the perambulation follows the modern boundary at all checkable points, and here a 1352 perambulation[7] helps with the identification of the 970 landscape. (The best Anglo-Saxon text is in E.O. Blake, ed., *Liber Eliensis*, 1962, p.113.) Leaving the

---

[7] Nathaniel Bacon, *Annalls of Ipswiche* (1654, ed. W.H. Richardson, 1884).

Orwell estuary at Bourne Bridge and following the bourne (*brunna*), we reach the ford-site now called Belstead Brook (then called *Theofford*, or Thetford, 'the ford of the people, or tribe'). We strike off up past Gosford Hall (and a great sprawl of new suburbs), on past a 'holy well', or spring (? at Firtree Farm), and then down the London Road and across to the Hadleigh Road Industrial Site; which in 970 was *Healdenesho* (? Haldane's, or perhaps Halfdan's *haugh*, his rising ground, or spur), and by 1352, below that spur, was called *Holdessie vally*, a more pastoral image than our modern one. From *Healdenesbo*, Ely's Stoke boundary ran back down the river past Pottaford, *Hagenefordebrycge* (Handford Bridge is thus our earliest recorded bridge in Suffolk) to *Horse wade* (another ford) and past a marsh mill to Stoke Bridge (the second earliest recorded Suffolk bridge).

The tree-shaded water-meadows and brick bridges and old plastered houses of Chelsworth are among the most idyllic experiences in all the Suffolk landscape. Furthermore, the village has the useful historical survey[8] it deserves. These boundaries of Chelsworth in 962 have now been triumphantly established by Dr Cyril Hart in *The Danelaw*, 1992, ch.15, 'The Earliest Suffolk Charter'. This is a monumental pioneering book. There is a reference to a *street* (a Roman road), but Chelsworth is one of the places where two Roman roads must have touched the parish; once, according to Anthony Syme, at Clay Hill, running along the west side of Chelsworth Park, and, secondly, where the Coddenham-Melford road may have framed the NW edge of the parish. We seem reduced to only one certain fixed point, 'the stream that runs into hollow fen, *culan fenne*'. After a thousand years, the meadows at the boundary opposite Nedging are still called 'Culfens'; and the entire boundary can still be followed, with Dr Hart's book and sheet TL94 of the 2½-inch OS map.

That grant of 962 was from the king to Aethelflaed. Her sister Aelfflaed, wife of Byrhtnoth, the hero of the unforgettable battle at Maldon in 991, did everything she could to ensure with the king their family's endowment of the *halgen stow*, the 'holy foundation', at Stoke (in this case, the church at Stoke-by-Nayland), where their ancestors lay buried. One thing Domesday Book revealed, only two or three generations later, is that despite her precautions almost all those landed endowments had been snaffled (should one say 'acquired'?) by another leading Essex family, that of Robert FitzWimarc, a Breton who skilfully anticipated the Conquest and served both the Confessor

---

[8] Geoffrey R. Pocklington, *Chelsworth*, privately published.

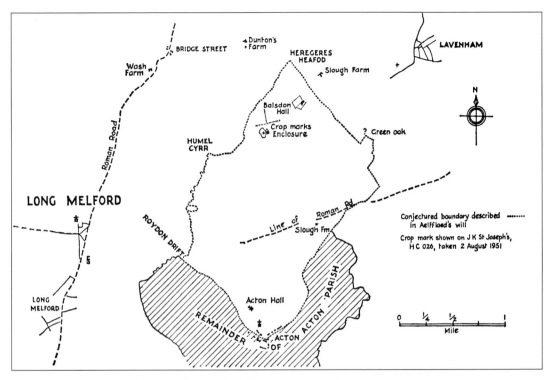

35 *The boundaries of Balsdon, a late Anglo-Saxon estate.*

and the Conqueror as sheriff. And the great church of Stoke spent the Middle Ages as one of the endowments of Prittlewell Priory, a 'holy foundation' of the FitzWimarcs.

An adjoining pair of those estates, four carucates in Withermarsh and four in Polstead, have their boundaries described in Aelfflaed's will, but, as at Chelsworth, many of the details so far defy all attempts to relate them to the very agreeable features of those places. However, the boundaries of Balsdon, one of Aelfflaed's family gifts the FitzWimarcs missed (it went to a thegn, Seward of Maldon), are much more identifiable, and we can walk them with confidence (see illustration 35).

Balsdon Hall, now little more than a cottage, stands within and beside magnificent moated enclosures not far from one of the winding roads that connect Lavenham with Long Melford. The estate was reckoned at five 'hides' by Aelfflaed. As described in her will, it occupies the northern half of the parish of Acton, and there its bounds coincide exactly with those of the parish. In Domesday Book, Balsdon is not mentioned, but must be contained in the large Acton estate, 12 carucates, held by Seward. Here the carucate seems to be equivalent to the hide, and Seward had added to Balsdon the poorer lands to the south, including Babergh Heath (whose name suggests that it must have been the meeting–place of the Hundred of Babergh). Babergh was extensive and counted as a double Hundred, so Balsdon, with five hides, would have found 'one-fortieth of Babergh's Danegeld'.

These were the boundaries of Balsdon at the beginning of the second millennium. We start at the stream at *Humelcyrre*. *Humol* is a rounded hillock, and *cyrr*, as in the surviving place-name Stanton Chair, means a corner, or bend. This exactly describes the location of 'the Humblechar meadows' given in a note in Parker's *History of Long Melford* (1873, pp. 241, 279, 285), so we know exactly where to start perambulating: the meadows lie at a pronounced bend in the stream that runs on down past Long Melford Hall, originally turning the Hall mill at the mill-ford. At this point a tributary stream runs in from the north-east. Its valley is followed by a path and by the track of the abandoned little Sudbury-Bury branch-line, whose trains puffed up this old boundary line for one of its long centuries of existence. As the boundary-path rises above the gully, it passes the invisible site of the earliest known settlement of Balsdon, a pair of irregular round ditches with what looks like a native farmstead, perhaps of the Romano-British period, tucked into the slope just below Hawk's Grove. The boundary continues to climb between Paradise Wood and Lineage (formerly Lenynge) Wood until it comes to two concrete strong points of World War II and the Lavenham-Bridge Street road. This is where the Gospel Oak stood.

At this point the Acton parish boundary comes to a head and turns at a sharp angle to the south-east. We have reached the next point in Aelfflaed's description. It is *Heregeresheafod* which means Heregere's *headland*, a point where the ploughs would turn. In a conveyance of 1305, two pieces of Humblechar meadows were described as lying between those of David of Hereford and those of William Bonde. Ordinarily one would suppose David came from Hereford, but here his name may be a contraction, after three centuries, of *Heregeresheafod*. Next year he witnessed another very local conveyance by Ralph of Dunton.[9] Dunton's Farm is only half a mile from this point at the head of the Balsdon boundary. Now we follow the Acton parish boundary along what was already known as 'the old hedge'. Alas, most of it has been grubbed right out. A bit survives alongside the 'Green Willows'

---

[9] Parker's *Long Melford*, pp.285-7.

Building Estate, one of the latest attempts to suburbanise Lavenham a little more. The old boundary wobbles just here, probably because it was marked only by 'a green oak', which might easily have been confused with others, and lost over the centuries.

'Then on till one comes to the paved road', the Roman road. Here its course is still plain, as a green lane beside School Farm and then as a most impressive hedge alongside Slough Farm (Acton), which looks for all the world like a Slough factory. At this point Aelfflaed's Balsdon boundary leaves the parish boundary and runs 'along the shrubbery until one comes to Acton-village', that is, along the present road into Acton. 'Then from Acton till one comes to Roydon.' This is still marked by Roydon Drift. 'From Roydon back to the stream.' We have completed the parallelogram of Aelfflaed's five hides. By extending his Acton estate to 12 carucates, Seward created the complete parish boundaries of Acton as they are today. When we look, now, at Domesday Book and find over 400 churches already recorded, it will be reasonable to assume that many of them will already have achieved boundaries that are identical with a large estate like Seward's at Acton. But we shall find some churches that are associated with small farms within a whole grouping of estates within a vill. How soon the boundaries of such a parish and vill were established is something that needs much more careful study.

The Domesday View of Suffolk
Many men have devoted their lives to the mysteries of the Domesday record. It has been studied as a record; and as a source of constitutional, social and economic history: by men interested in documents as such, or in manors, or in villeinage or sokeright. For the next county, Essex, the formidable J.H. Round displayed with great virtuosity what Domesday Book could do. For the whole of England, Professor H.G. Darby has elicited and analysed what he calls the Domesday Geography. What I look for is the Domesday Topography. I am less concerned with aggregates and wholesale distribution, more with actual location, to see whether we can get any picture.

Darby gives a vivid *overall* picture of the county, with the surviving woods recorded in just those parts which still retained the name 'the Woodlands' when Kirby was writing *The Suffolk Traveller* (1735): they were concentrated from Mendlesham and Thorndon across to Mendham and Bungay and Leiston. And he shows the highest density of plough-teams, four to the square mile, in the good strong claylands across the middle of Suffolk – indeed falling

36   *Watermill, open trestle postmill and smock mill beside the Lark at Fornham St Martin, c.1870.*

below three to the square mile only in the Breckland and Fenland of the north-west corner. Meadowlands he shows lavishly distributed in small acreages over every part of the county except the Breckland. Pasture, as distinct from mowing meadow, is apparently recorded only in the reference to the Hundred of Coleness (i.e. in the southern part of the peninsula between Orwell and Deben): 'There is a certain pasture common to all the men of the Hundred.' Usually, as we saw, grazing on commons was common to men with rights in smaller units than the Hundred.

   In terms of the configuration of the landscape, Darby's reconstruction of all the recorded mills on a map of all the Suffolk streams and rivers is most evocative. Windmills, whose sails gave mechanical movement to the landscape for seven centuries, were not introduced until a century after Domesday. All these mills in the record are therefore presumed by Professor Darby to be water-mills. (Can one rule out the alternative, slower, process of stones turned by plodding animals?) He counts them in 178 different settlements, as many as five and a half in Bungay. (Half a mill, like half a church, in this record means 'a half share, or right, in': the assumption is that there were six actual mills, but that one half-share, at least, has been missed by the recorders.) The most precise physical description that occurs is *molinum hiemale*: 'winter mills' certainly suggest a position on a stream so near the water-shed or in so level a plane, that there was enough water to turn the wheel during the wet months only. They were recorded in the middle-west of the county, from Rickinghall and Pakenham, down to Cockfield, Edwardstone and Groton. Pakenham's water-mill, among the sheep and the Roman remains at Grimstone End, with the tower windmill standing proudly on the ridge behind it, is one of the most picturesque watermills in Suffolk today. But standing as it does between Micklemere and Pakenham Fen, it may well have had trouble in getting going in 1086. All these mills were a sure index of heavy corn-production.

Suffolk's network of streams is vital to the draining off of her heavy clay cornlands. The perception of these (sometimes extremely gradual) water-courses, in the early stages of their run down to the Minsmere River, or the Lark, or the Stour, is a most delightful part of the process of getting to know the landscape: as essential to the discriminating tourist as to the working farmer. A most rewarding time awaits the person who undertakes to locate on the ground the likely sites of all these Domesday mills. None appears to be impossibly high and dry. On the other hand, the assignment in Domesday Book of a saltpan (for the processing of salt from sea water) to the small estate of eight sokemen at Hintlesham, inland from Ipswich, seems strange: the explanation probably lies with the Hintlesham sokeman called Suart who also held 30 acres in *Canapetun*, which seems to be the Domesday scribe's rendering of 'Chempton', properly spelt Chelmondiston. There, Pin Mill, beside the tidal Orwell, certainly had a saltpan. The saltworks and fisheries were naturally distributed round the coast in both east and west. Some of the most profitable fisheries were along the shore of the Fen, from Freckenham round to Lakenheath, where eight villeins held an estate with four 'fisheries' in Ely, and one fishing boat.

The farmlands themselves provided the great mass of the material of Domesday Book. In Suffolk over 2,400 estates are recorded (Mr. Welldon Finn has lately counted 2,481, excluding boroughs and the land attached to churches: my own count makes it 2,438, *including* boroughs, but not the church lands. The difference is unimportant compared with the availability of this rich quarry of detail.) These estates (holdings is really the best word: *tenementa*) vary extremely in size. In Coddenham, in an owl-haunted valley then known as *Uleden* but now unidentified, one of these holdings was only a quarter of an 'acre', 'worth 2d.'. A freeman held it of 'Brictmar the Bedel', and presumably had other holdings elsewhere, or he would have been dead from malnutrition. At the opposite extreme, one of the biggest of the 221 estates in Suffolk taken over by the Conqueror's trusted henchman William Malet, who built the castle at Eye, was Leiston. 'He held Leiston as a manor and as twelve carucates of land.' So it was identical in taxable size with Seward of Maldon's expanded Acton manor (with Balsdon), and suggests that these carucates were relatively rough assessments: also that a 'duodecimal system' operated. There is not much difficulty in showing that a carucate was, in Suffolk, reckoned at about 120 'acres'. Malet's Leiston estate was thus reckoned at 1,440 'acres'. But what is often uncertain in the text is when we are looking at a real acre, and when, as we mostly are, we are looking at a hypothetical acre, one that is just a unit of fiscal assessment. It is not necessary to try to resolve this here. If I refer to carucates, and translate them into equivalent 'acres', it is solely to gain an idea of the possessions of one holder, or one church, in relation to those of another.

It is astonishing that four out of every five of Suffolk's 500 medieval churches were already in being in 1066, that is, at the end of the Anglo-Saxon period. Few of them have retained any of their Anglo-Saxon features, possibly because most of them were wooden, like the famous little church at Greenstead, near Ongar, in Essex. With only one exception, those churches which do retain features (whether in their stonework or their dedication) that make it seem probable that they were pre-Conquest foundations, are found to be recorded in Domesday Book. That exception is Falkenham, whose dedication to St Ethelbert we have noticed. Domesday Book devotes much detail to a fuss at Falkenham. It had belonged to an unfortunate East Anglian, Brictmar, whose estates were being divided among three Normans. When Roger Bigot was sheriff he summoned two of the Normans to appear before the Hundred, who awarded it to the one who appeared. The other claimed he was never summoned, and so on. I mention all this because it might explain how the scribe failed to mention Falkenham's church.

There are, inevitably, omissions in the Domesday record. It has been shown, for instance,[10] that a church with 20 acres of land in Harpole, a hamlet now known as Thorpe Hall, in Wickham Market, was omitted from Domesday but recorded in the contemporary *Inquisitio Eliensis*. My own impression is not that this proves many omissions to the record, rather the reverse. This is why I labour the point about Falkenham. I incline to feel that omission from this record is a serious, but obviously not final, argument against the existence at that time of a church – even of a landless one, for a number 'without lands' were included.

Ignoring Falkenham's patron saint, and perhaps some small pieces of carved stone dug out from under the south aisle floor at Halesworth, it is hard to feel strongly that any feature of the 140 medieval churches omitted from Domesday Book dates from before 1066.[11] In subsequent years of prosperity, rebuilding has removed all obvious signs of pre-Conquest building except in 13 places: Little Bradley, Bungay (Trinity), Claydon, Debenham, Great Fakenham, Gosbeck, Hemingstone, Herringfleet, Little Livermere, Redisham, Syleham, Thorington (near Dunwich) and Thornham Parva.[12] Little Livermere, for years 'unsafe', still exhibits some early features in its fabric (illustration 50). I say no more here of South Elmham Minster, whose plan seems to be early Anglo-Saxon though the structure itself seems to be an 11th-century rebuilding. It incorporates in the fabric a piece of carved Anglo-Saxon stonework. Gosbeck has hitherto been counted missing from Domesday. People have forgotten that it was originally called Easton; it assumed the name Easton Gosbeck from its chief manorial lords to distinguish it from two other Eastons, in two other Hundreds. This one is recorded, with 14 acres, as Easton in Bosmere Hundred. It has dropped the word Easton only since the 17th century.

I reckon that 418 Suffolk churches were recorded in Domesday Book. Adding the 141 built later in the Middle Ages, we can see that there were at least 558 medieval Suffolk churches all told. Almost 500 remain standing, many of them now threatened with redundancy, alas, in our over-peopled,

[10] Victoria County History, *Suffolk*, Vol.II, p.9.

[11] See my article on 'Domesday Churches' in *Historical Atlas of Suffolk*, 1999 edn., which accompanied the map reproduced above on p.16.

[12] H.M. and Joan Taylor, *Anglo-Saxon Architecture*, Vol.II (1965), list only 11 in Suffolk. They overlook Bungay Trinity, Little Livermere, Redisham, Syleham and Thornham Parva. They include Burgh Castle (on inadequate grounds), South Elmham Minster, and Flixton by Bungay (on the evidence of Suckling's *Suffolk*, which may be acceptable; it is maddening that no satisfactory drawing seems to survive from before Salvin's rebuilding). In Herringfleet's admirably constructed round tower the Anglo-Saxon features are combined with Norman ones, and indicate a building of the end of the 11th century; which reduces the number to twelve.

37 *The landscape of scattered farms at Old Newton, near Stowmarket. Church Farm stands beside a tributary of the Gipping. 'The subtle beauties of the Boulder Clay lands depend on an awareness of the water-courses.'*

financially incompetent society.[13] Of the rest, the sites of 19 are at present lost. This leaves some 28 whose sites are known: like those at Fordley (in Middleton churchyard), or Creeting St Olave's, or Harkstead St Clement's[14] down beside the Stour. The sites of the nine Dunwich churches are now interesting only to aqua-lung enthusiasts (see pp.166-7).

But the rest, the sites of the 400 or so pre-Conquest Suffolk churches provide the true bone structure of the historic landscape. Nowhere else in Britain is it at all feasible to go out into the country, look around at so impressive an array of churches, and know that you are looking at points fixed on the human landscape even before that decisive battle on 14 October 1066, when Bremer, a freeman, of Dagworth, a hamlet of Old Newton, near Stowmarket, died fighting in Sussex. Norfolk's Domesday record of churches is a hundred fewer than Suffolk's. Nowhere but Suffolk can display so rich an Anglo-Saxon *pattern* of church buildings.

About the choosing of their sites, one can only speculate. The name Trimley, near Felixstowe, is spelt *Tremelaia* in Domesday Book. That means island, or perhaps clearing, of the tree cross (Old English: *treo-mael*). This suggests a site hallowed by a very early cross; and since two of the Trimley churches mentioned in Domesday stand together in one churchyard (illustration 84), the cross presumably stood there. One would love to know what was 'holy' about the 'stow' at West Stow: perhaps no more than the early establishment of a Christian church. Anglo-Saxon bishops, like later missionaries, made a point of establishing Christian altars on pagan holy places. Bede described the Wuffinga king who compromised with the bishops to the extent of combining pagan and Christian altars in one temple. Ellough's church, near Beccles, is another that might be thought to replace a heathen temple of the Norsemen: for *elgr* was a Norse word for temple. If so, it appears not to have replaced it by the time of Domesday Book, which records no heathen temples either. Churches built on Roman or Iron-Age earthworks or cemeteries may all be in this same category: they include Burgh (near Woodbridge), Ilketshall St Lawrence, Kedington, Stowlangtoft (very impressive), perhaps Ubbeston. Shottisham should probably be included in this group. Once a church was established it was seldom moved, for its site soon grew hallowed, not least through the Christian burial of the dead.

---

[13] See the Rev. John Fitch's magnificent manifesto, *The Churches of Suffolk: Redundancy and a Policy for Conservation* (1971), published by the Suffolk Preservation Society.

[14] A field in the tithe map of 1839 is called 'Myrtle bones' – perhaps meaning 'mortal bones'. This is the third field upstream from that marked on the 2½ inch O.S. map as being the site of St Clement's church.

It is often remarked that most of Suffolk's ancient churches stand isolated, out on their own. People brought up among concentrated Midland villages imagine there must have been some similar village near these Suffolk churches, and then usually postulate its extinction by the Black Death. Yet there is no evidence that these churches were ever accompanied by any such villages, were ever at the heart of some great uniform three-field agricultural system. Everything in Domesday Book suggests the opposite.

Let us look for a moment at Badingham church. It is sensibly fixed not more than a mile and a half from the farthest of the scattered settlements listed in Domesday Book under the heading of Badingham. This presumably means that the whole area of settlement was recognised as bearing this name. We would think of the area as some sort of civil parish. They thought of it as a 'vill', a component of lete and Hundred, and a convenient word, embodied in our own village. (The trouble with the word 'village' is that it connotes a *concentration* of rural houses along a 'village-street': such concentrations are not common in Suffolk, and are often 'late' developments in response to a market, in the 13th or 14th centuries, or later still.) Within Badingham, the names occur already in Domesday – such as that of *Colston*, now represented by Colston Hall. Badingham itself is presumed to mean the village of Bada's '*ing*', his descendant kin or folk. The site of that may easily be the great deserted medieval moat that once enclosed Badingham Hall. Like the original West Stow settlement it is a longish walk from the church. The name, like so many other Suffolk names, seems to go right back from us to Domesday Book, miraculously unchanged, and from Domesday Book back perhaps five more centuries or so to the time when Bada's kinsfolk got down to the business of clearing and farming these heavy but rewarding clay slopes on both sides of the steep little valley of the upper Alde. The valley may mark the way they first arrived.

At some stage, we can never know when, they or their descendants built the church, on a site called *Burstonhaugh*, the haugh (spur) of the settlement of the *geburs* (cottagers). Old Suffolk men have been heard greeting one another as 'bor' in the 1960s, it forms part of the word 'neighbour', and it was still relatively common form in the 1930s. Here, below the church, the cottages are still grouped. Just south of the church, the Old Rectory, with 60 acres in Domesday, now sports a small park. The church with its stout, square-built tower (Norman within) is oriented more north-east than east: see how the sundial on the south porch has had to be slewed to face south. The dedication is to John the Baptist, and the sun rises straight through the east window on his Feast, which is Midsummer Day. Perhaps, as Lilian Redstone suggested, Bada's folk were induced to replace their pagan mid-summer celebrations with a church ale.

Over and over again one notices in Domesday Book that there are several estates within a vill, some of them small manors, some just holdings of a few acres. In Finborough, for instance, which is now divided into Great and Little, and from which Finningham might in the early days of settlement have hived off, Domesday Book shows a cluster of nine estates. Here the church is part of the biggest estate, which is described already as a manor. This probably explains why Great Finborough today has the appearance of a 'traditional' English village, with church and Hall, pub and cottages forming a centre. But for a view of the true character of the Suffolk landscape, notice a more significant revelation of Domesday Book. This is the way the church is very often recorded along with one of the smaller estates within the 'village'. In Ilketshall, there is no record of a church associated with Burchard's manor of two carucates (240 'acres'), or with two other largish manors. But a freewoman with an estate of only 20 'acres' (and one and a half acres of meadow) had a church with 20 'acres'.

Whatfield, near Ipswich, provides an interesting example of a number of these 'Suffolk' characteristics, and we look at it, side by side with Aldham, in a moment. For anyone who expects to find archaeological traces of a former main village-site, in present-day 'scattered villages', in close proximity to the church, this association of the church with minor freemen, or groups of freemen, and women, within the vill is worth watching. It helps to explain the apparently rather haphazard scatter of the churches among the farms. There is also extensive Domesday evidence of *shares* in churches, which survives in the present-day practice of taking turns to present new incumbents to a living. It suggests the founding of a church by agreement between groups of farmers. In those circumstances, they might well have agreed to build it at a point mutually convenient and accessible to them all. In Worlingham, by Beccles, there were two churches (one of them presumably at what is now North Cove): 'others have part therein', says the Book. In Loudham (now in Pettistree), whose well-endowed church long stood as a picturesque ruin in the park in front of the Hall, 'several persons have shares therein, *ibi parciuntur*'. In Bedingfield, near Eye, six freemen with 80 acres had a fourth part of a church with six acres. And so on.

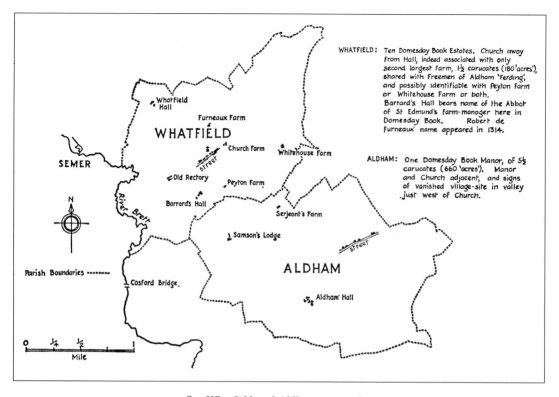

WHATFIELD: Ten Domesday Book Estates. Church away from Hall, indeed associated with only second largest farm, 1½ carucates (180 'acres'), shared with Freemen of Aldham 'Ferding', and possibly identifiable with Peyton Farm or Whitehouse Farm or both. Barrard's Hall bears name of the Abbot of St Edmund's farm-manager here in Domesday Book. Robert de Furneaux' name appeared in 1314.

ALDHAM: One Domesday Book Manor, of 5½ carucates (660 'acres'). Manor and Church adjacent, and signs of vanished village-site in valley just west of Church.

38   *Whatfield and Aldham: two settlement patterns.*

Now for Whatfield and Aldham, near Hadleigh. Whatfield's simple Anglo-Saxon name shows that *wheat* was grown in open ground (where the woodland had been cleared). This was before the Danes arrived, but how long before is something we shall not know unless datable Anglo-Saxon or earlier pottery or other objects are found.

In 1086, Domesday Book described a complex series of ten estates, mostly small farms of 15 or 60 or 100 'acres' (an eighth, a half or five-sixths of a carucate). But two were bigger estates, both belonging to St Edmund's abbey at Bury, and presumably managed by Berard, described elsewhere in Domesday Book as 'the abbot's man'. The first of the two may have occupied the west side of the parish, associated with what is now Whatfield Hall (see illustration 38): it amounted to two and a half carucates of arable (300 'acres') and seven 'acres' of meadow, down beside the river Brett towards Cosford Bridge and Kersey, where cress grew. It measured six 'furlongs' by five. Berard himself held 120 of these 300 'acres'.

The second of the abbey's large estates here was partly in the *ferding* of Aldham (that is, in the tax-group comprising Elmsett and Aldham), and partly in what Domesday Book calls *alia Watefelda*, 'the other Whatfield'. This amounted to 180 'acres' of arable, and was presumably located in the area of the Whatfield/Aldham boundary: it measured six 'furlongs' by three, and was held by six freemen in Aldham and ten in Whatfield. Forty of these 180 'acres' were held by Berard himself. (Berard also held 100 'acres' in Whatfield from a Norman called Robert-the-son-of-Corbutio. Barrard's Hall, moated, upon a ridge with fine long views east and west, presumably stands on the site Berard's Hall occupied in those early days of Norman rule.) The most interesting fact recorded of this second estate of St Edmund, lying partly in Aldham and partly in 'the other Whatfield', is that here was the church, with two 'acres' of land of its own. We know that this must be Whatfield church, for Aldham church, with seven 'acres', is recorded elsewhere in Domesday Book.

So Whatfield church belonged originally not to the whole vill or place called Whatfield with its ten estates in the time of William the Conqueror, but to the 180 'acres' farmed jointly by 16 freemen, six living in Aldham and ten in 'the other Whatfield'. This 'other Whatfield' is presumably represented by the neighbourhood of Whatfield Street, the homely line of cottages and houses, and the *Five Horse Nails Inn*, and so on, that leads up to St Margaret of Antioch's church. In the chancel roof, Edward III and friends appear to the life.

Looking from the white wooden gate across the mown grass of the churchyard to the plaster covered walls of the old building, one no longer sees anything earlier than about the year 1300. The church of those 16 freemen was presumably a modest wooden building, replaced *c.*1300 and 1370 by the fabric Whatfield people have gathered to worship God in ever since.

By contrast, Aldham's church went with Aubrey de Vere's large manor, five and a half carucates, 660 'acres', and the landscape confirms the picture. At the head of a small gulley, Hall and church stand together, the venerable round flint tower, with its small red-brick openings, glorious in evening sunlight, and the earthworks of a slightly more extensive settlement casting their faint shadows in the slopes below. Built into a window-jamb in the nave, part of the shaft of a stone cross is carved with interlace of perhaps the century before the de Veres came with the Conqueror. But Aldham means 'old farm', and there are presumably four or five blank Anglo-Saxon centuries of farming to trace.

Domesday Book's chief contribution to the record of the Suffolk landscape is its patient listing of over 2,400 holdings of land, in complicated ways that must have bewildered some Norman scribes, as they baffle all but the most dogged students. But it shows unambiguously that the plough had conquered all except the very peripheral woodlands of each parish. In displaying, in detail, the two chief forms of 'village' ('scattered' and 'nucleated'), side by side, and by showing the early forms of the ownership and development of our phenomenal inheritance of churches, it reveals the essential structure of what had now become the most densely settled of the counties of Norman England.

Even so, the landscape was by no means equally filled with people. The light sods of the Breckland in the north-west had only three recorded people per square mile. This probably means ten or eleven people in all per square mile: the generally accepted multiplier for the recorded population (mostly heads of households) is 3.5 to arrive at a total population, though Domesday statistics are the subject of endless argument. Still, nothing alters the fact that the most densely peopled part of the county, the Hundred of Claydon, had seven times as many people as the Breckland. Claydon Hundred begins at the north borough-boundary of Ipswich, runs through Claydon (where the Hundred meetings were anciently held: Claydon parish covers clay slopes above the Gipping river, and has an archetypal name), and stretches on northward to Helmingham and Debenham, through which the young Deben flows (illustration 62). The whole of the clay 'Woodland' country had sixteen to twenty recorded people (households) per square mile. These are the extremes: much of the remainder of the county was settled at an average density of ten to twelve households.

If we measure the degree to which the Suffolk landscape had been brought under cultivation by the number of plough-teams per square mile, it shows just the same wide variation. The central claylands had about seven times as many teams at work as the Breckland. The latter, with its multitudes of sheep, would never offer much more scope for human expansion in terms of taming the natural landscape. (Ironically, these areas of earliest woodland clearance are those in which the modern human economy raises the densest coniferous forests.) Clearly there was still room for movement into 'fresh woods, and pastures new', both in and beside the central uplands. The villages and parishes of 1086 continued to grow for perhaps a further 200-250 years (eight or nine human generations) before they reached their particular frontiers.

Some of Domesday Book's most telling, indeed sensational, descriptions concern the growth of towns. With their dynamic stories we turn to survey the medieval landscape.

Four

THE MEDIEVAL LANDSCAPE

Giant Pedantry also will step in, with its huge *Dugdale* and other enormous *Monasticons* under its arm, and cheerfully apprise you, That this was a very great Abbey, owner and indeed creator of St Edmund's Town itself ... that its lands were once a county of themselves ... that the monks had so many carucates of land in this hundred, and so many in that ... Till human nature can stand no more of it ... Another world it was, when these black ruins, white in their new mortar and fresh chiselling, first saw the sun as walls.

Thomas Carlyle, *Past and Present*

The Towns

Suffolk grew wealthy early. The natural resources were these: her closeness to the mainland of Europe and to the capital city of the realm, combined with her peculiar population and productive soil. The easterly position meant first that the land was entered and colonised by migrant farmers from across the sea in the Low Countries and the Baltic, and then – indeed almost simultaneously – was all ready to take part in trade with those not entirely foreign parts. The Sutton Hoo ship-burial gave proof of very wide intercourse: 'Frankish, Scandinavian, central European, Byzantine and beyond'.[1] An extremely early English coin has been thought to bear the name of Raedwald's successor, Eorpwald (?625-632). In their generation, Bury acquired a minster church and by *c.*700 Ipswich was taking shape. The landscape was being conquered by an active and unusually 'free' people, whose medieval customs, especially of landholding and inheritance, have close affinities with those of medieval Friesland (the seven *seelande* that formed the coastal strip between the Scheldt and the Weser). This is not surprising, but G.C. Homans' comparative study is not widely enough known.[2] For 'Dutch' influence in the Suffolk landscape is certainly not confined to buildings with stepped or curving gables.

Recovered after the Danish conquest, Ipswich, Bury and Sudbury assumed the form of *burhs*, towns with a ditch or other water-barrier that the whole

[1] *The Sutton Hoo Ship Burial: a Provisional Guide,* British Museum (1947). Vol.I of the definitive study appeared in 1975; Vol.II, 1978; Vol.III, 1983.
[2] *Econ. Hist. Review* (Dec. 1957): I think he only slightly overstretches his material.

township could defend against outsiders. The Norman idea was different. They at once started to build castles, primarily for their own families' defence within so many alien and 'free' communities. Then they produced Domesday Book, which gives an incomparable account of these communities.

Account-books are not everyone's favourite reading, and the English called this one 'the day of judgment'. It showed that Suffolk was the most thickly populated county in England, with as many people as Devon, where there was nearly twice as much land. In Suffolk only 909 slaves were recorded: invaluable to a colonising society, but a liability once it is stabilised. A more notable figure is that of the recorded freemen. With no fewer than 7,460, Suffolk had well over half the total recorded for the rest of England. Here is the measure of Suffolk's economic and social lead, a main ingredient in her physical difference. Taken with the fairly widespread custom of partible inheritance (equal division between children) and the freedom to alienate 'socage' land, it is easy to see how an active market in small pieces of land, of a fairly modern kind, was well developed by the end of the 13th century. In these circumstances, feudal and manorial ideas were slow to make headway against the Old English 'royal' and 'folk' customs of leet and Hundred. But feudal ideas were themselves an encouragement to prosperity in growing towns like Eye and Bury, at least to begin with.

So Suffolk was able to stay among the most flourishing English counties until the opening up of the New World in the 16th century put the Atlantic ports ahead and reduced the relative affluence of Suffolk's coast. In 1524, Suffolk (including Ipswich) was the fourth wealthiest county, coming after Kent, Devon and Norfolk, and equal with Essex. Among the provincial towns of England in that year, Ipswich ranked as the sixth or seventh richest, after Norwich, Coventry, Bristol, Exeter, Salisbury, and possibly, Newcastle, which was not taxed that year.

Though Ipswich was an exception, market towns usually developed before industrial towns. Domesday Book records markets in nine Suffolk 'towns'; and we can be sure the list is incomplete, and that they were already established in Bury, Ipswich and Dunwich, for instance. They were recorded at Beccles, Blythburgh, Clare, Eye, Haverhill, Hoxne, and Kelsale (a place-name the recorder made much play with, writing it *Kereshalla, Chylesheala,* which without the final Latin 'a' is nearest to modern pronunciation, *Kireshala, Cara(m)halla,* and *Cheressala*: discouraging to strict derivationists), and at Sudbury and Thorney (now Stowmarket). This is a long list of market towns compared with those recorded in other counties in 1086.

MEDIEVAL MARKETS

SHOWING DATES OF GRANTS & MARKET DAYS

Belton 1270 M

Flixton 1253 W
Oulton 1307 M
Lowestoft 1308 W

Carlton Colville 1267 F 1295 Th
Kessingland 1251 T

Covehithe 1298 M
Easton Bavents 1330 W
Southwold 1221 Th

Dunwich 12th cent ? Daily

Beccles DB. S

Brampton 1271 M
Sotherton 1226 Th then W
Blythburgh DB Th ? 1324 M
Middleton 1270 F
Kelsale DB ? 1312F 1391T
Leiston 1265 W
Saxmundham 1272 Th
Sizewell ?1237
Aldeburgh 1547 W 1568 S

West Hall 1229
Wissett 1267 F
Halesworth 1223 T
Bramfield 1270 Th
Kelton (Benhall) 1292 T

Orford c.1154 M 1256

Bawdsey 1283 F

Bungay 1199/1200 in use 1228 Th

Whittingham (Fressingfield) 1267 T
Stradbroke 1227 F
Laxfield 1226 S

Framlingham in use by 1270 T F S
Kettleburgh 1265 W
Wickham Market in use 1377

Pettistree 1253 Th
Woodbridge 1227 W

Croxton (Kirton) 1270 W

Sholey 1303 F

Hoxne DB.S then F 1227 W
Eye DB. S

Earl Soham 1307 Th

Clopton 1304 T
Grundisburgh 1284 F
Great Bealings 1227 T

Ipswich DB. perhaps daily after 1200

Erwarton 1254 F

Botesdale 1220 Th
Burgate 1272 M
Westhorpe 1372 T
Wyverstone 1231 F
Mendlesham 1280 T
Haughley 1231 S

Debenham 1221 F

Needham Market 1226 W
Earl Stonham 1327 W

Witnesham 1227 Th

Cattawade (Branham) 1247

Market Weston 1263 S

Walsham le Willows in use 1384

Woolpit

Stowmarket DB.1338 T

Ringshall 1270 S
Great Bricett c 1135-54 T

Raydon 1310 S

East Bergholt ? pre 1495

Stratford St Mary 1384

Ixworth 1384 T

Bury St. Edmunds DB, W, S &?

Felsham 1268 F

Lavenham 1257 T

Brent Eleigh 1260 Th

Bildeston in use 1348 W

Kersey 1252 M

Stoke by Nayland 1303 W

Nayland 1227/8

Brandon Ferry 1319/20Th

Long Melford 1235 Th

Sudbury DB S &?

Bures St Mary 1271

Lakenheath 1201 Th 1309 W
Mildenhall 1220 1412 S
Worlington 1270 W

Barrow 1267 S

Ousden 1254 W

Lidgate in use 1279 Th
Thurston (Hawkedon) 1290 T

Clare DB. F
Stoke by Clare c.1247-52 T

Freckenham 1218
Exning 1257 M
Newmarket c.1200 T

Moulton 1298 W

Great Thurlow 1272 T

Haverhill DB. W

Grey - MARKETS STILL IN USE IN THE 17TH CENTURY

Black - MARKETS OUT OF USE BY THE 17TH CENTURY

⬡ - MARKETS RECORDED IN DOMESDAY BOOK 1086

0 1 2 3 4 miles

39 *Medieval and later markets.*

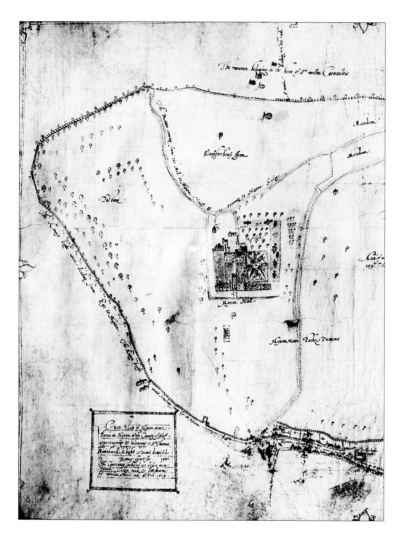

40 *Hoxne. The site of the bishop's Anglo-Saxon manor house, and market place on green at bottom right, 1619. (From map in East Suffolk Record Office; west is at the top.)*

It is much more than a list, it describes the places we see today. The best example is, perhaps, that of Hoxne and Eye, where the coming of the Normans created a crisis for Theodred's episcopal successor in his estate at Hoxne. At Hoxne, the site of the market is a small, wedge-shaped green at the heart of the 'village', to the south of the large medieval church of SS Peter and Paul, and to the east of the Anglo-Saxon bishop's manor-house. That house stood just in the crook between the Dove, on its way north into the Waveney, and the Goldbrook running into the Dove here from the east. In 1619, an estate-map (illustration 40) showed that the house had acquired a four-storeyed tower gatehouse in its main front. The west side of the old market green

41 *Eye, looking east. The town is shaped round the line of the castle's outer bailey. The motte on which the castle stood is marked by boscage and masonry just this side of the splendid church-tower. The former island site of the town is self evident. The priory's remains lie beyond the river Dove, top left. The market place lay outside the bailey in its bottom left corner, where the curve ends. The Victorian Town Hall is prominent with clock-tower on the left edge of the picture.*

formed the east boundary of the Park. The sad story of that market is told in Domesday Book:

> In this manor there used to be a market, and it continued after King William came. And it was a Saturday market. And William Malet made his castle at Eye. And on the same day as the market used to be held on the Bishop's manor at Hoxne, William Malet established another market at the castle at Eye. And thereby the Bishop's market has been so far spoilt that it is of little worth; and now it is set up on Fridays. But the market at Eye is held on the Saturday.

Saturday was obviously a better market-day than Friday in the 1080s, as it is still in the 2000s. William Malet died in 1071 in the campaign in the Fens against Hereward. So we have a date for the creation of the town of Eye, in the precise form we see today (illustration 41): it was all laid out, and built, on its island (which is what its name means) between 1066 and 1071, just nine centuries ago. The island is formed by the broad meadows of the Dove on the east, the stream from Yaxley to the north, and the 'Town Moor', a lovely willowy common, very 'Dutch' looking, across the south west side. This 'moor' may be partly artificial, like Framlingham's great 'Mere', on the north side of the Bigod castle. They would be produced as part of the defensive 'moating', in the course of quarrying thousands of loads of earth to create the steep motte on which the 'keep' of the castle stood.

Moat and motte are closely related words in French, and the idea of moats seems to have caught on quickly in Suffolk's Boulder Clay as a means of creating slightly raised platforms and useful drainage, and a plentiful water-supply for stock, round the hundreds of isolated wooden farmsteads that are so fundamental a feature of the landscape. These farmsteads were clearly scattered all over the landscape even before they appear in Domesday Book. But whether they were already moated is at present doubtful. In Suffolk over 850 moats have been recorded. (In Essex, I counted only about 300.) They are often fed by freshwater springs, which adds much to their value. Their owners keep them regularly cleaned out, and thus undateable. It was once thought that the peasants got their ideas about moats from barons, but who shall say whose needs were more pressing? The word 'motte' is still used in Normandy for moat, which proves nothing. I think the boulder-clay farmers saw the need to drain their house-sites just as early as the need for field-ditches.

To return to Eye Moor, 'moor', related to 'mere', means boggy ground in medieval Suffolk. Within his island, William Malet's men worked fast. St Peter's church, like St Michael's at Oulton (colour illustration V) among the ten

42 *Crows Hall, Debenham. A moated site, where farm buildings and a substantial part of the house remain. Many similar moated complexes characterise the Suffolk landscape – sometimes fully occupied, as at Helmingham Hall, sometimes deserted, as at Cotton.*

richest in Suffolk, occupied the eastern tip of the island. Next to it rose the great cone of the motte, and the inner and outer baileys were thrown out in a long loop to the west. There, at the entrance to the outer bailey, where the *White Lion* now is, the market place began. Broad Street marks its eastern edge, Cross Street its western. By 1086, Domesday Book could record: 'And in the market, twenty-five burgesses have their dwellings.' The outlines of this Norman market place can still be made out, built and encroached on by the descendants and successors of those 25 traders, but in shape exactly as it was laid out within five years of Hastings.

Their prosperity derived from their position at the gate of the castle, which was the administrative headquarters of the great 'Honour', a cluster of 220 estates in Suffolk alone, taken over by the Norman *en bloc* from a *Suffolk* man,

43 *Parham Moat Hall, built in early Tudor brick on local chocolate-brown crag foundations: see bottom-left corner.*

Edric of Laxfield (whose headquarters may have been there). The effect of Norman feudal ideas was to solidify this great estate, so that it was transmitted more or less intact right down through a series of medieval potentates, ending up with the de la Poles, who, after the Peasants' Revolt, built themselves a more fashionable stronghold beside the Green at Wingfield, where its splendid gatehouse-front survives. But this transmission of the Honour intact meant that there was much business to be transacted at the *caput* of the Honour here in Eye. The armed administration did the trick. By 1086 it was no longer worth the bishop's while holding his market at Hoxne. The bishop, who had been the Conqueror's chaplain and was now his chancellor, was also displeased to find that about one-third of Suffolk, the great liberty of St Edmund, was immune from his spiritual jurisdiction. In 1078 he removed the seats of the bishopric from North Elmham cathedral and St Ethelbert's at Hoxne to Thetford, on the very boundary of the Liberty. He reckoned without Abbot Baldwin. Archbishop Lanfranc came to Freckenham to arbitrate between bishop and abbot, fell ill, and was cured by Baldwin! The issue was not resolved in the bishop's favour, and by 1098 the see was finally established at Norwich.

44 *Bury St Edmunds from the south. The remains of St Edmund's abbey lie among the trees on the right. Its great rebuilding was begun by Abbot Baldwin (1065-98). It was probably continued under Abbot Anselm (1121-46). It grew to occupy much of the Anglo-Saxon town that had lain along the river Lark. Baldwin probably knew the tradition of laying-out towns in Normandy that started with Rouen in the 10th century, and proceeded to create a new planned town on a grid running west from the west front of the abbey church – the present Churchgate Street. In Suffolk, this was the first attempt at anything like the old Roman urban 'civilisation', a town that was more than just a place of industry and trade, though they were prominent. The Great Market was established in the north-west corner of the town: it and Moyses Hall, a late Norman building, may be seen by reference to the map (illustration 45). So may Angel Hill, scene of one of the great medieval European fairs, now chiefly occupied as a car-park.*

Three years later at Hoxne, it is perhaps significant that the name of the eighth-century East Anglian king and martyr Ethelbert had been replaced by that of the ninth century king and martyr Edmund at the bishop's old manor church. In his foundation charter for Norwich cathedral priory, dated 1101, Bishop Herbert made the first claim that his old seat at *Hoxne* was none other than the scene of Edmund's martyrdom at *Haegelisdun*. So Ethelbert's dedication was replaced by that of Edmund, and a small priory in Edmund's honour established a mile or so from the bishop's manor house. It never came within many miles of competing with Bury for devotion and pilgrimage to the saint. The bishops would have done better to cultivate Ethelbert, who had a genuine association with Hoxne.

Abbot Baldwin was not only a good doctor, he transformed the ancient royal town of Bury into the agreeable country town our generation has known, and which is being expanded into something twice as populous by the post World War II councils of the town (illustration 44). He came as abbot from St Denis outside Paris, in the year before the Conquest, and by the time of the bishop's withdrawal from Thetford he had rebuilt the east end of the abbey and translated into it the important mummy of King Edmund and the remains of Botolph and King Anna's son, Jurmin. Ten years earlier, Domesday recorded an increase of no fewer than 342 houses since 1066, on land that had been under the plough. It showed that some of the country gentry, the 'reeves over the land', had town houses in Bury, a sign that its character as a local capital had been established – as indeed at Eye, but on a more pronounced grand scale. The abbot had royal rights, and was much visited by medieval kings, ministers and legates. Bury continued as, in effect, a 'villa regia' all through the Middle Ages; and when the abbots were equal to their responsibilities, as in the days of Abbot Samson (1182-1211), the story of Bury reads like that of the capital of a principality, with the abbot's lodging a real palace. For all the *panache* of the Crofts at nearby Saxham in Charles II's time, and the very active loyalty of some of the Herveys of Ickworth in Hanoverian days, Bury's provincial, small town career, delightful enough, began with the Dissolution of the abbey and the extinction of the cult of the last pre-Danish king of East Anglia.

That large recorded increase of houses in Bury, taken together with the survival of a number of (late) Norman stone houses at the far limits of the medieval grid-pattern of streets, enables us to attribute to Baldwin's abbacy the design of that grid – the framework of life in Bury from the 11th century right through to our own (illustration 45). One main street ran

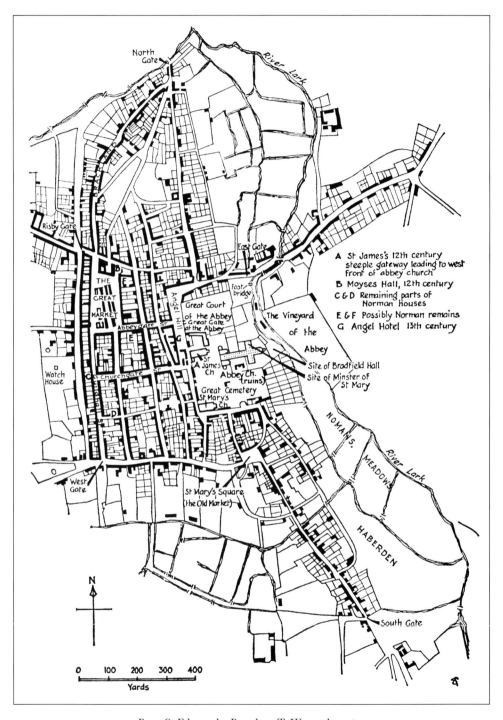

45   *Bury St Edmunds. Based on T. Warren's map, 1747.*

due west from the line of the presbytery and nave of his great new church. This is now called Churchgate Street from the monumental gate-tower built in the 12th century to lead triumphally through to the abbey church and at the same time serve as bell-tower to the new church of St James the Greater (the cathedral of the 21st-century diocese) planned originally to recall St Edmund's chief European competitor (at Compostela) in the business of popular pilgrim attraction. A little to the north, opposite the abbot's palace another street was laid out westwards, parallel to Churchgate Street. At the far end of Churchgate Street, the west edge of the medieval town is marked by the structure of a Norman house built into the core of 79 Guildhall Street. Guildhall Street runs north and Abbeygate Street runs west, to meet in the more open area of the Great Market (illustration 46), another of the creations of the Baldwin régime. Standing forward from the market place's original north side, Moyses Hall, now a museum, represents a very early encroachment. Whether it was originally one unit, or two, it is certainly one of the most perfectly preserved Norman secular buildings in England. Its plan, with the first floor devoted to domestic life and the ground floor in the form of a vaulted undercroft for various other functions including presumably the commercial ones, reminds one first of Harold's famous manor house at Bosham in the Bayeux tapestry, and second of so many shops in so many market places and High Streets where the supermarket has not yet taken over the entire town and shop-keepers are still content to live on the premises. (Ironically, the first dreaded Comprehensive Development Area in Bury was planned to rise alongside Moyses Hall: it has, happily, been rejected.)

As in so many market places all over Europe, and certainly all over Suffolk, one indication of increased prosperity is the way the open space laid out for the original 'forum' gradually diminished as stall-holders acquired permanent rights and built permanent buildings. St Edmund's market at Beccles provides a delightful demonstration of this encroachment. At Eye and Clare one has to look carefully before realising the extent of the original layout. And so it is at Bury, with the west side of the Buttermarket (facing the *Suffolk Hotel*) and both sides of Skinner Street and the Traverse, with the Corn Exchange, Library and Adam's Town Hall all representing encroachments on Baldwin's open rectangle. Jocelin of Brakelond, writing as an official of the abbey at the end of the 12th century, showed the process well under way. The passage, like most of the book, has a familiar theme:

46 *Bury Great Market: Corn Hill, Town Hall, Shambles and Cupola House. Picture painted c.1700, when Cupola House was newly built. It is the tall house on the right, and had been finished five years when Celia Fiennes described it in 1698: 'the new mode of building, 4 rooms of a floore, pretty sizeable and high, well furnish'd, a drawing roome and chamber full of China and a Damaske bed embroyder'd …'. It belonged to an apothecary.*

> We made complaint to the abbot in his court, saying that the business turnover of all respectable towns and boroughs in England was increasing and growing to the benefit of their owners and the prosperity of their lords, all except this town, which pays its regular £40, and never the slightest increase. And we said the burgesses were to blame, for they had so many and such large encroachments in the market place, in the shape of shops and booths and stallage, with no agreement by the Convent and solely at the gift of the Town Reeves, who were answerable to the abbey's Sacrist, and removable at his pleasure.

The planned expansion of Bury under Baldwin kept well within the economic territory prescribed for the town by the king back in 945. His expansion of the abbey and the monastic site must have involved destroying much of the old layout of the town. A fragment of that old town seems to survive among the wretched stumps of the ruins of the infirmary and 'Bradfield Hall' immediately east of the site of the Lady Chapel. It is aligned on the stream of the Linnet just before its confluence with the Lark at the Abbot's Bridge, and seems to reflect the layout of the 'villa regia' of the Wuffingas. Everything else within the precinct, and to the west outside, bears the stamp of Baldwin and of Anselm who ruled as abbot 1121-46. But in the lime-lined walks among the graves of the great medieval cemetery, we must be crossing the site of some of the Anglo-Saxon town. And when we walk further south, to Honey Hill and into St Mary's Square, where Wesley preached and Clarkson lived, we are in the Anglo-Saxon market place. It is traversed now by motor traffic of which we long to see it rid. But what slow, slow centuries of history this beautiful small square still manages to suggest.

After Baldwin took the main market business away to the west side of the town, the old market kept one trading function, that of horse market. Indeed, the documentary confirmation that this was truly remembered as the 'Eldmarket' is a rental of the Sacrist in 1433, recording that William Baker's holding abutted to the north on 'the old market, called Horsmarket'. As the Horsemarket, it still appears on 18th-century maps.

Baldwin was supported by the Conqueror against the bishop; he may have been embarrassed by the Conqueror over a sumptuous late Anglo Saxon-foundation at Clare. There Aelfric, Wisgar's son, with his own son's consent, gave the entire manor (24 carucates, almost 3,000 'acres') to St John the Baptist, and 'put in Ledmar the priest and others'. This must have been a most splendid collegiate church of secular canons. Aelfric entrusted his foundation and 'the whole place' to the joint care of his own son and Baldwin's predecessor as abbot. But in 1066, the Conqueror had no compunction in seizing 'into his own hand' what was far and away the most richly endowed church in Suffolk. By 1086, the manor was in the hands of Richard de Clare, son of the Conqueror's old guardian, Gilbert de Brionne. Clare was soon the headquarters of an even greater Honour than that of the Malets at Eye.

No more is heard of St John's church. The parish church on the south side of the Old English market place is dedicated to SS Peter and Paul. A lofty motte-and-bailey castle went up among the floodable water-meadows of the Stour, and the Norman market place was created between bailey and parish church.

There is reason to think Aelfric's lavish foundation was part of an attempt to avoid the confiscation of his estates in the event of the Normans conquering. For among the most prominently well-endowed churches in Domesday Book, after St John's at Clare, the next richest was his church of St Peter at Ipswich (760 'acres'), and then came the church at Long Melford which he presented to St Edmund's abbey and which Baldwin contrived to keep for the saint.

Finally there was his pair of churches at *Deseling* (180 'acres' between the two), which went, like Clare, to Richard FitzGilbert. *Deseling* has become Desning, an interchange of 'l' and 'n' such as may be supposed in the name Icklingham. Desning Hall, a formidable rebuilding of 1845, ugly and dilapidating, stands within the remains of a great moat in the rolling chalky landscape west of Bury. Above it, an old hard flint bridle-way leads over dry flinty fields to the earthworks of FitzGilbert's castle, an outpost of Clare. Both castle and Hall-moat lie within the present parish boundaries of Gazeley, whose village church is probably one of the two Aelfric endowed. The other must have been at the site of either the Hall or the castle. It is not certain that the castle-site was occupied before the FitzGilberts built it, and the hall-site seems the likelier. The castle stands close to the parish-boundary and indeed the church of Denham, but Domesday Book records a separate church already there.

This interlocking of town and country estates is of course closely related to the growth of towns like Clare, whose prosperity depended upon one great family, so long as that family endured. Adversity, too. Ipswich's plight, like Norwich's, in Domesday Book, was grim. Sometime between 1066 and 1086, it had been devastated, and in 1086, three-fifths of the town still lay waste, and another fifth was still much depressed.

> In the borough there were in the time of King Edward 538 burgesses rendering custom to the King ... but now there are 110 burgesses who render custom, and 100 poor burgesses who can render to the King's geld only a penny a head ... And 328 burgages [*mansiones*] within the borough lie waste.

In 1085, the Conqueror was threatened by a great invasion from Scandinavia. The implacable Domesday commission was one response. Another was 'scorched earth'. 'The King gave orders for the coastal districts to be laid waste.' Ipswich lay almost flat, but not its 13 churches.

Ipswich had tremendous natural advantages, its harbour, and its healthy abundance of fresh water, and doubtless soon recovered its strength. The earliest water-supplies were registered in the names like Brook Street (the main north-south thoroughfare of the town (illustration 73), crossing the aboriginal line of Tavern Street next to the Great White Horse: this ancient way led from Westgate Street past St Mildred's church through Tavern Street to Spring Road and St Helen's Wash (now just 'St Helen's') and 'the Washes' (now Greyfriars Road). From the tenth century to the 13th, like all the early boroughs, it had its own mint and moneyers to supply the needs of the tradespeople for ready money. If the Normans built a castle to keep an eye on the town, it seems likely to have been just outside the town, beside what is now the Henley Road and immediately opposite the Ipswich School. The site is part of the delightful arboretum of Christchurch Park, and the mounds could be early unrecorded landscape gardening. But old maps show a meeting of four ways here, and the name 'Great Bolton', which suggests a house of some importance. And the continuation of Christchurch Park north over Park Road was called Great King's Field. Wherever the castle was, Hugh Bigod the earl seized it in 1153, but was besieged by King Stephen and forced to surrender (illustration 28).

The Bigod ambition led to the creation by Henry II of the castle and new town of Orford, complete with market place and church, in the 1160s. It had the latest kind of polygonal keep, and its landward picture is much published. It survived an 18th-century move to demolish it, for its service as a landmark to coastal shipping. Only from the river, as one sails past, does one become wholly aware of the majestic and sculptural qualities of this early and incomparable demonstration of vertical ('high-rise') living. The adjoining shingle beaches bear abundant current estimony to the use of this corner of the coast for national defence (illustration 78). Bigod already had a castle within the Roman fort down the coast at Walton-Felixstowe (illustration 21).

Bigod's great keep at Bungay, rising neck and neck with the royal stronghold at Orford, retained the old-fashioned square design, with corners vulnerable to the enemy's explosive miners (as may be seen under one corner). The mortar had scarcely hardened round the flints when he was involved with the earl of Leicester in the rebellion of 1173. The rebellion was 'chronicled' in a ballad in Norman French by a loyal church-official called Jordan Fantosme ('the Thin'). It contains our one reference in contemporary literature to the shape of the prosperous 12th-century sea-port of Dunwich, which rivalled Ipswich before it fell, dramatically, in 1328, a victim to the siege of the implacable sea.

What survives now at Dunwich, on the top of the crumbling cliff, is the line of the westward edge of the town rampart, which is presumed to have been surmounted, like all medieval earthen town ramparts, by a stout stockade of wooden pales (illustration 66). Where St James's Street continues east past the *Ship Inn*, one comes to the point where the 'Bridge Gates' provided passage through those ramparts. Outside them, and on top of some of the rampart, the Grey Friars later built their stone skirting wall (1290), which survives with an impressive gateway. (And there is still the ruin of the Romanesque leper-chapel of St James naturally some way out in the former suburbs, with the site of its own spring welling out under the hillside just across the road.) The medieval rampart in action was brought into close view by Fantosme. When Bigod blustered to the Dunwich townsmen that Leicester was their friend, but that they would all hang if they refused to join him, they shouted back their defiance and got ready for the siege.

> That day you could see tradesmen like trusty knights hurrying out to man their defences, each knowing his job, some as bowmen, others with lances, the strong helping the weak to have frequent spells of rest. Inside the town there was not a girl or a woman who was not carrying stones to be hurled from the palisade ... The earl of Leicester went off, humiliated.

A study of the Bigod estates from 1066 to 1306, when Edward I finally got the better of them, would show details of fundamental developments in the landscape. For instance, the minority of the 4th earl produced, in 1228, an account of the revenues due from their various estates. It leaves out Framlingham, their headquarters, one of the most rewarding examples of a baronial market town: St Michael's magnificent church is secluded from the market place by the walls of the former guildhall, and stands at the approach, over two great lines of moating, to the castle whose walls and flanking towers circle the top of an immense artificial mound (illustration 47). Apart from Framlingham, the dues from the other Bigod estates suggest that towns were not necessarily more profitable to their owners than well managed country estates. Their manor at Walton (Felixstowe), which did not acquire its market until 60 years later, was due to pay £45, whereas Bungay-cum-Ilketshall was assessed at only £34, of which £15 was due from Bungay market. Walton Manor largely comprised the successors of the small groups of Domesday freemen farming 50 small estates scattered through the seven or eight parishes of Coleness Hundred (Nacton parish alone lay outside the manor). Those fifty very small, but clearly very profitable Coleness estates mostly survive by name as farmhouses and farms with ancient boundaries today: in Morston Hall, Grimston Hall, Kembroke Hall, Candlet, Gulpher, Alston Hall, and so on (so, in this small peninsular corner do many of the Domesday farmers: Woolnough, Thurston, Surman, Levitt, Gooding). Grimston, Candlet and Alston appear in illustration 84. The relationship of the 50 small joint farms to the landscape, on average about six to a parish, would be worth following in microscopic detail. The pattern resembles Whatfield, not Aldham. Incidentally, as at Whatfield, the name of one of the Norman immigrants is preserved among these English, or occasionally Anglo-Danish, farm-names: at Burnaville Hall in Levington,

47 *Framlingham Castle, a baronial stronghold, headquarters of the Bigod earls of East Anglia, and later of the Mowbrays and Howards (who added the chimneys, most of which are show-pieces, without fireplaces beneath). A 12th-century chimney of an earlier hall rises against the inside of the skirting wall. The series of flanking towers round the wall were the latest deterrent of their day, anticipated only in the royal stronghold of Dover. A mere to the left of the willows is conceivably the result of making the huge artificial mound?*

William de Burnaville had by 1086 managed to get the holding of ten freemen with 32 acres, some meadow, and Levington church. It is likely that by 1228 much of the profit of the manor was coming from the Deben side of the peninsula, where the small riverside settlements like *Guston*, vanished now from beside Kirton Creek, collectively formed a port called Goseford. It included all the creeks at the mouth of the Deben, formerly the Wuffingas' estuary.

The story of this port has been told by W. G. Arnott.[3]

> The Anglo-Saxons gave it its name of Goseford when they settled about the estuary and penetrated inland to found homes at Falkenham and Kirton, using a ford across the arm of the river we now call the Kingsfleet. To them it was the ford haunted by geese, or the goseford, so descriptive of the lonely valley with its wide horizons where the welling tide ran in over the land to the higher ground.

He shows, and so does M. Oppenheim in the *Victoria County History*, how Goseford flourished, and sometimes 'outshone' even Ipswich and Harwich and managed to expand with the decay of Dunwich, but began to decline in the 15th century when perhaps the bigger ships were unable to cross the Deben bar, and when Woodbridge with its shipbuilding was able to monopolise the trade of the estuary.

The Spread of Markets Across the Countryside

Domesday Book recorded nine markets, and may have overlooked at least three others. By 1547, the year Aldeburgh's market was granted, there were no fewer than 98 towns and villages in Suffolk, about one in every five, that had had a market, or at least a grant of one. Seventy of these grants were made between 1227, the year the minority of Henry III ended, and 1310, the beginning of the political rifts of Edward II's reign. If we could imagine the towns and villages of Suffolk at the beginning of the 14th century, we should be astonished at the activity and wealth.

The map (illustration 48) shows the geographical distribution of all these places. Here it will be possible to look at only one or two, that have either left a characteristic mark on the landscape or have vanished (illustrations 51 and 67). Plainly, one cannot be sure how many of these markets were being held in any one year. A few succeeded one another, as Westhall's succeeded Sotherton's in 1229, after a presumably abortive start. Others may soon have decayed altogether. One difficulty is that, though grants required permission from the Crown and were thus recorded, failures did not and were not. Grants that

---

[3] *Suffolk Estuary* (Ipswich, 1950).

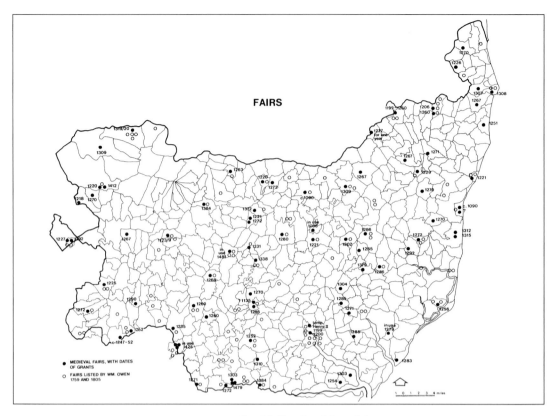

48 *Medieval and later fairs.*

were not taken up would probably have been annulled. And many of the smaller markets, which flourished in their local way before the Black Death, dwindled and died in the century or so of declining trade and population that followed the repeated epidemics of the 14th century. In any case the map tells a tale that may be a little further elaborated here.

The parish of Kelsale lies just north of Saxmundham on the A12 between Ipswich and Lowestoft. Its claylands spread just over a mile to the west of the main road, and two miles to the east. In the east, several claypits have been dug for distribution over the lighter soils. All the way through Saxmundham the road has been following the shallow valley of a tributary stream running south into the Alde. Only when you look at the map (illustration 49) do you realise how significant the 100-foot contour has been in the settlement of Kelsale, with the Hall and the lodge of the medieval Park each sited beside a different feeder of this stream, and the church up on a spur projecting into the dale. Away to the east, East Green was laid out on the eastern edge of the

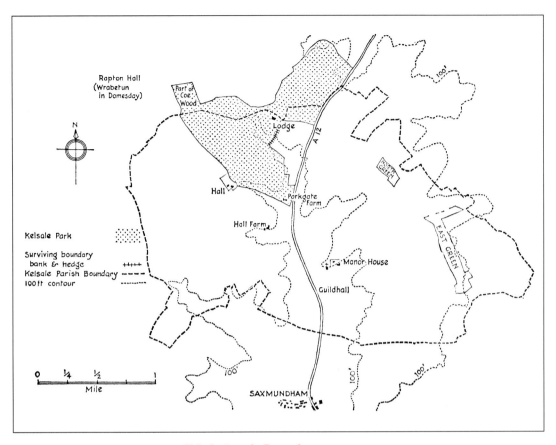

49 *Kelsale since the Domesday survey.*

same clay table. On the north-west side of the parish a medieval park was also set within great boundary banks that relate closely to the course of that 100-foot contour, and incidentally spilled over the Kelsale boundary into Yoxford and the Minsmere valley. And somewhere there was once a market place.

The stream and the main road together divide the original clay arable lands of Kelsale into two; those in the west, round what is now called the Hall, and round Kelsale Lodge, which was set in the instep of the shoe-shaped park, and those in the east, around the church, and two Greens. These two 'wings' of the parish, or vill, were very clearly depicted, as two main manors, in Domesday Book, which also recorded the overall dimensions of the whole vill as one and a half 'leagues' by one. Today Kelsale covers what I take to be the same area, measuring approximately three miles by two: these are the same proportions, at any rate.

Of the two main manors, the first is the one based on the manor house up alongside the church, which appears as part of the same entry, with its own endowment of 30 'acres' only a little above the average, but comfortable. The manor farm was a good big one, 480 'acres', and well wooded enough for 60 swine, a relatively big wood. A flock of 25 sheep had grown to 100 in 1086. The men working the (presumably still open) fields of the manor, and its woods and sheepfold and small stockyard, had almost doubled in number from 17 to 32, with three ploughs for the lord's demesne, and ten ploughs of their own.

Continuing its account of Kelsale, Domesday Book describes the second manor, in which Roger Bigod had displaced a woman, Ulveva: rather smaller than the first, 240 'acres', some meadow, two ploughs on his demesne, five of the men's, nine men had increased to sixteen. I have no doubt that this manor was the one to the west of the stream (and the A12). There the Hall, now a delightful Regency, bow-ended, white-brick house with a lovely crinkle-crankle walled garden and let to American service families, is approached up a long ancient ride, among cornfields, and great scattered oaks surviving from the park. It commands views over miles of cornfields, and one can imagine Ulveva's anger and dismay at the loss of all this.

At this point Domesday Book returns to the first manor, 'which Norman had had before the Conquest'. 'In it are thirty-five freemen having power to sell and give their lands.' Kelsale was outside the Liberties of both Edmund and Etheldreda, so the ancient royal dues of these 35 freemen, sake and soke, and other customs, went to Roger. 'And they have three carucates of land' – only one less than Roger on this manor. 'And they have twelve ploughs, as they had in 1066 and an acre of meadow. *And now a market, of the King's gift.*'

Domesday Book rounds off its account of Kelsale with its increase in value. Ulveva's old manor had risen from £3 to £8. Norman's manor had been worth £5 and the freemen £4: together they were now worth £74.

Those 35 freemen, who could sell and give their lands, what sort of landscape did they farm? This is a fundamental question that requires much more intensive research into the early history of Suffolk land-tenure. With Mr Charman's work on Mutford and Lothingland, and the work of Mr John Ridgard and Dr David Dymond, our ideas are gradually clearing. Here in Kelsale, one inclines to think they may have had something like a village settlement, the precursors of the cottages in Bridge Street, alongside the Guildhall, and that that might explain their apparent involvement in the

Domesday account of the new market that the king gave his efficient henchman Bigod. But equally, they may have been in scattered farms linked to that fine strip of common grazing: East Green. We cannot yet be sure.

There should be traces of that market, for market places were laid out as a clear open space, and were usually first built round, and then encroached on, as we saw at Bury and elsewhere. At Kelsale, the most convincing site is certainly in the area of the 'Spar Foodmarket' and the Guildhall, a handsome timber-framed building of the later 15th century, which has been studied by Mr Cedric Holland[4] and itself seems to have fulfilled the need for a shop in that neighbourhood in the later 16th century. What became of the Norman market? The answer lies in the fortunes of the Bigods, which can be traced in ruined castles in the landscape, but not just in ruins. The towns of Bungay and Framlingham were their creation, and they are a legacy to be proud of. But the Bigods had crossed Edward I, who succeeded to the throne in 1272. That year, a market and fair were granted at Saxmundham, just a mile down the road from Kelsale!

That Saxmundham's market got going is plain. In 1311, the Close Rolls record an order to pay its lord 'the profits of a market and fair held on seven acres in Saxmundham'. It continues, in a small way, and has expanded into a lively little 'thoroughfare-town' of a recognisable Suffolk type. It may be reasonable to date the decline of Kelsale's market from about the beginning of the 14th century. Before leaving the Bigod's market at Kelsale, let us glance at their deer park there. When they made it, to the north of Ulveva's Hall (see illustration 49) seems not to be recorded. Its limits are preserved in two maps. The first, by John Middleton, surveyor, 1616, shows 'the late disparked park of Kelsale and Yoxford now divided into divers enclosures'. A rough sketch of the manor house, as it was then, marks a 'bleaching yard', a dovecote, and so on. A more extensive survey was drawn out in 1638 by Thomas Waterman.[5] The outlines of the ancient park boundaries conform in every detail to field boundaries and footpaths shown on the 2½ inch O.S. map of 1956. One stretch of the original boundary earthwork survives about 300 yards south of Kelsale Lodge. A farmer here told me he removed another length of it from the north side of the little valley running from Coe Wood towards the Lodge. The surviving stretch is as formidable as Dunwich's town rampart, and supports a dense hedge of at least five species, including stout

---

[4] *P.S.I.* (1965).
[5] Original in the possession of Mr H.T. Bush of Bramfield.

oaks. We remember how, at the end of the 12th century, Abbot Samson of Bury, according to Jocelin, 'made a number of parks which he filled with animals [presumably deer], and he kept a huntsman and hounds; and when he had grandees to entertain, he would sit for a while with his monks in a glade under the trees, watching the hounds in pursuit; but I never saw him touch venison'. The park he made on his manor at Melford occupied the northern tip of the parish; on the left as you enter from Bury. One never travels that road without that picture in mind, and the earthen and hedgerow outlines are still there.

At Kelsale, the Lodge presumably served the park keeper. In 1486, at the awkward transition period from York to Tudor for the Howard dukes of Norfolk, who then held the estates of the Bigods, John Martyndale managed to get the Keepership of Kelsale Park secured to him for life. Was he an adherent of the Howards' immediate predecessors, the Mowbrays? For a splendid barn, alongside the Lodge, has gable-ends of diapered brickwork and small terracotta roundels containing the rampant lion of the Mowbrays, and of the Bigods before them. The brickwork otherwise appears to date from John Martyndale's time, shortly after the Mowbrays had merged, like the Bigods, into the forgotten past.

Deserted Villages

Despite the inventiveness of the Domesday scribe in spelling Kelsale, it remains true, and amazing, that almost every one of the 500-parish names familiar in Suffolk today is fairly easily identifiable in the record of 1086.

Furthermore, among over 2,400 'holdings' recorded, of every size, there is a wealth of not so readily identifiable names. This provides the main starting-point for researches, in the landscape, into what are known to archaeologists as D.M.V.s – Deserted Medieval Villages.[6] Largely through W.G. Hoskins's pioneering work in Leicestershire, the sites of entire abandoned Midland villages such as Ingarsby – its street and croft-sites still thrown up into relief in the grazier's grass by the low evening sun – are now sought eagerly everywhere. In Suffolk it must be remembered that the basic patterns of parishes vary greatly, as between one parish and another (Aldham, say, and Whatfield), and that indeed there is a great variety of pattern *within* settlements, as at Kelsale, or Walsham-le-Willows. Even so, there are examples very

---

[6] The splendid book by Beresford and Hurst, on *Deserted Medieval Villages of Britain*, listed 23 known deserted sites in Suffolk as against 148 in Norfolk.

50 *Livermere deserted village. At the bottom right is the abandoned church, which retains Anglo-Saxon features, and shares its churchyard with two Herefordshire bulls. The mere, involved in a great Georgian 'landskip' scheme, remains idyllic.*

reminiscent of the Midlands, especially in the north-west, where the Midlands are close and the circumstances right for 'Desertion'. J.K. St Joseph's air photograph (illustration 50) of the field just west of churchyard and mere at Little Livermere shows the unmistakable outline of a former very long village-street with regular croft-sites on either side. Domesday Book records a fishery at a Suffolk Livermere. But before imagining nets and boats in this picture, notice that the Livermere with fishery lies in a different Hundred, further to the west, and is vanished even more utterly beneath the Forestry Commission's conifers at the edge of Wangford Fen.

In Suffolk, where villages and hamlets have disappeared in this way, one of two explanations generally applies. They are found to be either in the light lands, the marginal soils, or else in parkland, having been removed as part of the 'improvement' of the landscape by the owner of a big estate. Sometimes, as at Little Livermere, both rules apply. Dr Dymond tells me that in the Breckland he sees evidence of 'lost villages' at Euston, Little Fakenham, Fornham St Genevieve, Wangford and Wordwell. In the same area Mr J.T. Munday has with admirable clarity uncovered the history of the two Eriswells right through their parallel careers from their separate pagan Anglo-Saxon origins beside two wells, or springs.[7] Perched between the fen-edge and Breckland it is not altogether surprising that one of them has grown indistinct, though not invisible. Mr Munday reconstructs the crofts and the fields and the warren with its Lodge as they were in the Middle Ages. Emparking is usually the explanation of 'lost villages' on heavier lands. St Joseph's photographs show that something has gone from Ickworth, for instance, and Little Glemham, and Heveningham and Redisham: it may be a farmstead or a hamlet rather than a village.

Domesday Book is, as usual, full of suggestion. We need not bother to comb through Wangford Hundred for traces of *Wichedis*: it means an elmy ditched enclosure (? moat) where a freeman held a mere 'acre' worth fourpence. But what about *Chiletuna*, *Cheletuna* or *Keletuna*, in Plomesgate Hundred, no end of a place, with 500 'acres' of arable, ten of meadow, a mill, sheep and no fewer than 43 recorded households, all in an area measured, superficially, as nine 'furlongs' by four, and belonging to the Malet lord of Eye? That can hardly have vanished, though its name has. What makes its disappearance doubly improbable and provides the first clue to its rediscovery is the grant in 1292 'of a fair in Benhall and a *market and fair* at Kelton within the same manor'.

A place called Kelton, somewhere near Benhall? The people of Benhall, just south of Saxmundham, recently found medieval pottery turned up by the plough in the field immediately east of their church, and, upon hearing of lost Kelton, concluded that it was there. But luckily, Joseph Hodskinson's marvellous map of Suffolk in 1783 clears up the whole question. The southern part of what we call Silverlace Green, in the south-west corner of Benhall parish, on those heavy clay slopes at High Wood just north of Benhall Street, looking down to the south and west over the upper Alde to Marlesford and Great Glemham, is blandly labelled Kelton End by Hodskinson (illustration 51). Now it all seems perfectly obvious. The huge clay pit dug into the westward slope is accompanied by extensive kilns marked 'Pottery' on the first edition, 1 inch O.S. map, 1836. The likeliest meaning of the Domesday place-name is at once clear:

[7] *P.S.I.* (1965).

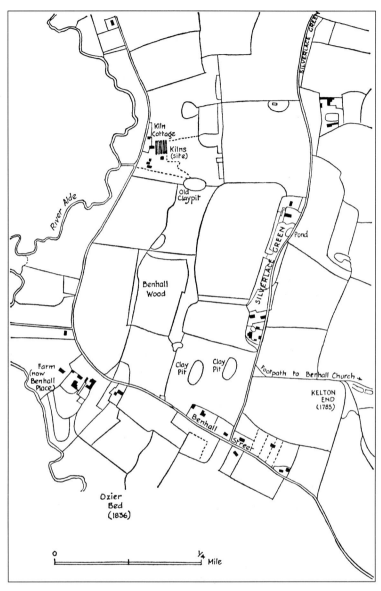

51 *Kelton: a vanished medieval market. Based on Joseph Hodskinson's Map of Suffolk, 1783, the O.S. map of Suffolk, 1836, and Benhall Tithe Map, 1846.*

kell is the East Anglian word for kiln, as may be verified in the Supplement by W.T. Spurdens to Forby's *Vocabulary of East Anglia* in Part IV of the 'Reprinted Glossaries' edited for the English Dialect Society by Walter Skeat, and published for them in 1879. It looks as if in Kelton we have unearthed not only a lost settlement of considerable size, but also an Anglo-Saxon industrial site (for small scale kilns probably existed in most parishes). There is no difficulty in placing the unusually large amount of Domesday meadow. And Lord Cranbrook tells me he thinks a possible mill-site on the river would be above Kiln Cottage, where the river flows faster. I suppose the old-looking settlement-sites of Benhall Place and Benhall Street may have been the main farm-settlement of William Malet's men. Silverlace Green provided a strip of common grazing. The field immediately west of it yields plentiful early medieval pottery, which suggests early squatters round that Green. A large depression in the southward slope suggests an early clay pit. Odd that the name Kelton should have vanished so utterly, but at Silverlace Green it gave way to something more poetic. Again Spurdens' Supplement to Forby's *Vocabulary* explains: 'lays' are 'ponds in the midst of coppice'. Sure enough, beside the road through Silverlace Green, a pond in a very small coppice reflects like a silver mirror the light of the Suffolk sky. Two or three peaceful old cottages survive on the Green, and several down in the valley, in Benhall Street.

But what became of the market and fair of 1292? Guy Ferre, to whom it was granted, died childless in 1323, his widow in 1349, perhaps of the Black Death. After much dispute the De Ufford earls of Suffolk got the estate, but seem not to have bothered with Kelton market. 1349 was a bad year, except in the market for shovels and dirges for the dead. In 1314 there were 80 stalls in Sudbury's market place. In 1340 there were 107 stalls. The Black Death struck in 1348-9. Its dismal effects may be read in the court-roll of Cornard, an adjacent rural manor.[8] We can guess at its work in the town. In 1361, 13 years later, there were still only 62 stalls in Sudbury's market, suggesting about half the business of 20 years earlier.[9] How far the Black Death was directly responsible for the shrinkage of such markets as Kelton, or of Monk Soham Green, or Hestley Green in Thorndon – there are countless examples – still awaits the joint study by archaeologists and historians working together that alone can supply the answers. Edward Martin has supplied a very useful map, number 38, of Suffolk's 'deserted, dispersed and small settlements, medieval and later', in the *Historical Atlas*, pp.88-9.

A characteristic feature of Suffolk's landscape – its isolated country churches – is popularly ascribed to the wiping out of the hypothetical villages that are supposed to have clustered about all those churches. At present this must be classed as a 'popular misconception'. There is sometimes evidence of medieval habitation near such churches, at Depden, for instance, and Gedding, and, as we have just noticed at Benhall, where there must have been a substantial

[8] Augustus Jessopp, *The Coming of the Friars* (1889), p.201.
[9] C.G. Grimwood and S.A. Kay, *History Of Sudbury* (1952), p.86.

late medieval house. So far, these finds do not seem to represent 'lost villages'. The subject urgently needs coordinated research. So does the story of the abandonment of dozens, scores of isolated farms – often represented in the landscape now only by overgrown moats. The parish of Cotton contains several. But at least we now know that medieval Suffolk settlement patterns were the opposite of uniform. If they resembled Midland 'street-villages', it was mostly in West Suffolk. But in West Suffolk parishes, the Bradfields, for instance, or Denham, or Rede, there was nothing of a uniform, 'nucleated' pattern. Several of Suffolk's 'scattered' villages, market-villages and 'thoroughfare' villages were given new changes of shape from about 1300 onwards by the spectacular expansion of the clothing industry. We look at that in a moment.

The Fields

Robert Ryece[10] reminds us how the fields of Suffolk were looking in his day, at the end of Elizabeth I's reign. The soil was not everywhere the same. Among the enclosures of Central Suffolk 'it is heavy with clay, and sometimes intermixed with chalk in other places, as nearer the champion' (the unenclosed fields between Bury and Newmarket). 'Where the ground is so heavy, the best husbands without six strong horses in one plough will not till their land, so that generally the country in winter time, out of the common roads, is very foul.'

He proceeded to describe the land use of his day. 'Those parts inclining to the east, having sufficient tillage, abound with all meadow and pasture, by reason whereof their greatest commodities are raised by feeding and grazing'. He was describing the eastern side of the Boulder Clay, watered by the upper reaches of Blyth, Minsmere, Alde and Deben, with lush grazing indeed, and dairying that Arthur Young, Secretary to the Board of Agriculture during the Napoleonic Wars, was very ecstatic about when he found it two centuries later. Ryece ended by describing the rest of the Central Boulder Clay, in the heart of which he himself lived (at Preston, near Lavenham): 'The middle parts of the country are rich in pasture and plenty of meadows, but their chiefest is corn-grounds, from all which riseth the grain that filleth their purses.' On another page he has an even clearer phrase or two for the central clay: 'our deep, miry soil … our manifold enclosures, severed with so many deep ditches, hedges, and store of wood, bushes and trees.'

We can fill out Ryece's picture with endless detail from numerous estate-maps that survive from his day, a great period for estate-surveys. But since his

[10] The 20th-century editor of Ryece's *Breviary of Suffolk* unfortunately spelt his name Reyce.

picture is not unfamiliar, indeed there are still a few farms very closely identical to their portraits drawn by his contemporaries, let us not spend too much time in 16th-century rural Suffolk. We will try, cursorily, to imagine those same fields in the medieval centuries. No difficulty with the 'champion', open field parishes west of Bury: textbook large fields with a patchwork of little strips. In the Breckland corner there were complications (as there still are). The hungry soil 'looked up' and was fed by large flocks of sheep: the system of fold courses and 'in field and out-field' is described by M.R. Postgate.[11] Traces survive, especially in J.K. St Joseph's photographs, some of which can be related to old estate-maps, drawn before the great parliamentary enclosures. These traces are limited mainly to meer-baulks. (Some of the larger estates arranged private enclosures earlier.)

What is more complicated is the story of the medieval Boulder Clay fields, so largely enclosed by Ryece's day. Mr Derek Charman showed how farmers could enclose here when they liked, since there was no custom of grazing in the stubble after harvest: the Greens were capacious enough for all the grazing. He quotes one of Ryece's contemporaries from the Lowestoft area: that the farmers 'time out of mind used to sever and divide their copyhold land with ditches, hedges or pales, at their pleasure, without licence'.

G.C. Homans, comparing medieval East Anglia with Friesland, emphasised the effect on land of the very widespread custom, in both societies, of 'partible inheritance'. It is true that the children of a freeman or sokeman could share out their inheritance equally without dividing the land physically and often did so. One can point to several examples of brothers agreeing to farm their inheritance together, perhaps sometimes even agreeing to share the farmhouse. (It is this truth to early medieval Suffolk farming custom that makes H.W. Freeman's novel about an early 20th-century farm at Badingham, *Joseph and His Brethren*, 1928, so particularly stirring. He tells me he knew nothing of the antiquity, in Suffolk, of partible inheritance.) It would certainly contribute to the early enclosure of arable holdings. How early this was may be seen by reference to Mr John Ridgard's study of the estates of the nunnery at Flixton-by-Bungay. In an extent of 1306, 150 acres were named enclosures, while only 50 acres were unenclosed. On another manor, between 1400 and 1450, '41 per cent of all grants were grants of closes'. (Dr Dymond adds his impression from documentary research over a number of years, now fortified by botanical dating, that the early 15th century was the time of most enclosure

---

[11] *Agric. Hist. Review* (1962).

52 *Sibton: the Cistercian abbey's ruined refectory and fishpond.*

of the arable fields of Central Suffolk. More recently, he has published studies of two Elizabethan surveys of Walsham-le-Willows – *Proceedings*, Suffolk Institute of Archaeology, XXXIII, 1975, p.204 – in which the Walsham field book of 1577 'best reveals both the existence of open fields and their break-up'.) Mr. A.H. Denney, in his study of the *Sibton Abbey Estates, 1325-1509*[12] found that on two of their Granges, at Cookley and at the North Grange in Sibton, the area of enclosed exceeded that of the unenclosed lands. At the South Grange, on the other hand, the unenclosed greatly exceeded the enclosed. These hedges and ditches of the clay farmlands to the north and south of the upper Blyth valley can be found intact today. And what is of the very greatest interest, in view of Ryece's description of the rich dairying of precisely this district of sticky clay closes, is the Cistercian monk's account of the dairy at this North Grange, in 1507, in the care of Katherine Dowe. Mr Denney shows us the late 15th-century Suffolk cows in those lush closes. They were called 'Countryware' and were already being improved by the introduction of 'Northernsteer'.

One of the clues to early enclosure in Suffolk, then, is the distribution of Greens, either as part of the very early arrangements of the Hundreds, or, on

[12] Suffolk Records Society (1960).

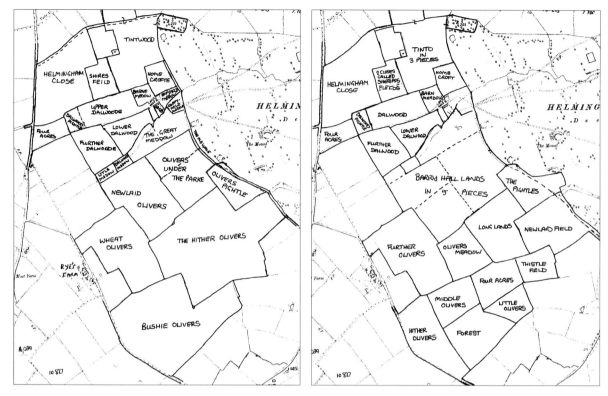

53 *and* **54** *Helmingham estate: the changing shapes and names of enclosed fields.* **53** *shows enclosed fields in* c.*1630.* **54** *shows them in* 1729. *By courtesy of Lord Tollemache.*

a small scale, of the manors. In interpreting the Suffolk landscape, one of the first things we look for is the Green (illustration 23 and 30). Many of them have now been enclosed, over centuries. But often one sees at once its original bounds from the line of old encroachments round the perimeter. The ancient perimeter is usually still fixed in the landscape by lines of ditch and hedge. The most impressive Green in Suffolk is not Greshaw, in South Elmham, for all its importance. It is the Green at Mellis, stretching one and three-fifths of a mile to the east from the manor house of Pountney Hall.

The enclosure of the Greens themselves has been going on steadily since the 15th century: many encroachments on them are already detailed in the Hundred Rolls, c.1275. Most of the survivors are now registered as common land, and reasonably safe if public interest is maintained. In 1957 Walter Tye noticed that East Suffolk had 103 commons, still, with 4,000 acres, in 65 parishes,[13] and that Stratford St Mary's, lately enclosed, was the only common

---

[13] *Suffolk Review*, Vol.I, p.5.

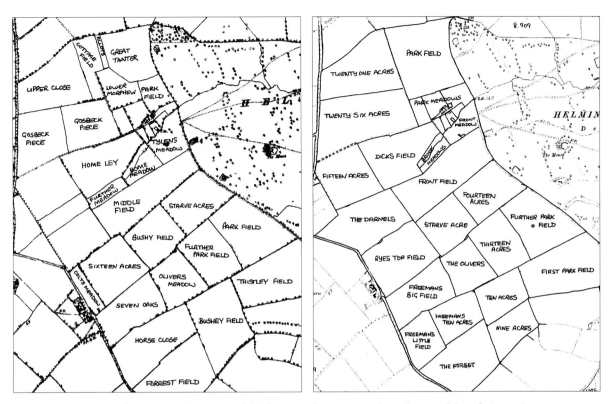

55 *and* **56** *Helmingham estate, field-shapes and names.* **55** *shows them c.1865.* **56** *shows them c.1980. Stephen Podd's researches.*

(dole meadows) that had preserved its strips through all the centuries. There now seems to be only one other bundle of surviving medieval strips in Suffolk: four in a row in 'The Carrs' in Westhorpe Field. Mr Barker of Westhorpe Lodge is lord of the manor. Mr Reg Cattermole of Cotton remembers these strips being ploughed with 'a pony and horse'. On the tithe map of 1840, they are numbered 240, 293, 239, 164. Many years ago, Professor Diarmaid MacCullough, then of Wetherden, kindly took me to see them. In the Westhorpe Court Rolls he has traced their last years, and noted the admission of Sheppard Frere into some of these lands in 1771. (That eminent archaeological name goes back, in the next parish, to 1664.)

We sometimes think of fields being enclosed and retaining their hedged framework 'for good'. It is instructive to look at these four maps of a part of the Tollemache estate at Helmingham at intervals between *c.*1630 and *c.*1980, drawn by Stephen Podd in the course of his studies of the neighbourhood. The map of *c.*1865 reveals fields rationally remodelled by the Victorian

1st Lord Tollemache, who built excellent brick semi-detached cottages for his farmworkers, each with a large garden and enough land to sow their own corn, to be threshed at home. In the map of *c.*1630, the name Olivers predominated. It just managed to survive into our own time. In 1327, Benedict Olyver was one of the two leading landowners in adjacent Ashbocking.

John Ridgard has been studying the late medieval records of Suffolk. When a dark sloping field, at Poplar Farm, Hollesley, was excavated to reveal an extensive pottery, an activity on an industrial scale, using the heat of huge bonfires fuelled from Hollesley Common a few yards away, Ridgard dated the manufacture to a couple of years in the 1280s, and was confirmed by the pots. Looking at the account-rolls for Fritton (1317/18) and Flixton by Lowestoft (1355/7), from which Oulton was formed, he found that 76 per cent of the manorial income at Fritton and 31 per cent at Flixton was derived from 'turbary', the extraction of peat. It is now well known that the Norfolk Broads were created in this way, by the digging of peat. Fritton produced over half a million sods of peat in that one year (illustration 7). Ridgard has given a clear indication of the approximate date of the completion of the enchanting lake-decoys in both Fritton and Flixton.

Ridgard's most indelible contribution to the story of the medieval landscape emerged from his study of the nunnery at Flixton-by-Bungay. After noting that 350,000 'Breketylls' (bricks) were being made on the bishop's South Elmham manor in 1464-5, and sent to Hoxne, either to that struggling market or to the bishop's manor house, he came to 1469 and perceived a delightful new activity and what he called 'this revised function of the landscape'. For the first time fishing was recorded as a pastime for a gentleman: '*Et quod Thomas Bateman, gentilman, per diversas vices piscavit in seperales riparias domine apud le Melledam.*' This certainly reveals a revised picture of the medieval Waveney valley.

The 'Woodland'

If one lives on the Sandlings or the Breckland or Fielding, on either flank, one knows that steady climb on to the dividing central clay tableland, called, down to the last century, 'the Woodland'. But the woods are reduced now to such small patches, and it seems incredible that they may have been a part of a wide woodland that started to grow perhaps 8,000 years B.C., when the ice finally melted. Yet Staverton Park, on the Sandlings, is now known to be that kind of survivor. There are probably others, all over the clay belt, at

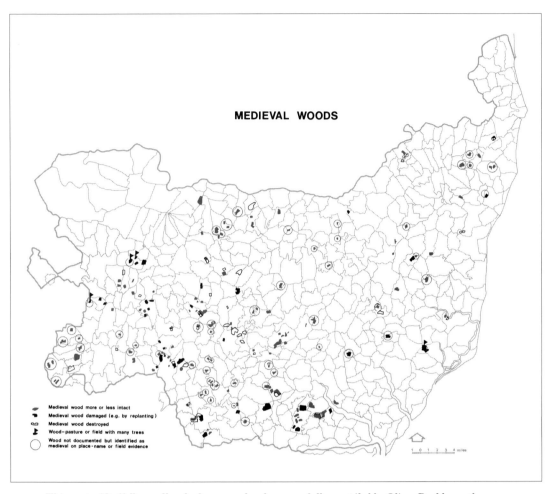

57   *This map of Suffolk woodland after 1350 has been carefully compiled by Oliver Rackham, the leading authority, from the separate histories of hundreds of individuals woods. See particularly his commentary on this map in* An Historical Atlas of Suffolk, *1999.*

Hintlesham and Barking, for instance, and Helmingham and (till the other day) Letheringham. A specially important one, because now being preserved, and in full cultivation (coppicing) and of great scientific interest, and provided with the most agreeable walks, flourishes on the final watershed between east and west Suffolk, whence the Lark flows north and west to Bury and the Ouse, and the Ipswich river flows east. Here, between the capitals of east and west Suffolk, between two different cultures, on a narrow, flat–topped watershed only a mile or two across, some very early English settled in a broad open space which they called Bradfield. Two large settlements of this open area

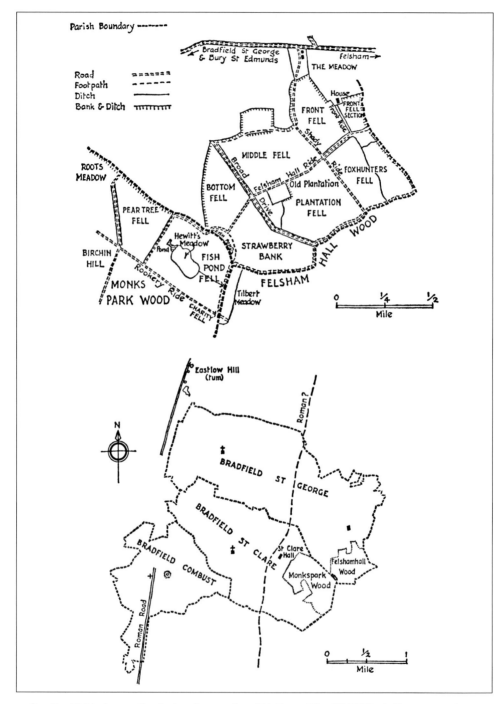

58   *Bradfield: the woodland edge of an ancient feld. Part of Bradfield Woods Reserve may be seen on application in advance to the Wardens at Felsham.*

were given to St Edmund's monks in the first half of the 11th century (see illustration 58), and that is Bradfield's first appearance in written record. The woodland edge of this great clearing is still substantially there to see.

There is so little to be sure of before those grants of *c*.1005-9 and *c*.1039-43. There is the place-name. There are two parallel Roman roads running south-north, one of them a major road, Peddars Way; the other minor, presumably an estate-road running from the Cockfield direction, also towards Ixworth. Looking at the western boundary of Bradfield St George, one sees that it took its shape and line from Peddars Way. One knows that at that point, called Eastlow Hill, just over the north-west corner of the parish, some dignitaries of the late Romano-British period were buried in great conical mounds, and that a settlement, perhaps their great house, lay near the adjoining lake. Could the 'broad field' of the first English settlers be a large arable farm left, or perhaps merely run down, by the Romano-British, and then reclaimed and cultivated by the incoming English? There seems to be no other satisfactory way of explaining this trinity, three pre-Conquest farming communities related to one original broad space. A more detailed version of illustration 58, Bradfield Woods, was published in 1976: Oliver Rackham, *Trees and Woodland in the British Landscape*, pp.80-3. Rackham says the Bradfield woods are 'among the richest of all British woods in plant life, with some 350 flowering plants, including 42 native trees and shrubs'. This may be partly due to their 'probable derivation from the Wildwood'. (This may have been in Bradfield St George, or have overlapped all three modern parishes.) Left alone, on this land, without some cultivation, the space would have reverted to woodland in twenty years, and the name would never have occurred to the English. They were probably describing what they saw when they moved into this landscape – a broad (open) piece of country. And it seems almost certain that Mickfield – 'the great field' – over by Debenham, has the same meaning in terms of an older estate 'rediscovered' and revived by the earliest English newcomers. Stanningfield and Cockfield, too, back in the Bradfield neighbourhood; they have evidences of Romano-British farming and living all around them. The Great Green may have been the original 'field' at Cockfield.

Samson's *Kalendar*, *c*.1186, makes it clear that the one Bradfield church recorded in Domesday was Bradfield St George's. Two of St Edmund's tenants there in Samson's day were Adam the Huntsman and Godwin the Carpenter, proper names for the wooded village whose vestiges survive. Samson granted several Bradfield tenements to someone called Bacun. That name is equally

interesting in terms of the shaping of Suffolk. A Robert Bacon was taxed in
Bradfield St George in 1327. St George's tower was built a century and a half
later, only 66 feet high, but a noble object from the west, and bearing a
Gothic inscription in stone on its buttresses to say that it was John Bacon's
doing. The Bacons of Bradfield are likely to have been in some way related
to the Bacons in the neighbouring parishes of Hessett and Drinkstone, one
of whom took to the law and became Elizabeth I's Lord Keeper. Nicholas
Bacon was solicitor in the court through which all the monastic lands of
England passed, and his own estate-management, in its way reminiscent of
Abbot Samson's, conservative and profitable, gives an idea of the way the
landscape of monastic Suffolk went on long after the Middle Ages.

Outside one of the three Bradfield churches (Bradfield Combust), beside
Peddars Way, lies Arthur Young (1741-1820), one of the most influential
moulders of farming landscapes this country ever saw, and one of the most
voluminous describers of it. His picture of the Suffolk farmlands during the
Napoleonic Wars is an indispensable authority. There had been a continuous
series of Arthur Youngs here from 1620. But his feelings for his native
woodlands were those of a strict economist:

> The woods of Suffolk hardly deserve mentioning, except for the fact that they pay
> in general but indifferently ... Rough pastures ... and broad hedgerows were
> nurseries of timber. These have been cleared and ... timber has declined, a
> circumstance not at all to be regretted, for corn and grass are products much more
> valuable. Underwoods are not generally productive in this county.

What he says is, so far as it goes, incontrovertible. What he did not begin to
see was the possibility that all hedgerow trees and all copses might be wiped
out in the interests of a total corn and grass landscape. Like Mr Reg Harvey,
of Braiseworth Hall, Tannington, he might still, today, have preferred a wide
sweep of prairie, interrupted by a few rather exposed farmhouses and a church
or two. But it would be pleasant to walk him through Monks Park Wood, in
his own Bradfield neighbourhood, and show him the coppicing that has been
practised there since at least the 13th century. Coppicing is the lopping of
trees, practised at Bradfield now on a seven- to ten-year cycle, to produce
various posts and poles, rakeheads and handles, and, formerly, the 'wattle' for
the stiffening of the mud walls of the timber-framed houses. (Coppicing can
be practised on longer cycles of up to thirty years.) Oak, ash, maple and birch
are the chief species being cultivated. For the botanists, over 300 species have
now been counted in these ancient woods.

59 *Green Farm, Wetheringsett. Black poplars along a 'late enclosure' road, made c.1846. 'No other native tree can compare with it in rugged grandeur … more than almost any other tree, black poplar reminds us of the splendour of the medieval countryside' – Oliver Rackham, 1986.*

Cloth-Making Country

The first picture of Suffolk cloth-making comes inevitably from Jocelin of Brakelond, *c.*1200. Delineating his own job, and incidentally deploring the way the monastic lands had been sub-divided into so many parts (presumably through freemen and sokemen selling as they pleased and being often subject to the system of partible inheritance), he told how he would summon the fullers of Bury and forbid them to use the waters (the Linnet to the south, the Lark along the east and north sides of the town), and would seize the webs he found there, if they failed to furnish cloths for the carriage of his salt. This statement points straight at the importance of water for the fulling (or thicking) process. (It also shows how salt was carried.) With scarcely one exception, the clothing towns lay on a stream, the great majority of them built beside the river Stour and its little northern tributaries, the Box and the Brett, and their tributaries draining that fruitful landscape. A look at a map shows the convenience of Ipswich as a vent for cloth intended for export, and Sudbury was using Ipswich for this purpose by the middle of the 13th century.

60 *Hadleigh's medieval bridge (Toppesfield Bridge). The only survivor of its kind in Suffolk. From 1252, a Monday market was held in the street leading (from the right in this picture) to Toppesfield Bridge, and so to the villages and small clothing towns to the west.*

Bury, dependent on road communications till the Lark was made navigable in the 17th century, tended to get left on one side by that trade. The westernmost cloth-towns, like Clare, dealt direct with London. At the end of the 13th century, the name of the leading cloth manufacturer of London was Fulk de St Edmund. And Bury's main business was centred on her own Great Market. Apparently London merchants actually came to buy the merchandise of Flanders and Italy in Skinner's Row (now Skinner Street) and 'the Frenchmen's Quarter' (*vicus Gallorum*: a part of what is now the open Angel Hill, it seems to have been cleared by the early 15th century, presumably to make more room for Bury Fair, held every summer). That king of taste,

Henry III, himself sent William the royal tailor to Bury Fair to bargain for some new scarlet and black furred robes for himself and his sisters, from the looms of Flanders. But by the middle of the 14th century, the looms of Suffolk were stepping up production for export. Bury concentrated on her own big trading market, and the Fair on Angel Hill. But in the 15th century her *industrial* output was only next below Lavenham's, and was well above Ipswich's. Here, then, is the economic base of those elaborately carved timbers, streets-full of them, and those hillsides and valley bottoms enriched to profusion by late medieval traceried and embattled churches.

By 1381 we find – from a maddeningly damaged, incomplete medieval list – that Hadleigh was well away on her impressive early career as an industrial town. She had started as a market town with a grant in 1252 on the Toppesfield manor, adjoining the Archbishop of Canterbury's manor along the north boundary of that incomparable Close, the churchyard. There flush with that boundary-line, before 1438, the doubly 'jettied' guildhall was erected (colour illustration IX), and there the market flourished in the street leading to Toppesfield bridge, the one massive medieval bridge still in use in Suffolk. The Canterbury officials were not backward, and it looks as if it was on their main manor that the clothing industry expanded into an exporting one by about 1305. In that year four tenants were fullers, and one of them, Vincent, had a dye-house.

That was in 1305. By 1568 only Ipswich and Bury were richer than Hadleigh; and Lavenham was no more than half as rich as Melford, having had three times Melford's wealth according to the assessment of 1524. Lavenham owed its late 15th-century eminence largely to the famous clothier Thomas Spring III. Without him, it resumed a modest career. His widow was assessed at £1,000 in goods in 1524, and his son became a landed gentleman.

In Hadleigh, the leading townsman of 1524 had a more moderate 400 marks in goods, and his son had £30 in lands. Their name was Forth, and two decades later, in 1544, they were established in the glorious gatehouse of Butley Priory, among the gentry. In 1524 there were in Hadleigh 110 'artificers, labourers and servants' earning between twenty and forty shillings and each taxed fourpence. There were only six aliens, including Robert Forth's 'Iceland man servant, taking no wages'. Only one of these was connected with weaving. How bored one gets, on being told by people who admire timber-framed houses 'constructed of old ship's timbers' that they were of course inhabited by 'the Flemish weavers'. Two more ludicrous notions never caught on among relatively intelligent people. What one now awaits, from the admirable surveys by Mrs Sylvia Colman for the West Suffolk County Council,[14] is some correlation of the enrichment and the geographical spread of these old 'urban' timbered houses, with the fluctuating economic fortunes of the individual small and enchanting townships. Mrs Colman will need the utmost assistance and collaboration. There are questions for historians working with rentals and surveys, as well as archaeologists examining crown-posts, chamfering and joints.

In the very next year, 1525, the people of Hadleigh, Lavenham and Sudbury rose in uproar against Wolsey's excessive new tax and the coincident spasm of unemployment. It was said 4,000 of them assembled at Lavenham and had the 'bells rung to rouse the district'. That massive, magnificent *campanile* had been going up ever since 1486. A number of bequests towards its completion were made in 1520, and a last one of £200 came in Spring's will, 1523. How strangely ironical and symbolic that those bells should have rung out in 1525 – when the great steeple had perhaps just reached its present state of near completion – to rally an industry in distress, giving a first intimation of mortal vulnerability. As if stricken then with a coronary thrombosis, those towns have gone economically steady ever since.

---

[14] Mrs Colman's comprehensive surveys of the historic buildings of Woolpit, Walsham le-Willows and Clare have been published by the West Suffolk County Council.

Five

THE MODERN LANDSCAPE

As far as agriculture and the countryside are concerned, the true end of the Middle Ages is not the accession of the Tudors but the introduction of the internal combustion engine.

George Ewart Evans, *The Horse in the Furrow* (1960)

Elizabethan Landscape with Figures

The modern landscape of Suffolk is still essentially a medieval one. Five hundred churches, ten thousand 'listed' houses of 'architectural or historic' interest, old 'Hundred lanes' of the tenth century that may be based on pre-Danish boundaries, over ninety market places (or at least their sites), and innumerable hedged and ditched cornfields and pastures, have all survived, more or less intact, from the Middle Ages into the 21st century. Compared with all this, it should not take long to indicate the contribution of the 17th, 18th and 19th centuries, and even less long that of our own, other than the steady erosion that we are learning, only too late, how to mitigate and modify. But the 16th century did make a distinctive and substantial contribution, not least in providing the first maps and surveys, the first real pictures of the land. It also provided the first detailed description of the whole county.

Robert Ryece's *Breviary of Suffolk* is usually supposed to be a work of 1618, since the published version was based on a copy made in that year. In fact it was largely written in 1603, and may be regarded as a true product of the end of the Elizabethan age. Its author thought his ancestor had come to Suffolk from Wales with the Tudors in 1485. His recent biographer has found that ancestor charged with 'breaking and entering' in Preston, near Lavenham, *before* the Tudor victory at Bosworth, in court rolls of the manor of which Ryece himself was subsequently lord.[1] The name seems to be a fairly common old

---

[1] C.G. Harlow in *P.S.I.*, Vol.XXXII (1970).

local one, sometimes spelt Ryes, or even Rush. The manor house next to the church was rebuilt in his own day without a moat: the Tudors had reduced the incidence of breaking and entering. The brick fireplace in the hall is fronted with a Jacobean overmantel carved with the arms of his great-grandfather's marriage (and brought in by the present owner from Parsonage Farm opposite). His heraldic window-glass from the house is gone, but in the church much of what he had painted by a Lavenham glazier survives, together with superb paintings on wood of the Commandments and Royal Arms to show the strength of his adherence to the Queen and her church.[2] As a builder, and as a writer about this county, he epitomised his age's contribution to the landscape.

We have already noticed Ryece's division of the clay belt into a more easterly part devoted to pasture and feeding, and a more central part 'enjoying pasture and meadow, yet far more tillage'. Of corn, Ryece thought Suffolk must always have had enough to feed 'the populous number of their own inhabitants, even in the scarcest years', or when 'the greedy covetous merchant' cashed in on shortages abroad, and exported 'by stealth'. After corn, Ryece described a sort of hop-rush, with people dropping their former occupations to drain 'unprofitable marshes and moors' when they saw how the 'countryman Hop Merchants' were making their fortunes. 'The influence of the heavens and the unkindness of the seasons' demonstrated the uncertainty of profits, and by 1602 the hop-fields had 'come to decay in these parts'. But they have been revived intermittently; and old hop-grounds are still to be seen down by the river at the Abbots Hall open-air Museum of East Anglian Life, at Stowmarket. Ryece noted the shrinkage of coppice woods (of the Bradfield kind), and consequent rise in the cost of hop-poles, as a deterrent to the hop-rush. On the subject of forestry proper, he uttered a very familiar warning. The 'multiplicity of curious' timber buildings and costly ships 'hath almost utterly consumed our timber'. But there was no public concern about replenishing the woods, 'since generally there is more respect to a present private benefit how small soever than to the great advantage of the common wealth hereafter.'

Ryece's notice of rabbit-warrens indicates a very common feature of the landscape of his day, and earlier days. One of the earliest maps of a part of Suffolk shows the country at precisely the point where the Ipswich-Bury road crossed the east-west Suffolk boundary (till it was dissolved). The map (illustration 61) I believe to be early Elizabethan.[3] The boundary between the

---

[2] The arms are labelled *ELIZABETHA MAGNA*.
[3] It is in the library of Lord Stafford at Swynnerton Park, and used to be thought pre-1500.

61 *Elmswell – Wetherden – Woolpit, c.1568: boundaries, roads and other old landmarks. All wording (except that in brackets) transcribed from photocopy, in West Suffolk Record Office, of original map in Staffordshire. Notice the post-windmill on the heath, and the prosperous chimneys on the warrener's lodge. Also the relatively late strip-fields.*

East Suffolk 'geldable' and the Liberty of St Edmund was marked, as it still is, by 'The alde diche called the Fraunchise bancke'. Just to the east, on the south side of the road, where Haughley Park now begins, stood a windmill; so we see how much more open this neighbourhood was then. All signs of the mill seem to have been obliterated by an army camp of the Second World War. On the north side of the road, opposite another ancient ditch, dividing 'Grass field' from Woolpit Heath, a note on the map records that 'at this verie corner a Gospell was wont to be said by the parson of Wolpett'. (The reference in the past tense helps to confirm the map's post-Reformation date.) Going west along the north side of the main road, just west of the county boundary, 'the Warrener's Lodge' stood on a small hill. It was provided with a prominent chimney-stack, a sign that the warrener was a man of parts, for it was only in the course of Elizabeth's reign that chimneys became at all common. This site, too, is now lost; taken by a great gravel pit. But, to demonstrate the general unity of the Elizabethan landscape with our own, a large oval on the map, over to the west near the site of the late Woolpit brickworks, was already labelled 'a great gravell pitt'. And the unity of both periods with that time, before 1013, when Woolpit's name was first recorded (*Wlpit*) is apparent enough.

The point of this diversion is to demonstrate the help maps give from now on in interpreting the landscape's story, and also to illustrate Ryece's comment on

> the harmless Coneys which do naturally delight to make their abode here ... with rich profit for all good housekeepers ... whence it proceeds that there are so many warrens here in every place, which do furnish the next markets and are carried to London with no little reckoning ... There is none who deem their houses well seated who have not to the same belonging a common wealth of coneys.

From coneys, Ryece moved on to deer parks, and explained why they were thought wasteful on good land, and why so many more parks were being 'disparked' than newly enclosed. Saxton's map of Suffolk, 1575, plots in the deer parks with a symbol, a circle of pales. Three parks were noticed in Domesday Book, at Bentley, Dennington and Ixworth, and the Malets had one at Eye very soon after. St Edmund had parks at Melford, Chelsworth, Bradfield and elsewhere. We traced the Bigods' Kelsale park in the landscape. It seems likely that the Domesday park at Dennington was later merged with the vast Bigod park at Framlingham, the boundaries of which can still be traced by great discontinuous banks and hedges. Edmund Farrer published brief articles on 103 Suffolk parks.[4] His list was not complete, omitting for instance the pleasant parkland at Bramford. Parks have been a delightful feature of the Suffolk scene since before 1066, and have survived and flourished, most notably of all at Helmingham, despite Ryece's worry that they were uneconomic.

In a brilliant study of Lord Keeper Bacon's own personal estates, Alan Simpson observed that sheep-farming was in the Bacon blood (we saw them at Hessett and Drinkstone, and Bradfield), and he went on to describe the

---

4 *East Anglian Daily Times*, January-June 1925.

adjacent champion country, west and north of Bury, as 'one vast sheep-walk; every village had its flocks'. Again, this was true, on a smaller scale, in Domesday Book and right through to the 19th century. Ryece noticed that, for size, Suffolk sheep did not compare with Midland breeds, especially in the poorer 'heath and barren Champion, where our greatest numbers of flocks be'. These animals make their own characteristic grey-white patterns in the fields, sometimes folded in squares by hurdles or wire netting, sometimes adopting single file along the marsh walls and fen banks, or advancing in extended order for a yearly feed through the grasses and vetch and campion of our lonely beaches (illustration 78). More than any other physical feature, even the plough-furrow, the sheep add to the landscape a sense of the endlessness of time known, and it is intensified by that weird, gregarious, dry-throated cry. But they nearly vanished from the Suffolk scene after 1925, when subsidised sugar-beet began to take over from the traditional root-breaks. They are back, also pigs in small pig-size Nissen huts.

A Few Late Enclosures

From what has already been said about the extremely early enclosure of pastures and cornfields, it will surprise nobody to learn that only 115 Parliamentary Enclosure Acts related to Suffolk, and over half of them were concerned exclusively with the enclosure of commons. Those parishes with open fields still left to be enclosed in this way were for the most part in the Fielding, west of Bury (illustration 3). Apart from a couple of hundred acres in Finningham and Gislingham, the only exceptions of any consequence were all away to the east of the central clays, and close to the seacoast: almost exclusively in the Waveney valley and the area immediately north and south of Lowestoft. A photograph of the Enclosure Award map of 1817 covering a handful of small fields beside the Waveney in Mettingham (reproduced by W.E. Tate in *Proceedings*, Suffolk Institute, vol. XXV, 1952) demonstrates the negligible extent to which the Parliamentary Enclosure movement affected the ancient fields and pastures of Suffolk.

On the other hand, some thousands of acres of commons and waste were enclosed by Act in the late 18th and early 19th centuries (illustration 77). For instance, the road from Woodbridge through Martlesham to Trimley and Felixstowe runs along the edge of what on Hodskinson's map of Suffolk in 1783 was accurately delineated as Levington Heath and Foxhall Heath. Together they formed a band of heathland stretching all along the southern boundaries of the parishes of Bucklesham and Foxhall. A private Act in 1803 resulted next year in an enclosure award that turned these heaths (amounting to 760 acres) into trim rectangular fields. That Woodbridge-Felixstowe road runs alongside the eastern edge of the new enclosures in Bucklesham; but to the east of the road, towards the Deben valley, the older enclosures, studded with ash and oak, look only a few degrees less rectangular. And the thorn hedgerows of the new enclosures (the kind that make the Midland fields so comparatively monotonous) are here fairly well interspersed with holly and oak. In fact, one would not suspect this of being an area of late enclosure at all if it were not for the prominent road-sign labelling one of the Bucklesham branch-roads *Tenth Road*. Of the ten public roads 'set out and appointed' in Bucklesham and Foxhall under the Act, only the sixth and tenth were new creations, aligned to accommodate the new fields. The rest exactly followed the lines of the ancient heath-tracks. In the case of Ninth Road, in Foxhall, known now as Straight Road, it is hard to believe that this was not newly laid out after the 1804 Award notwithstanding the great girth of the oaks that still over arch it and make it a green tunnel in summer.

One of several invaluable services performed by Joseph Hodskinson's fine map of the county[5] is that it presents an accurate picture of the old Greens and heaths of Suffolk before so many of them were enclosed. On the ground, the former Greens may often still be detected by the otherwise rather meaningless grouping of collections of old houses and cottages: they were originally ranged round the edge, and so continue to mark it. David Dymond illustrated the effect of this in Elmswell with a composite map (in *East Anglian Studies*, ed. Lionel Munby). Among the encroachments noted in 1845 on a small Green at the south end of Debenham (Cherry Tree Green, see illustration 62), were three cottages and gardens, an iron foundry, the National School (1834) and an osier ground. So here was an example of enclosure of a Green piecemeal, by agreement. By that time, the horse and lamb fair, formerly held on the Green, had to make do with the field behind the *Cherry Tree* inn. This Midsummer Fair at Debenham is one of 68 Suffolk fairs listed by Ryece (in an unpublished version of his *Breviary*), which in his day 'do furnish the inhabitants of their household provision and necessaries, by which a great part of the country's trade and intercourse is continued'. At Aspall, nearby, a fair was already in being in 1086. Being held only annually, fairs have made a less permanent

---

[5] An exemplary edition by D.P. Dymond of Hodskinson's map has been published as Vol.XV of the Suffolk Records Society, 1972.

62 *Debenham from the south. The road follows the stream of the Deben down from the top of the picture. The stream curves away to the east above the church (which has Anglo-Saxon masonry and stands on an eminence). In the wider part of the street, south of the curve of the stream, are the former market and guildhall. Cherry Tree Green is at the bottom of the picture.*

impression on the landscape than markets. The most famous of them, the month-long autumn fair at Bury, accounts for Angel Hill, one of the most beautiful urban spaces in England. Its final decline was ascribed to peacetime affluence by William Bodham Donne in 1847: 'Now, a dropsical Mayor followed by four scarecrows in blue and yellow liveries, and preceded by a tame lunatic with a bell, informs the four corners of the town of the opening of the Carnival.' There were about ninety grants of medieval fairs in Suffolk (illustration 48, above and *Historical Atlas*, pp.78-9). (Bury Fair first held in July; later, in October.)

There is no old tradition of cricket on the Greens of Suffolk. Poaching and shooting, fishing and hunting, seem to have been the chief traditional sports apart from 'camping', which usually took place on the local Green, and is recorded as early as 1466, in Cullum's *Hawstead*. It was a local medieval ball-game. Among the Articles preferred against the rector of Eyke by the Puritans in his parish in 1644 was that 'he hath been present with such of his parish as have been at the same time camping on the Lord's day, and showed no dislike thereof.' Many of the field-names of villages and towns include the 'camping-piece'. An advertisement by the publican of Eye *King's Head* in the *Ipswich Journal*, 30 September 1752, announced that on the day after Old Michaelmas Day, in a large field adjoining Lanthorn Green (now Langton Green), five guineas would be given, 'to be CAMP'D for by twenty men, the ten winning men to have half-a-guinea each: each side to choose their goalkeeper and sidesmen – the ball to be thrown exactly at half-past three, and to play the best of half-an-hour.' The antiquary D.E. Davy, brought up at Rumburgh, remembered that when he was a boy, in the 1770s, 'the young people met two or three times a week on Rumburgh Common during the summer evenings for this amusement. Matches sometimes used to be made between parishes, which sometimes became real battles' (British Library; BL19171, ff.368-9). He then described the game in detail; as Forby did, rather differently, in *The Vocabulary of East Anglia*, 1830.

The most interesting 'town camping-close' in Suffolk is that of Walsham-le-Willows. There, on the north-west corner of the main crossroads in the village, diagonally across the main street from St Mary's church, the camping close site of 1509 is identifiable with that of an Elizabethan open-air theatre of 1577, known then as the Game Place.[6] The Walsham Field Book of that date has been transcribed by Kenneth M. Dodd, of Lakehead University, Ontario:

> The sayd game place in the tenure of divers men to the use and behofe of the towne of walsham aforesayd is customarye ground holden of the sayd manor of walsham and a place compassed round with a fayer banke cast up on a good height & havinge many great trees called populers growinge about the same banke, in the myddest a fayre round place of earth made of purpose for the use of Stage playes.

The round plan of this earthwork seems to be recorded on Ordnance Survey maps as late as 1904. What is so particularly challenging about the

---

[6] Kenneth M. Dodd, 'Another Elizabethan Theatre in the Round', *Shakespeare Quarterly*, Shakespeare Association of America, Vol.XXI, No.2 (Spring 1970).

identification is that the site of so rare and remarkable a theatre in the round should coincide with a natural amphitheatre (behind a new large house opposite the cemetery lychgate).

Buildings

Since the Anglo-Saxon centuries, the wooden churches have all, with the partial exception of one, been replaced by stone buildings.[7] These include some of the best achievement of the entire history of the county, and their contribution to the landscape has already been touched on. It is hard to think of post-medieval buildings to compare in splendour and richness with the churches of Blythburgh, or Southwold, or Eye, or Stoke-by-Nayland, Lavenham, or Melford, or St Mary's Bury, or Mildenhall.

Their story is familiar from Munro Cautley's book, *Suffolk Churches and their Treasures*, though his Victorian belief that only medieval Gothic would do to worship God in blinded him to the interest of Euston St Genevieve, largely of 1676, with Baroque detail; or Shelland, a pretty church in the Georgian Gothick taste. Cautley and Pevsner and my own Shell *Guide* say most of the things that need to be said, and yet there is still much more to discover about these 500 centres of age-long worship and (it is worth remembering for the bleak future) of much other social activity. New facts about their building constantly come to light, and, in terms of the landscape, some of the most interesting are being uncovered by Mr Peter Northeast of Rattlesden. He is going methodically through all the surviving late-medieval wills to see what bequests relate to work on church fabrics. The results have a general interest, in terms of the local prosperity as well as the dating of some of the chief features of the landscape.

Of Woodbridge, he wrote to me: 'The whole neighbourhood was intent on tower-building in the middle of the 15th century: Bredfield 1452, Melton Old St Andrew's 1446, Eyke 1450, Bromeswell 1450, Woodbridge 1441-51, Martlesham 1450, Great Bealings 1445-51, Wantisden 1448, and Woodbridge's splendid flushwork north porch 1448.'

A single will, or a record for one year, is naturally not enough by itself. The documents are mostly indications of intent. Setting them beside the buildings themselves, a more complex story develops. For instance, Melton Old Church, idyllic beside the water-mill from which the original settlement was named, retains superb 14th-century window tracery in its tower. The will may refer to

---

[7] The exception, Crowfield's chancel, is unexciting, late medieval and much restored.

63 *Gipping Church was built as a chantry-chapel, probably in 1484-5, the year before Bosworth, by a leading Yorkist, Sir James Tyrell. It celebrates, with heraldry and monograms, his marriage alliance with Anne Arundel of Lanherne. Limestone was expensive in Suffolk, the quarries distant, but local flint was plentiful; and so this combination was devised, of delicate 'flush patterns'. Of all the masterpieces of flushwork masonry all over Suffolk, in church-towers and porches and clerestories, this is the most sustained and brilliant. It would originally have been battlemented: the high-pitched roof and the tower are later additions.*

a new west doorway and a set of flushwork battlements. All Eyke now has is the base of a 12th-century central tower. The fact remains that 1450 was the approximate date of a very large number of Suffolk's finest towers.

From such building-accounts as we have, it is known that a flintwork tower would go up at not more than ten feet a year, to give it a chance to set solid (even though flint is the toughest of stone, it is held by mortar which is most vulnerable to weather). So a 70-foot steeple (this is the 15th-century Suffolk word for church-tower) would be building over a period of at least seven years. The master mason at Helmingham was allowed ten years for a 60-foot tower. It is no uncommon thing to find bequests spread over ten or more years. The 15th century was certainly the great period for Suffolk church-building – not only of towers. Some of the most beautiful displays of canopy-patterns in flushwork have gone into the outside walls of clerestories, at

64 *Helmingham church-tower, 1488-c.1498: its proportions are modelled on Framsden's. The parapet was added in 1543. The plinth is inscribed in Latin, 'She ascends to Heaven, the Virgin Mother, of Jesse's stem.'*

Coddenham, at Wilby, almost all over Suffolk. In two dimensions, the *trompe l'oeil* effect of three was achieved.

When Mr Northeast has finished his researches, the quantity of the church-building datable to specific years in the middle of the 15th century will, I imagine, reveal a proud building industry. We know too little about it. The master builder of Helmingham's handsome steeple, 1488-*c*.1498 (illustration 64), was Thomas Aldrych of North Lopham, in south Norfolk. What his contract with John Talmadge and the Helmingham churchwardens shows about tower-building in Suffolk is that emulation was the basic principle. They wanted their steeple to be 60 feet in height, and 'after the breadth, wideness and thickness of the steeple of Framsden', the adjoining parish (illustration 65). The fabric should be 'a black wall wrought of Flint'. Later, they used the alternative word for flint, which was calyon: the churchwardens 'shall lay or do to be laid in the churchyard' all the freestone, calyon, lime, sand, bowls, shovels, hod, rope, windlass, hawser and boards that Aldrych or his workmen should need. The only other design-specification was that the west door, lower west window (with niche either side, for an image) and all other windows and buttresses of the steeple should be 'after the fashion of the steeple of Brandeston' – the next church on beyond Monewden, at most four miles from Helmingham. Here was healthy local rivalry, nothing pretentious. They were not eager for egregious Midland spires of the kind the Victorian diocesan architect supplied at Woolpit and at St Mary Tower in Ipswich; nor for eclectic 'Gothic' of the kind the cathedral church of St James has lately been enlarged with, in Bury, a town with a most pronounced character of its own, that is essentially uneclectic, East Anglian, and 'Suffolk'. The late Birkin Haward, a retired very distinguished architect, made measured drawings of all the church arcades with moulded piers: altogether 112 in Suffolk. This showed links between the works of known master-masons: *Suffolk Medieval Church Arcades* (1993). He also completed a photographic survey of carvings on hammer-beam roofs: *Suffolk Medieval Church Roof Carvings*, 1999.

Richard Russell of Dunwich, master mason and MP for Dunwich, worked with a Blythburgh master mason on the steeple at Walberswick, one of the four best towers in Suffolk. They were not instructed to eclipse all other towers in the district. On the contrary, they were told to copy the proportions of Tunstall (towards Woodbridge), and the details of the west front of Halesworth. If Russell and his Blythburgh partner did better, as they did, and it is no empty compliment, then it was probably that they had it in them, and were given the

65   *Framsden church-tower: the traditional East Anglian design of the second half of the 15th century. It looks as though the belfry louvre was enlarged after the building of Helmingham, to go one better.*

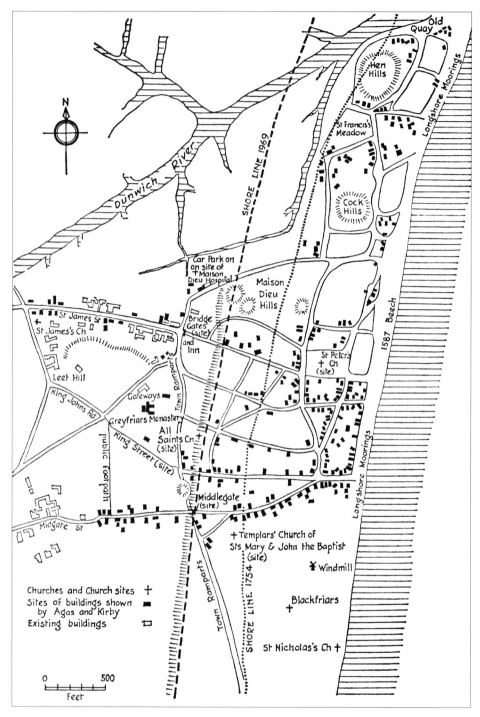

66 *The remains of Dunwich.*

right encouragement, or inspiration. (They may have done Kessingland's steeple, also.) At present, the dignity of the parish steeple is all the evidence we have of the prosperity of innumerable Suffolk villages in the 15th century; at Covehithe, very notably, which in the desolate splendour of its great church-ruin almost eclipses the surviving medieval suburbs of Dunwich. It is an indicator less of particular than of general former well-being.

After the early 14th century, the decline of Dunwich, that 'city of chilblained monks' continually battered by the steel-grey eastern sea, apparently encouraged

---

66   *The remains of Dunwich.*

In its heyday, about the time of King John, Dunwich was a gated town on a hill about forty feet above the sea. Within its gates stood eight, possibly nine, parish churches and a number of religious houses. In its market places, markets were held every day of the week. One begins to get an idea of the former site of the town by climbing the hill to the west of the 19th-century church of St James and looking towards the sea.

Already at the time of Domesday Book, the sea's advance was recorded. The mother church of East Anglia, founded by St Felix, is presumed to have been the first church submerged. St Leonard's followed, c.1300. The sea's most damaging advance, on 14 January, 1328, completely choked the ancient harbour with shingle, and forced the river mouth away to the north, towards the territory of Blythburgh. By 1350, 'upwards of 400 houses', with shops and windmills, were reported overrun by the sea. The parish churches of St Bartholomew and St Michael disappeared c.1331. The last priest was instituted to St Martin's church in 1335, and to St Nicholas's in 1352. However, we know that St Nicholas's long remained standing 20 rods south-east of the Blackfriars, and that in 1573 men remembered that both St Nicholas's and St John's churches were cruciform in plan, with central towers. St John's stood near the Great Market Place, and was dismantled c.1540 to prevent the materials sliding away with the cliff. The sea entered the market place in 1677 when the townsmen sold the lead of the market cross. St John's church presumably stood near the 1587 shore line on the map, to the north of St Nicholas's, and south-east of St Peter's. St Leonard's is thought to have stood east of St John's.

1570 was a disastrous year, when the town's Gilden Gate and South Gate were swallowed. St Peter's, 'near as long as Blythburgh', was dismantled c.1700, and was well out to sea by the time Gardner's History of Dunwich *appeared in 1754. All Saints, the last of Dunwich's medieval parish churches, tumbled down to the beach early in the 20th century.*

Figure 18 is based on Joshua Kirby's plan of Dunwich published in Gardner's History *in 1754. Kirby collated his plan with Ralph Agas's, done in 1587, by which time the Dunwich river was entering the sea as far north as Walberswick. The former scale of this river is seen west of St James's church, where it has eroded the hillside. Here, a fresh water spring, 'St James's Well', now rather torpid, presumably supplied the medieval leper hospital of St James in the suburbs.*

From Agas and Kirby it seems that the sea has gained about a quarter of a mile in the four centuries since 1587. Roughly threequarters of that loss occurred during the first half of the period, and only a quarter (i.e. half a furlong) in the two centuries since Kirby's day.

The site of the town's western gate, Middle Gate, in 1968-69 disappeared down the edge of the cliff. Just north of this, a small stretch of the town's rampart joins up with the south-east corner of the Greyfriars wall. The present village represents the western suburbs of the medieval town.

the growth of the lesser Suffolk ports, as well as Ipswich, its chief rival, sitting smugly at the head of an estuary instead of lying at the weak, irresolute mouth, as Dunwich did. Blythburgh, Walberswick and Southwold felt the immediate benefit of the move close up to them of that distorted mouth. Easton (now almost entirely eroded), Cove and Kessingland (tower 1439-49) achieved some maritime prosperity. Kirkley's first recorded appearance was in 1322. Not that Dunwich was deposed without a struggle. She was rallying bravely in the 16th century, when one of Ryece's contemporaries wrote a description, the first reliable one, of the mortally wounded town (illustration 66). Even in the time of Henry VIII, Dunwich (what was left of it) was paying more in tax than the clamorous town of Birmingham.

In the same way, buildings epitomise Aldeburgh's history. The early Tudor moot hall (illustration 81), familiar all over the world now from the celebrity of the annual Festival of Music, stands literally beside the beach, showing that the town has come within an inch of its death by drowning. The little moot hall, timber-framed, and brick and stone, utterly idiosyncratic (and thereby most truly 'Suffolk') was presumably built in the middle of the market place when the market was first granted in 1547, at a curiously late date. The market was originally held in an open ground floor under the moot hall, which explains the external stair. The church was rebuilding a generation earlier. This pair of buildings represents a release from the moribund fingers of Snape priory at the Dissolution, and also a growth at the expense of Orford, which had monopolised the trade of the lonely tidal Alde river from the 12th century, when the royal castle was built. Aldeburgh's characteristic north-south length represents a stretch between two havens: one, the familiar sailing mooring on the river at the site of Slaughden (a hamlet taken by the sea in our lifetime), the other to the north, half-way to Thorpeness. Until the marsh was drained in the 19th century, Thorpeness Mere extended south as far as Aldeburgh, was fed by the Hundred River (the south boundary of the Blything Hundred), and maintained an outlet into the sea thus providing an inlet for ships, until the combination of shingle shoals and bigger 16th-century ships made Aldeburgh's northern harbour useless. It is now a marsh and a camping-site (tented and caravan variety).

The emergence of Lowestoft as a seaport behind the precarious shelter of two offshore shoals, or ridges – Holm Sand and Newcome Sand – marked the beginning of a prolonged and deadly struggle with Yarmouth. The two shingle-banks, usually visible as a line of 'breakers', still shift and give trouble to

Lowestoft's shipping, and the rivalry with Yarmouth remains, like Grimsby's with Hull. Out of all this competition for trade, Ipswich emerged easily ahead. She seems never to have had much difficulty in establishing her rights over Harwich to all the trade of 'Orwell Haven', the control of all the business of the estuary. (Medieval references to the port of Orwell, as to the port of Goseford, have misled people into believing they were places, actual towns with streets.)

To return to buildings in the landscape, the most remarkable recent discoveries have been a whole series of elaborate, and again surprisingly idiosyncratic 14th-century timber-framed houses. The oldest surviving Suffolk houses are stone buildings of the 12th century in Bury: incomplete, except Moyses Hall, but very precious, not least because they are probably a tangible link with the world of Jocelin and Samson. Then there are two houses of the 13th century. One of them, Little Wenham Hall, is well known, and incomparably romantic and beautiful. What an embattled skyline as one approaches from the west in the evening sunlight! It retains the 12th-century principle, for security, of having 'services' and guardroom on the vaulted ground floor, and living rooms and chapel above. The other, much less well known, and only recently discovered, is called Purton Green Farmhouse, in the parish of Stansfield, near Wickhambrook: it is a timber-framed aisled hall, and has been restored by the Landmark Trust. (The postholes of a medieval aisled hall have been found on a moated site at Brome, near Eye.)

Forty-two years ago, when my *Shell Guide to Suffolk* went to press, nothing was known of any timber house that was earlier than the 15th century. Or rather, two 14th-century aisled halls were just being uncovered. One was Abbas Hall, Cornard, close to Sudbury, the other Edgar's Farmhouse, Combs. Since then, it has been found necessary to rescue Edgar's Farmhouse, to make way for a housing estate already planned in those suburbs of Stowmarket. It has been dismantled and removed to the security (and the now more appropriate setting) of the East Anglian Life Museum in Stowmarket. Since the 19th century, its name has been Edgar's Farmhouse. By good luck, it has been possible to identify the farm as one owned by the Adgor family in 1437, and a rebuilding of the house may have been the result of the new acquisition of holdings there of farmlands and a house by John and Ascelina Adgor in 1342 and 1346. The structure had already indicated a building of precisely that prosperous time, when rich incidental subsidies came from the embattled squires in France, where the war was going well – as it continued to do for some years, almost regardless of the Black Death.

67   *Fressingfield, the former market place. A lease of 1741, preserved in the* Swan, *describes this as 'the common street sometime being the market place'.*

The most impressive of the 14th-century timber halls exemplifies this: a part of the old nunnery at Campsey Ash, patronised by the De Ufford earls of Suffolk. Close to a great fishpond, and beside an idyllic mill stream, it was probably erected for some canons, in a short lived experiment in monastic desegregation. The nuns disliked it, and complained successfully. But this marvellous building survives, as a private house. It is not precisely an aisled hall: in structure, it is as if the truss of an aisled hall were lifted up to the first floor, and supported on a gigantic tie-beam, a truly massive tree-trunk. Only one example of this kind of building was known, and lay just across the Essex border in Felsted. Then one more was found in north-west Essex (Wendens Ambo Hall), and five more came to light in Suffolk, so that the structure looks as if it may be the special design of a Suffolk house-carpenter. The others are Boynton Hall, Capel St Mary (the ancient moated manor house to which Capel's church was originally attached, though it lies some way across the A12); Choppings Hill Farmhouse, Coddenham; at Fressingfield Church Farm, a cow-house, in the occupation of cows, has this structure, and one supposes it may represent the 14th-century Church Farmhouse; Wingfield College Farmhouse, representing the structure of the college hall, and therefore presumably datable to 1361-2 when the college was founded by the

Black Prince's Chief of Council, Sir John Wingfield; and The Elms at All Saints South Elmham. Less than two miles from The Elms stands South Elmham Hall, in the parish of St George. Its pleasant, rather Victorian front conceals the great first-floor 14th-century hall of the manor house of the East Anglian bishops – the room in which the local followers of Wycliffe were presumably tried before the bishop for heresy. The ruined minster lies, within its (presumed) Roman precinct, in the little valley below.

Five hundred churches, ten thousand listed buildings and more being 'discovered', but do these things really make the modern landscape essentially medieval? The churches are little changed in external appearance, except that most of the medieval glass was smashed by the Puritans, and replaced by Victorian coloured glass or sensible modern plain glass. The nine timber-framed houses I mentioned in detail because their remarkable antiquity was totally unsuspected. Their basic framework was so effectively concealed within an external cladding that had, by its nature, needed renewal; this had led to a slight change of identity. But the bulk, the shape, the dimensions still occupy their corner of the Suffolk countryside as they have for six centuries. They had merged with the thousands of later medieval buildings, mainly of the 15th, 16th and 17th centuries. Some of the 15th- and 16th-century timber trusses, too, are spectacular, as fine in conception and execution as many of the contemporary churches; the work, presumably, of the same carpenters. What is perturbing is that not one of the timber domestic buildings I have just mentioned was identified, in the making of the enormous lists of the Ministry of the Environment, as being in any way out of the ordinary run of local old buildings. Some were even Grade III, which means that they were on the 'Supplementary', not the 'Statutory' List, and so virtually subject to no control as to alterations, or even demolition, unless a Preservation Order were obtained. One would have thought that the experience of a dozen years in uncovering nine hitherto unidentified important 14th-century timber buildings would suggest a more intensive professional check on the lists. Mrs Sylvia Colman was employed part-time by West Suffolk on this urgent work, and her valuable Reports were published on the buildings of Woolpit and Walsham-le-Willows. But this meticulous survey is not going on rapidly enough to cover even West Suffolk in our lifetime. In East Suffolk, whose record on conservation is otherwise fairly good, this job was not even started except in 'threatened areas', when an architect from the Department of the Environment descended.

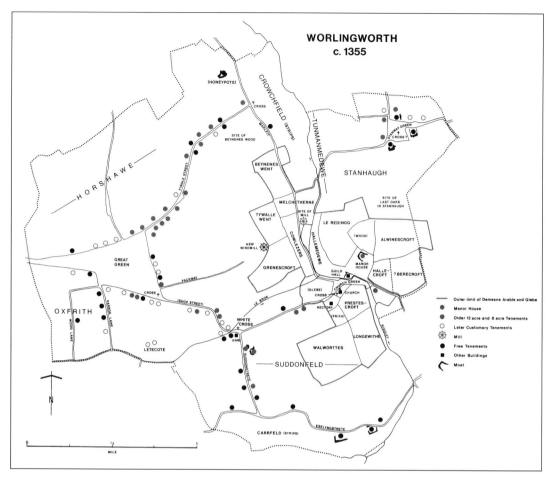

68 *The unusual structure of this medieval manor is examined by John Ridgard in great detail in* An Historical Atlas of Suffolk, *1999.*

However, David Penrose and Peter Hill set a valuable precedent by publishing in *The Suffolk Review* (Bulletin of the Suffolk Local History Council, Autumn 1971) their remarkable survey of 'The Houses of Stonham Aspal'. This enabled them to reconstruct a map of the buildings of the parish as it must have been in the middle of the 16th century (illustration 69). It shows a fairly characteristic scattered settlement with at least seven nuclei of habitation, and three fairly central long narrow Greens. Two of the house structures ('Symondes', next to *The Ten Bells*, and 'Elseys in the Fields') go back to the 14th century, each still bearing the name of the family that originally built it. It would be very valuable if these researches were extended to the adjoining Stonham parishes, Earl Stonham and Little Stonham, so that

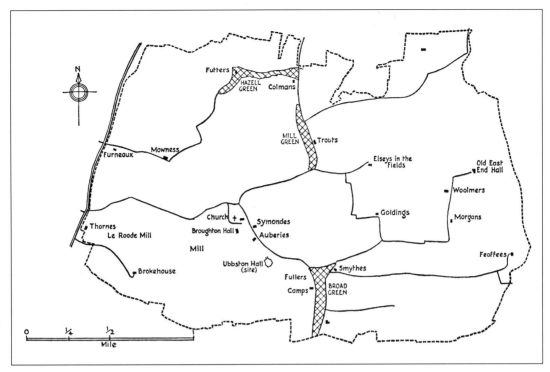

69 *Stonham Aspal: the pattern of dwellings in the 16th century, reconstructed by D. Penrose and P. Hill.*

we had a complete anatomy of all the surviving ancient dwellings of Stonham, with all that that might tell us about the overall pattern and history of the settlement. More recently in the *Historical Atlas*, John Ridgard has published his remarkable reconstruction of the manor of Worlingworth, *c.*1355. And then Leigh Alston is devoting himself to a full-scale study of our enormous legacy of old houses: it will be extremely rewarding. There is now a whole team of experts, including Philip Aitkens, Mark Barnard, Sylvia Colman, Timothy Easton and Edward Martin.

Of course, many of the ten thousand old houses are not as exceptionally interesting as those 14th-century ones, but at present we cannot be at all sure about the majority of them. One knows many old Suffolk farmhouses whose interest anyway lies not in their unusual structure, or high antiquity, but in their quality of being 'unspoilt', preserving their old plasterwork and colour, having been lucky enough to avoid the stain of solignum on the oak beams and studs, and not having had the external lime-plaster and pargetting ripped off, exposing timbers that nobody wants to see after they have once been covered: for they have lost their looks in the process, and need to be cared for under a sleek, smooth plaster of lime and sand (illustration 59).

The 'hall houses', whether aisled or not, were originally open to the roof: a fire burnt in the middle of the floor, and the smoke found its way out of a louvre in the roof. Brick chimneys were the symbol of the most general improvement in domestic comfort. They came in fairly fast in the second half of the 16th century, which meant that the whole house, and not just the wings, could be divided into two or more floors. But for a long time yet, down to about 1700, it was very unusual for a house to be built, like Basts, at Grundisburgh, more than one room thick. Until *c.*1700, the characteristic width of a house, as of a church or barn or any other building, was governed by what could be comfortably spanned by a single beam, from a single tree.

It was a Suffolk custom for copyhold tenants to have the right to fell timber on their land for the making and repair of their buildings, and to fell and sell timber one tenant to another for the same purposes. An example occurs in the court roll of Flixton-by-Bungay in October 1584 (I am indebted to John Ridgard for it). John Dade, a copyholder in St Peter's South Elmham, was allowed to take down 'one ruinous tenement or mansion house' wherein he then dwelt, also a little house adjoining it at the corner. His house was 47 feet long. Within the next two years he was to 'build again and set up there one new, sufficient and well-built dwelling-house', 47 feet long. From the specifications that followed, it was obviously going to be in one of the commonest of the surviving standard forms of Elizabethan Suffolk yeoman farmhouse. Happily one still finds hundreds of them all over Suffolk, though this one seems to have been lost. 'Standard' though the basic formula was, when it came to be put into practice, then the materials and the sites and the individuals concerned imposed their agreeable variations – initials of farmer and wife pargetted with the year-date, a series of small carved capitals on the posts below the strengthening brackets if the house was to have a jettied first floor, and so on. One constant was that the dairy was always sited on the north side, as Bloomfield knew:

> Streams of new milk thro' flowing coolers stray,
> And snow white curd abounds, and wholesome whey.
> Due north th'unglazed windows, cold and clear.

John Dade's formula, at South Elmham, was that the new house should, exactly like its predecessor, be 47 feet long, a clear indication that the rooms would be end-to-end in the usual way, and the width of the whole house governed by the length of the main tie-beams. By implication, there was to be an upper floor, so it may well have been a jettied house (i.e. with the upper floor projecting out over the walls of the ground floor, so that the joists could be bracketed and strengthened, on the cantilever principle, against any tendency to lean). It was to contain: 'in the nether floor, a parlour, a hall, a third room that, being divided, may serve for a buttery and a little chamber or other rooms.' This is the essential plan, on which of course there were many variations, with projecting wings and so on. Towards his rebuilding, John Dade was given licence 'to fell and cut down ten oaks and three elms now standing in or upon his copyhold'. Nothing was said about chimneys, but at this time there is likely to have been a stack running up at the partition between central hall and parlour, with bricks made locally. Thus was the Suffolk landscape self-contained. From about 1570 to, say, 1640, there was a 'Great Rebuilding' in Suffolk as over most of England. Old houses were replaced, as we should expect in a landscape so densely occupied for so long; or they were enlarged and pretty well disguised. Often, too, completely new houses were built, not only by wealthy magnates, but by thriving yeomen.

A marvellous example of this, in Suffolk at the beginning of the 21st century, is Rookery Farm, Monewden, one of a series of three on lands that in the 1590s were part of a thriving farming district from medieval times. My friend Stephen Podd has found, by field-walking, at least five medieval sites in the neighbourhood of the Clopton-Monewden road. He sees Rookery Farm as the holding of a yeoman farmer, already consolidated by 1656; a small farm, probably mixed, in an area of comparatively large dairy farms; and evidently profitable enough for John Stebbing to be able to rebuild his house in 1593, when his neighbours were doing likewise. Initials on the chimney-stack show that John Stebbing and his wife built it in 1593. A map was made for Mr George Stebbing in 1656, by Nathaniel Fuller. It shows that the present house had another wing running at right-angles between it and the road, and that the little front court was approached through a fanciful gate (of the type that went almost too far at Erwarton Hall, near Shotley). There also seems to have been a cartway leading into the farmyard through a vertically-timbered gabled barn. The surviving house, with the Stebbing initials in the chimneystack, retains almost exactly the form specified for Dade's house at Elmham. Inside the front door, a 'screens passage' leads straight through into the back yard, where, when Mr Frank Martin showed me it in 1970, a small flock of chickens ranged and pecked about in a Chaucerian way. The screen is made of solid oak, vertically panelled. The buttery and other service-chamber lie to the left, the 'hall' to the right, and the parlour beyond that. The original Elizabethan cock's-head hinges fasten the door of the cupboard beneath the stairs.

None of this is exceptional, happily. What is quite remarkable is the way the entire setting of this yeoman farmhouse has been preserved from the time when Nathaniel Fuller mapped it, and presumably from the time of the building, 1593. Here truly is a landscape with figures straight out of Ryece's *Breviary*. Fuller's map shows tree-studded hedges enclosing small fields (three five-acre, one seven-acre, two eight-acre, one ten-acre, one 11-acre, and so on) corresponding very closely to the hedge-pattern today, which has been altered only in small detail. Mr P.J.O. Trist, Conservation Officer of the Suffolk Trust for Nature Conservation, reported on the farm as follows (I abridge).

> The farm extends to ninety acres, all arable except three grass fields of about twelve acres. The 1971 crops are wheat, barley, beans. The farm's two important features are an almost unspoilt field boundary system compared with that of 1656, and a unique collection of plants in a type of habitat now rare, two permanent pastures. Of the three permanent pastures, it is likely that two, near the farm yard, have never been ploughed. They have probably been cut for hay for generations. Certainly no chemical sprays or fertilisers have been applied. The third meadow, flat and less well drained, has a probably unique collection of old pasture plants, typical of the former farming of wet sandy clay loam.

Among the plants growing in this meadow Mr Trist names Autumn Crocus, Fritillary, Green winged Orchid, Adder's Tongue, the Yellow Rattle and the Wild Daffodil. It would make a stage-set for Bottom and the fairies in *A Midsummer Night's Dream*. The Lesser Knapweed, Ox-eye Daisy, Meadow Foxtail and Quaking Grass are also 'present'. Naturally, several of the hedges contain four or five species of trees and shrubs. Finally, next to the road and the house is a small orchard of elderly fruit trees. This was the orchard in 1656.

John Nunne, of Tostock Old Hall, died in 1540 of the current epidemic of 'sickness'. His will,[8] besides illustrating that cloth-making was by no means confined to the famous 'clothing towns' like Kersey and Hadleigh, gives some idea of the complexity of a prosperous weaver's house. Basically of the 15th century, it acquired its main staircase and wall-panelling in the early 17th. This is how it was when he left it to his wife:

[8] Mr Peter Northeast has very kindly sent me his transcript of this and many equally interesting wills.

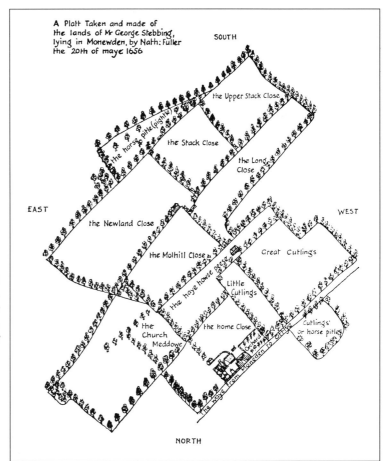

A Platt Taken and made of the lands of Mr George Stebbing, lying in Monewden, by Nath: Fuller the 20th of maye 1656

SOUTH

the Upper Stack Close

the horse pitle (right)

the Stack Close

the Long Close

EAST

the Newland Close

WEST

the Molhill Close

Great Cutlings

the haye house passe

Little Cutlings

the Church Meddowe

the home Close

Cutlings' or horse pitles

the waye from Monewden to Otley

NORTH

70 *Rookery Farm, Monewden: a late Elizabethan development. Re-drawn from the original map in East Suffolk Record Office. Colour version (original) at plate XXIV. And see p.176 opposite.*

My wife to have her dwelling in the new parlour and the chamber over it in my mansion where I now live and the house called the 'Brekinghouse' and the solar over the clockhouse: the oil house and the solars over it and all the little houses and solars at the end of the said parlour towards Russhebrooks, with the little yard called the ironstone yard and free liberty in the foreyard and ingress and egress at the foregate and carriage for herself and her servants, so long as she remain unmarried. She and her servants to have an easement at the 'withdrawte' in the yard … My wife to have the occupation of my dyehouse with all the woad, vats, leads, cisterns etc., necessary for the occupation of dyeing, together with the occupation and easement of the waters adjoining and also of my tenters and tenter yards and all things thereto belonging necessary for cloth making.

Tostock Old Hall, impeccably preserved among the silvery willows upstream from Little Haugh Hall at Norton and Grimstone End at Pakenham, still has a remarkable group of timber-framed outhouses across the back courtyard: it occupies perhaps the original settlement site of Tostock, whose oldest spelling, *Totestoc*, might mean 'the dairy-farm with the look out'. (The church stands above, where the land rises to a spur.)

Ryece described the grander houses built in his day in terms that make it hard to think of examples: 'placed where they may be furthest seen ... best prospects, rooms square, raised high, commonly with three, and often with four, storeys.' Can he have known Thorpe Hall, Hoxne? Probably he was 'sniffing' at the Springs' 'New House' at Pakenham. He could hardly be thinking of the Lord Keeper's house, Redgrave Hall? That had been built to replace a lodge in one of the Abbot of Bury's parks. But Bacon was not one for the latest fashions. Stone from Bury from the dissolved St Saviour's Hospital, that Samson built and West Stow helped to feed, went to the making of that house, as did the old 'superstitious' altar-slabs from Wortham, Rickinghall, Hinderclay and Redgrave itself, perhaps to pave the Lord Keeper's modest hall. In its day it looked like nothing so much as the Withipoll mansion, where the young Queen Elizabeth stayed, in Christchurch Park in the heart of Ipswich. But the Redgrave house is gone. As its historian, Alan Simpson, wrote:[9]

> In 1946, after enduring an ordnance dump in one corner of the park and a camp for prisoners of war in another, the house was totally demolished except for a single doorway, which the wreckers had exposed, and which the owner could not bring himself to pull down. This was Bacon's front door; but it will fall down in a year or two, and the monks will have the last laugh. There will be nothing left but their magnificent oaks.

Ryece complained of the fancy new buildings (that would certainly not have included Bacon's but might have included his son's, at Culford) that 'wasted our wonted plenty of timber' and forced the builders to devise a new kind of timber-framing, with almost half the timber formerly used, 'and far stronger as the workmen stick not to affirm, but the truth thereof is not yet found out so'. If he was reporting his own experience in the rebuilding of Preston Hall, then the workmen were not wrong. Ryece turned to 'the poor cottager', and since so many of the 'poor cottages' have survived, too, what he says is relevant:

> He thinks he doth very well to ... raise his frame low, cover it with thatch, and to fill his wide panels (after they are well splinted and bound) with clay or culm enough well tempered; over which it may be some, of more ability both for warmth, continuance and comeliness, do bestow a cast of hair lime and sand, made into mortar and laid thereon, rough or smooth as the owner pleaseth.

---

9 *The Wealth of the Gentry*, p.55.

XVIII *Denston church, by masons who built Long Melford church.*

XIX *Woodbridge: St Mary's church and Thomas Seckford's Elizabethan house, provocatively masked from school playing-field.*

XX Ufford's church tower, near the ford at the heart of the early East Anglian kingdom of the Wuffingas.

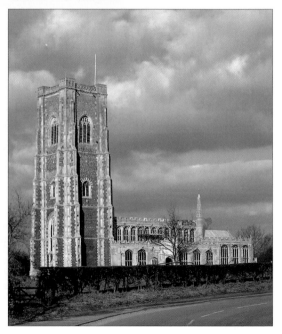

XXI Lavenham church, reflecting combined wealth of earls of Oxford and Thomas Spring, Lavenham clothier.

XXII   *Ickworth House in snow.*

XXIII   *Southwold from the harbour.*

XXIV *Heveningham Hall. Kim Wilkie's contribution to Capability Brown's great landscape. This low green amphitheatre replaces too steep a slope behind the house and its James Wyatt interior.*

XXV *The landscape at Sutton Hoo, the scene of a famous ship-burial. One of the mounds has been carefully reconstructed to its original proportions. It overlooks the Deben estuary in a frosty dawn.*

XXVI *Linstead Hall, moats and pond.*

XXVII *Stradbroke, Battlesea Green: the Rookery garden canal and moat.*

XXVIII *Framsden post-mill: Chris Hulcoop at work on stock (timber to which two sails are fitted) in July 1968.*

XXIX *Lowestoft Denes: smoke-houses and nets drying beneath North Light.*

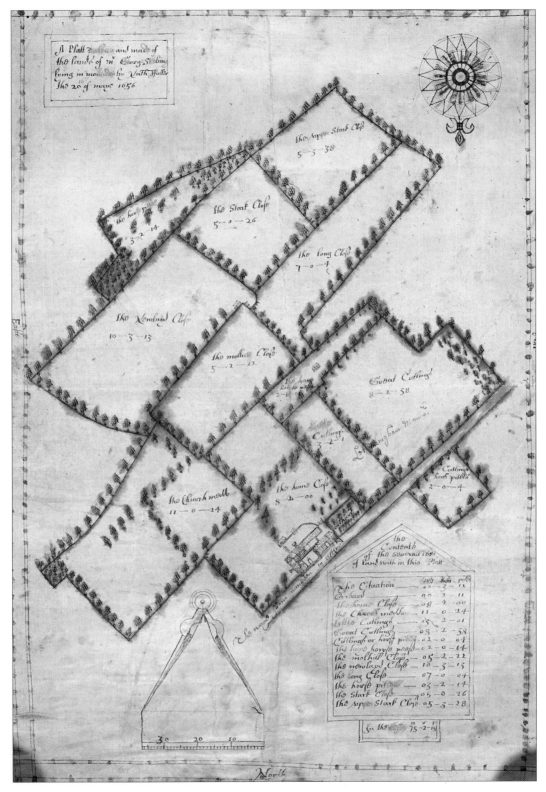

xxx *Monewden, original Rookery Farm map, 1656 (see also illustration 70, p.177).*

XXXI   *Chelsworth 'Peacock' from bridges over the Brett bearing initials of R. Pocklington, 1754, squires for two centuries of this village of beautiful water-meadows.*

XXXII   Golding Constable's Kitchen Garden *by John Constable: his father's back garden at home in East Bergholt, looking east to their mill on the common. See David Lucas's mezzotint, p.188.*

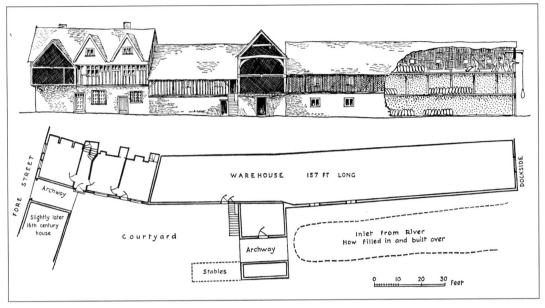

71   *Elevation and plan, drawn by Bernard Reynolds, of 80 Fore Street, Ipswich.*

The over-coat of lime plaster was described more appreciatively by Ryece's Essex contemporary, William Harrison: 'finally cover all with the aforesaid plaster, which, beside the delectable whiteness of the stuff itself, is laid on so even and smoothly as nothing, in my judgement, can be done with more exactness.' Nowadays, there is a mad craze to strip off this creamy lime plaster, and leave the timber vertical studwork naked, or else recoat it with a cement rough-cast, very injurious to it.

Among the most important ingredients of the landscape are all the varied farm buildings, barns, byres, stacks, dovecotes. John McCann's book, *The Dovecotes of Suffolk* (1998), describes the thirty or so survivors with a rare comprehension. John Weller of Bildeston has written invaluable guides to the future of the farming landscape. Such fundamental components of Suffolk as the maltings and the shops of the village tradesmen we have room to describe only in one illustration (illustration 71). The same is true of that most characteristic, and mechanically most remarkable, 'of all the features of the Suffolk fields, the windmill, and especially the post-windmill (illustration 77).

Some of the most complex timbered house-structures are to be found in the towns: Clare, Bury and Sudbury, Hadleigh and even Ipswich, where Fore Street still retains a few of the merchants' houses backing on to the quay.

72 *Ipswich Unitarian Meeting House (1699-1700) reflected in the glass cladding of Norman Foster's adjacent Willis Faber Office building of 1974.*

There the *Old Neptune Inn* is preserved in splendid order, and No.80 (illustration 71) was, in the 1970s, still lived in by the Corn and Coal merchant herself, Miss Lord: a most notable example of continuity in the landscape of an ancient sea-port.

'Landskip'

Ogilby's map of Ipswich in 1672, Pennington's map in 1778 like Warren's Bury show those ancient street-patterns evolved by the Old English in Ipswich and the Normans in Bury. They also show the provincial town background that both Gainsborough and Constable knew. Gainsborough was born in Sudbury in 1727, and baptised a Dissenter. 'Meeting-Houses' were a new addition to the landscape from the late 17th century. The oldest and most remarkable, at Walpole, is, like its name, an old house for meeting. There are several handsome ones – in Bury and Ipswich, Wrentham, Southwold, Horham, Rishangles, Rendham. Architecturally, two of the most interesting are at Fressingfield and Tunstall. They are specifically designed as auditoriums for the sermons.

Gainsborough's love of landscape appeared early in this book. His famous picture of an oak wood near Sudbury, traditionally at Cornard ('Corn earth': the name could hardly be more aboriginal), was begun when he was 13 and was the means of his father's sending him to London (*c.*1740). There, his association with Gravelot, the French engraver and first draughtsman of his day, and Hayman helped him to find his language and respond to the charm of nature in a universal, but not 'grand', manner. Hazlitt once called Watteau the French Gainsborough. What moves one most about Gainsborough is that his most sophisticated paintings (for instance, the *Harvest Wagon*, with its bold references to Rubens's *Deposition*) spring from the realities of a farm-cart frolic and a team of horses. He really meant it when, in 1768, he said 'I'm sick of Portraits and wish very much to take my viol-da-gamba and walk off to some sweet village where I can paint landskips'.

He spent the 1750s in Ipswich, newly married, and able to do just that. The attraction of the old town of Ipswich was, until the 1940s, that it was a place still pleasant to live and work in, as the consultants, hired to turn it into a 'New Town', and double it, recognised in the 1960s, before the scheme foundered on the Government's shortage of funds. Unluckily, a degree of expansion goes on, equally without guarantees for the provision of adequate roads, and without a balanced scheme. The Corporation should be asked to

73 *Hengrave from the air. 'Kytson the Merchant' built this ravishingly handsome white-brick house in 1525, and his son's Dutch gardener landscaped it in time for the Queen's visit in 1578.*

study Pennington's map of their town, and Gainsborough's pictures of the environs, and then asked to explain what went wrong. Pennington's map is crammed with pleasant human scenery, orchards, a botanic garden, bowling-greens, ordinary gardens, and the sparkling estuary a few minutes' walk away. Now, the swans at Stoke Bridge (the second of Suffolk's recorded Anglo-Saxon bridge sites) have to be hauled out of the water from time to time, and the survivors serviced with detergent.

Gainsborough's letters, as fresh as Mozart's, reflect his mind, as he got on with the business of painting. He laughed at the English gentleman's passion for building Italianate houses in the English countryside. The landskip he saw from Ipswich in the 1750s was natural English parkland and farmland, as it still, most happily, is. His pictures of it were painted with the relish of a 17th- or 18th-century Dutchman (and with the delicacy of Fragonard). Before

74 *Hemingstone Hall, apparently given much of its present delightful appearance by William Style in the 1620s.*

he left for Bath, he celebrated the descending series of welling ponds in the Ipswich park named Holywells after them. (Colour plate 27. The windmill on the horizon stood on Stoke Hills.) At Agnews in 1992, I was able to identify the landscape at first sight, and to encourage the Ipswich Museums and Galleries to secure it. (Previous owners thought it was Hampstead.) I'm proud that the book now wears it on its front cover.

His 'unclassical' view of the landskip was shared by most of his Suffolk contemporaries, and forebears. The leading figures had, as usual, relatively simple tastes. 'Kytson the Merchant', a leading London cloth-merchant who kept a staff at Antwerp, began to build his beautiful white-brick house at Hengrave in 1525, the year the bells first rang from Lavenham steeple (illustration 73). More lavish than the Lord Keeper's later house at Redgrave, it nevertheless stuck to the traditional quadrangular moated pattern (the

75 *Livermere Park, c. 1730, painted probably by Tillemans. Built of red brick for a branch of the Coke family in Charles II's time, when Euston and Saxham and Newmarket flourished in this part. The park, 1,000 acres of light land, may have been landscaped by Kent. Little Livermere church lies off the left side of the picture, and the great mere (see illustration 50) to the left beside the house. In 1795, Repton thought this 'good-coloured' water 'wanted clothing near the house', though in other parts wood and water were beautifully connected with each other' (Sketches and Hints). By 1820, the old red-brick front had been encased with white Woolpit tiles to resemble stone. House demolished 1923. Park now arable. Ampton Water stretches back to the right. We look due south.*

moat was levelled in the 18th century, but a very big fish-pond survives). The old main approach, now a walk with single avenue, was by a long straight causeway with deep ditches on either side and a triple avenue. It sounds Dutch. And when the builder's son, in 1575, wanted to improve the setting of his house, he got a 'Dutchman gardener' over from Norwich to look at the orchards, gardens and walks, dip the knots, alter the alleys, and re-plant. Three years later, the Queen and Leicester and the entire court were here in late August, and treated to a spectacle 'representing the fayries, as well as might be'. Whether Bottom performed is not recorded, but there were plenty of weavers about, and probably a bellows-mender. There was a mill and a forge on the estate, kennels for the hounds and the spaniels, and mews for the hawks. There were butts on an artificial mound that might still be traceable. For antiquaries, there is a most tantalising series of earthworks, invisible except from the air.

At the end of the 17th century and beginning of the 18th, Celia Fiennes and Defoe travelled through Suffolk and described a landscape very close to ours. Both were sympathetic to Dissenters and admired the mercantile developments they saw. Defoe was nearly lyrical about Ipswich: 'upwards of 600 country people on horseback and on foot, with baskets and other carriage, who had all of them brought something or other to town to sell.' He guessed he saw 20,000 people at a launch of a new ship on the Orwell. He commented on one of two large and splendid French-looking houses in the light lands: missed Livermere (illustration 75), built by a member of the lawyer Coke's dynasty, but knew Brightwell, built near Ipswich by Sir Samuel Barnardiston, a great East India merchant, of the Puritan family seated over at Kedington. Livermere came down in 1923, and only the mere remains. Brightwell came down *c*.1760, its site marked by a grassy platform; and some daffodils keep coming up where the garden was. Kip engraved Knyff's drawing of this sandy valley when it was laid out as a great formal garden, a triumph of Art over Nature, which nevertheless won in the end. At Livermere, regular miles of broad vista were created between regiments of trees, in the manner of Versailles – the kind of thing attempted nowadays only by the Forestry Commissioners or by the designers of runways for friendly aircraft armed with nuclear bombs.

The impulse to create 'landskip' is the impulse to garden in a bigger way, and landscape 'architects', so called, would do better to revert to their old name. Horace Walpole's famous tribute to Capability Brown gives the clue to much that is best in the Suffolk, and in the English, landscape: 'Such was the effect of his genius that when he was the happiest man he would be least remembered, so closely did he copy nature that his works will be mistaken'.

This is it. England's most original contribution to the whole history of art lies in the landscape, and was an affair of creating harmonious pictures with the land itself. Capability Brown visited Euston over most of his working life, and the benefit we all see, as we drive through that 'Bloomfield' country, today. The Duke of Grafton feels the benefit most, not only as a connoisseur of landscape himself, but because Brown managed to persuade the level of the lake to settle, at last, *below* the level of the ground floor of the house. To ride from Barnham to Euston and on to Rushford through broad avenues of grown trees is an ennobling experience; it is matched in the roads about Henham. Tom Williamson's book, *Suffolk's Gardens and Parks* (2000), based on wide and lively researches, is thoroughly informative on the most delightful aspects of the Suffolk landscape.

Brown's most famous work in Suffolk was designed for another London merchant with Dutch connections, Sir Joshua Vanneck: the park at Heveningham contains one of his characteristic serpentine lakes, and one of his happiest architectural inventions – the stable shaped like a horse-shoe round the stone-paved yard. One would love to know if he was responsible for the serpentine walls in the kitchen garden (known locally as crinkle-crankles, or ribbon walls). They are extraordinarily common from about this date in Suffolk gardens (and appeared *c.*1809 in Jefferson's Charlottesville). The most reckless profusion of these walls is found in the gardens of Gorleston and Yarmouth, so we may have to seek a Dutch source. Some of Brown's more ambitious ideas were never carried through. Heveningham's present owners, John and Lois Hunt, are celebrating the 21st century by completing Brown's plans to approach the house by a substantial bridge over the lake. It is hoped the bridge will match the nobility of the house, and add to the distinction of perhaps the finest of Suffolk's man-made landscapes. It is in the very capable hands of Kim Wilkie, who has already celebrated this century here by creating a magnificent grass amphitheatre behind the house (colour illustration XXIII).

Ipswich, like Yarmouth, had very much the smack of the Dutch towns of the 17th century, with the hospitals for the old and the sick. That came to an end in the middle of the 19th century. When John Evelyn was here in 1677 he noticed 'a thing very extraordinary. There is not any beggar asks for alms in the whole place.' He also saw a Flemish affinity: how the mansion of Christchurch 'stands in a park near the town, like that of Brussels'. During the Napoleonic Wars, on fine summer's evenings, the park was 'as crowded as Kensington Gardens'. It is often so in our own day.

Gainsborough's life-long friend Joshua Kirby was the son of John Kirby, whose *Suffolk Traveller*, 1735, was the first guidebook to Suffolk. A new, expanded edition followed in 1764, well edited by the Reverend Richard Canning, whose portrait by Gainsborough is in the Christchurch mansion. Canning was one of the originators of the rural union workhouse, the first for a rural union in England. In its day, 1756, it seemed a good, even humane, idea and it was

76 *'Stratford Mill'. Stratford is only a mile or two up the Stour valley from Flatford. Constable's famous picture, painted in 1820, shows the fishing that goes on at this identical spot to this day, and the wheel of the water mill now vanished (though its site is still obvious). He also recorded the degree to which the river was 'canalised' by the slimy posts and props that gave him such pleasure to paint, and one of the barges for which the system of locks was necessary. The Stour Navigation was begun in 1705. It enabled the barges to reach Sudbury, 25 miles above the estuary. Here one sees only men on the 'haling ways' (towpaths). In other pictures, Constable immortalised the 'leaping horses' that not only towed the barges but had to leap on and off them to cross the river whenever the haling ways changed from one bank to another. The Navigation's period of high prosperity lasted from c.1780 to 1848, the coming of the railway. It struggled on till 1892, and finally expired in 1913. This picture was bought, in 1987, for the National Gallery.*

followed in other East Suffolk unions and one West Suffolk one. They were based on the ancient area of the Hundred, and some of their buildings survive. That at Onehouse, near Stowmarket, was built at a cost of £12,000. In 1836, one of the Poor Law Commissioners noted wryly, not savagely, that 'it eclipsed some of the neighbouring mansions'. By then, the over-emphasis on cornfields had done its work, and the most famous painter of one, Constable, was writing (1822): 'My brother is uncomfortable about the state of things in Suffolk.

77 *East Bergholt Common under plough. 'Spring. A Mill on a Common. Hail Squalls' was one of the captions Constable devised for this sky-lit mezzotint by David Lucas. It first appeared in their joint work on* English Landscape *in 1830 and is based on Constable's oil sketch (Victoria and Albert Museum No.144). The Act for enclosing Bergholt Common was passed in 1815, and the sketch was probably made in the spring of 1816 (Ian Fleming Williams,* Burlington Magazine, *June 1972). Constable's father owned this post mill, now gone. It was visible from the back of their house (also gone). Constable was especially anxious that in the print the sails be seen to be able to catch the wind.*

They are as bad as Ireland – "never a night without seeing fires near or at a distance". The *Rector* & his brother the *Squire* ... have forsaken the village ... these things are ill timed.' Another of Constable's famous pictures shows East Bergholt common being ploughed up (illustration 77), which, in view of the enclosure award, was probably painted *after* 1815.

The Seaside
Kenneth Clark once wrote: 'The delicate music of the Suffolk coast, with its woods straggling into sandy commons, its lonely marshes and estuaries full of small boats, still had more charms for me than the great brass bands of natural scenery, the Alps or the Dolomites.'

The whole Suffolk coast from the mouth of the Stour and Orwell estuaries right up to a point just south of Kessingland, has lately been declared an Area of Outstanding Natural Beauty. This means that the Local Authority now has

78 *The coast at Shingle Street: sheep and shingle and Martello Tower for defence against Napoleon.*

special responsibilities and powers (within its financial means) to preserve one of the most 'unspoilt' pieces of England. The secret of its not having been infested with ten thousand bungalows lies simply in its curious structure, which has always dispelled any idea of building a coast road. One has only to go to Langer Road, Felixstowe, and look up at the old cliff-line, or to almost any part of the road between Lowestoft and Yarmouth, and see what a mess we make, daily, of our natural visual and recreational assets.

But between Bawdsey and Benacre there are places that are lovely to visit because they are hard to reach. One has to abandon the car and walk, which is good recreation for the legs. There were some obstacles: a so-called radio research installation on Orford Ness, now owned by the National Trust, who provide a delightful guided tour. We owe our survival in the Battle of Britain partly to the beginning of radar both here and at Bawdsey, so we are interested. They can be thought of as potential features of historic and even architectural interest, like Burgh Castle, and Orford Castle, and the Martello Towers put up between Felixstowe and Aldeburgh from 1808 onwards (illustration 78): at least three years *after* there could possibly have been a military need for them. They continued to be manned well into the 19th century. White's *Directory* of 1855 records that the five towers in Hollesley Bay were 'now occupied by

79 *Bromeswell encampment, water colour by G. Quinton, 1803, shows the Napoleonic War gunners' camp on the heath above the Deben, camp followers washing and ironing in foreground, where Sir John Moore had his first sight of mounted artillery, 1797. Kit layout and drill still seem familiar. The Suffolk Yeomanry galloped here in 1914. There have been great airfields nearby.*

coast-guard men'. These were first and foremost Inland Revenue men, in the age-long war to prevent smuggling; but on stormy winter nights they would be in the thick of the action to save lives with their rocket apparatus on shore and in their lifeboats at sea.

The shores must have been infinitely more exciting then, with barges and fishermen and every other sailing craft literally crowding the coastal shipway. I treasure a watercolour of Aldeburgh beach in the 1830s, with Thomas Churchyard's wife and infants sitting by the waves, and all the beach yawls drawn up beyond. They were perhaps directly descended from those ships at Snape and Sutton Hoo. A model of the most famous yawl, *Bittern*, is to be seen in the Southwold 'Sailors' Reading Room.'

Three main resorts have developed along this beautiful, bleak, sunny shore. Southwold was owned by St Edmund's abbey in Jocelin's day. It developed a market and fair and fishery and boasts one of the most breathtaking of all Suffolk's medieval churches, and one of the ugliest modern water-towers. It is rather treeless, but this is being remedied. A dreadful obliterating blaze wiped out 238 houses in 1659. It is sometimes said that one of Southwold's chief delights, her series of open Greens interspersed through the streets, derives from this fire. But Thomas Gardner, writing in 1754, implied that they were already part of the landscape. Before 1659, 'the town was in a flourishing condition, and spacious, as is apparently conspicuous by streets, lanes, and Greens partly built'. It never recovered its 'ancient Greatness, either in Trade or Buildings'. He recorded only 140 dwellings in the town in his day.

Carlyle recommended Aldeburgh to his wife in 1855. 'A mile of fine shingly beach, with patches of smooth sand every here and there; clear water shelving rapidly, deep at all hours; beach solitary beyond wont, whole town rather solitary … never saw a place more promising.' Engravings and paintings show it in their day, a scene completely identifiable today.

Felixstowe as a seaside resort grew later, though an early friend of Gainsborough had a picturesque cottage of which a few details survive on Cobbold's Point. The great merit of the place as a resort is its south facing relatively sheltered wide bay. This its Edwardian creators knew exactly how to develop to best advantage, with promenade and tamarisk, hebe, a 'dripping well', a very long pier for fishermen and coastal pleasure steamers, and so on. More recently the gardens have been prone to fairy-lights. The enormous successes of the town have been scored at the other end, beside the Orwell estuary, where roll-on, roll-off imports and exports have expanded in a prodigious way.

The Changing Countryside

Some of the most effective alterations in the social and economic landscape of Suffolk since the days of Defoe and Kirby have been brought about by changes in communications, mostly improvements. The roads Kirby travelled had been considerably improved a century later. Turnpike records have survived very incompletely (illustration 80), but there is plenty of other evidence. François de La Rochefoucauld stayed with Arthur Young in 1784, and while Young was complaining that the Sudbury-Bury road, beside which he now lies, was one of the worst in the kingdom, his very intelligent young French visitor was recording his own astonishment at the number of travellers always to be met on English roads.

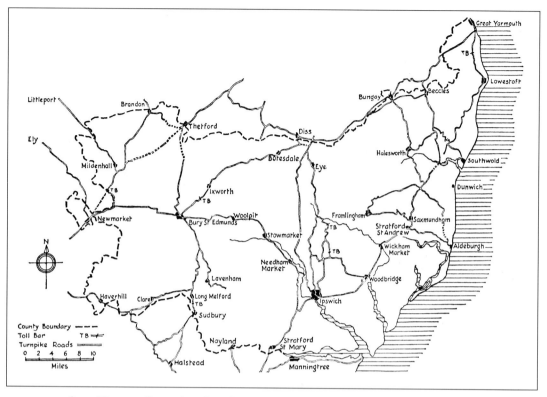

80 *The turnpike roads, 1831. Based on C. and J. Greenwood's survey and map. There were many more toll bars, but the evidence is incomplete and needs much more research. I have shown here only those recorded by the Greenwoods. I see that they were misinformed in including Framlingham in the network: cf, Dymond and Northeast,* A History of Suffolk, *p.88 and the* Historical Atlas.

> Bury is on the London-Norwich road, but this is the only road that goes through it. There are 125 horses available in the town for the service of post chaises and diligences … Over and above this large number of horses, you may reckon at least fifty hacks, let out either as saddle horses or for cabriolets … It is quite a simple matter to go from one place to another and, what is more, to go in comfort.

Young himself later remarked (1797) that the roads were 'uncommonly good in every part of the county … the improvements in this respect in the last twenty years are almost inconceivable'.

On the other side of the county, the improvements were slightly later. White's 1844 *Directory* shows how the life of the Woodbridge neighbourhood was affected in the first half of the 19th century.

> Fifty years ago only one daily coach and a weekly waggon passed through the town to and from London; but more than twelve *conveyances* (coaches, omnibuses, and

81 *Aldeburgh moot hall and the beach, crowded with boats and fishing gear. This aspect of the Borough is little changed since Crabbe published his verse-stories in 1810. In 1854, the moot hall was heavily restored by R.M. Phipson, and given new chimneys in the flamboyant local Jacobean style. The pattern of stud framework is original. See p.168. The town halls of Aldeburgh, Ipswich and Sudbury have sometimes, for no clear reason, been called moot halls.*

carriers' waggons and carts) now pass daily between the hours of six in the morning and twelve at noon; and persons may travel from Woodbridge to London in five hours, for 10s., instead of paying three times that amount, and being thirteen hours on the road, as was formerly the case.

(An intensely vivid account of a journey from King's Lynn to London by road waggon in 1864 is given by W. H. Barrett, in *Tales from the Fens*, 1963.) Till August 1972, the course of the ramped turnpike meandered prominently across the south end of the Melton playing-field in the half-mile between Woodbridge and Melton. Its metalled surface can yet be seen in the lane running behind Edmondson's historically well-sited garage. Two pubs, within a few hundred yards of each other, are still called the *Coach and Horses* and the *Horse and Groom*. Half way between them, an iron 'milestone' of 1818 made by J. Garrett in Ipswich, says 'MELTON to LONDON 78'. What worries me most about our roads in the early 21st century is that we may be overdoing it; or rather, that we have not yet got the balance right between major and minor roads. Despite much improvement, the main roads are still very dangerous and full of obstacles. Our small country lanes are getting too encouraging to the motorist: hedges are lowered and lay-bys created in the quietest of rural lanes, which are increasing lined with concrete kerbs. Local Authorities are supposed to be economising.

When Wilkie Collins wrote of Aldeburgh in *No Name*, in 1862, the villainous Captain Wragge 'sauntered through the gate of North Shingles Villa to meet the arrival of the coach which then connected with the Eastern Counties Railway'. The modern growth of Lowestoft would not have been possible without the development of the Railway and Harbour Company. Nor would Ipswich have developed so extensively without its dock and railway facilities, the work of the 1840s (marked by a handsome Custom House). These and Felixstowe, and now Haverhill, are the only places in Suffolk that Kirby would find it physically hard to recognise.

But ominous plans were made by the West Suffolk County Council. Their document, *Rural Planning in West Suffolk*, published in January 1968, showed the appalling estimates that, between 1966 and 1981, three of the best historic towns in England would be virtually doubled (Bury from 23,000 to 40,000: Hadleigh from 4,400 to 8,000; Sudbury from 7,000 to 16,000). This seemed bound to render their entire basic structures precarious. Fortunately, these plans were not fulfilled. Instead of reaching 40,000 by 1981, Bury had reached only 35,000 by 2001; Hadleigh was not many over the 7,000 mark last year, and Sudbury last year was still under 12,000. These are more realistic figures; perhaps they can be reached only by aiming too high.

In Ipswich, the great expansion had begun three or four decades before the arrival of the railway, but the development of the modern suburbs is directly related to the introduction of horse-trams in 1880, electric trolley-buses in 1903, and the availability of bicycles and then motor-cars. Felixstowe's latest phenomenal dock-expansion is an affair of massive lorries, by-passing the railways. Despite the valiant efforts of the little branch lines that have left trackways, and Halts like diminutive cricket pavilions, in various parts of the county, there can

82 *Helmingham estate cottages. Between 1852 and 1881, Lord Tollemache built and rebuilt nearly 150 of his cottages in the Helmingham neighbourhood.*

be few places less transformed by railways than Suffolk. Ipswich was altered. Lowestoft was altered. It meant the end of the little canal ventures. Yet somehow the railway has never supplanted the road in the county as a whole.

James Wilding, a farm-worker in the scattered village of Monk Soham, was going to emigrate to America with his wife and large family in the middle of the 19th century. A few days before his departure, he was asked how he was going: 'Oi doon't fare to know roightly. But we're a goin' to sleep the fust night at Debenham, and that'll kinda break the jarney.' Debenham was four miles away, and vaguely in the right direction. A 71-year-old farmworker in Akenfield lived about a yard from a Roman road. Ronald Blythe described him as doing his utmost to comprehend the foreign place in which he happened to have been born. Grandchildren arrive during the university holidays. Nephews and nieces fly in from Canada, while the ash at the end of the road, which marked the last point at which soldier and emigrant sons could turn and wave before walking to Ipswich to catch the train to Gallipoli or Quebec, still blocks the view.

Our view of the Victorian villages is still partly blocked by our being too close to them. The farmers themselves suffered badly, went bankrupt, and their widows were left on the parish. These were respectable, not improvident, farmers. The Metropolitan Police recruited well among their sons. But the surviving farmers, perhaps inevitably, hardened their hearts. They dispensed with the labourers who had large families and wanted more wages. The ricks that were burnt were usually those of farmers who were Poor Law Guardians. Things were so bad in the winter of 1843-4 that Sir Henry Bunbury, whose family are now based on Rendlesham but then lived in West Suffolk, wrote to *The Times* that, after the Poor Law Amendment Act, he had imagined the farmers would have employed more men at better wages.

> I deceived myself. The new scheme ... has been brought into operation with a cold harshness that is revolting to the feelings of the labouring class. Let land and cottages to labourers at reasonable rates, pay them wages in proportion to the work they do, discharge them not because there comes a day of rain or a day of frost, talk to them, talk with them, and you will have no more fires.

At that time, two-bedroomed cottages were found to have nine, ten and eleven persons sleeping in them. The big landowners could, and did, put their cottages in order. Part of Lord Stradbroke's survey of his cottages in 1874 is printed by Joan Thirsk and Jean Imray. Lord Tollemache spent £16,092 on his estate cottages between 1852 and 1881. Fifty-two were rebuilt, and 91 newly erected at £278 a pair. 'A chimney between the two warmed both, and in sickness each had neighbours to call on for help' (illustration 82).

Country cottages are now so much sought for by weekenders and commuters that 'estate cottages' such as these, that still catch the eye and not just in the Helmingham neighbourhood, do so more because they are of a model pattern, grouped together, than because of the general good repair, and the neatness of gardens and fruit trees. More recently, many new 'estates' of cottages have been provided, mostly by the Rural District Councils. But the 'rural' feeling is seldom so well captured as it was in the 'model' estates at, say, Brandeston, or at Woolverstone, or in the old Bunbury territory round Barton, where the flint-textures are so visually satisfactory and so appropriate. In the building of modern estates, no Rural District has yet managed to compete with the Rural

83 *The mechanisation of arable farming: reaper-binder at work in ever-broadening field — well before the advent of the combine-harvester that has brought about the prairie landscapes of Tannington, for example, and Mickfield. Such revolutions are not in mind here, at Holly Tree Farm, Yoxford. Or, are they?*

District of Loddon, just north of Bungay, and in Norfolk, where Tayler and Green, a Lowestoft firm, managed, between 1946 and 1974, to create a countryside that neither William Kent, nor Capability Brown, nor Humphry Repton, would have faulted.

Changes of a most complex kind occurred throughout rural Suffolk in the 19th century. They cannot well be understood without reference to the detailed Census returns, and this is no place for a statistical study. What is clear, from such a study, is that in almost every Hundredal district (for that was, naturally, the neighbourhood unit still used by the census officials) the majority of rural parishes increased in population down to the middle years of the century. The maximum population was reached in 67 parishes by 1831, in 83 more parishes

84 *Trimley in 1971. This photograph was taken from the air during the building of a by-pass designed to take vast 'container lorries' from Ipswich to the new 'roll-on-roll-off' port in the Orwell mouth at Felixstowe, perhaps the biggest of its kind in the world. The picture also shows the lines of the railway (on the left) and the (probably) Roman high road running towards the fort (illustration 21). That road runs past Trimley's two medieval churches contained in one churchyard (lettered A: see p.105). This is the landscape of intensive farming by groups of freemen in Domesday Book. B, C, and D show three of their farms (see p.127). Finally, the picture shows the clusters of suburban dwellings, little Lutons spreading gleefully into our villages an indirect consequence of the fact that much over 80 per cent of us are now born in towns or suburbs.*

by 1841, in over 150 more by 1851, and again in 50 more by 1861. That is to say, the decade ending in the year of the Great Exhibition marked (with entire appropriateness) the climax of the growth of the typical Suffolk country parish. Whether they got back to, or even exceeded, the sizes they had attained in the early 14th century is a question that calls for yet another programme of detailed local studies. Laxfield's local history group, for example, made a beginning. But so far we have little more than guesses and impressions.

Then, mechanisation (illustration 83) was followed, after 1879, by the deepest depression. And since then, mechanisation and a rationalisation have gone on steadily.[10] With them has gone a steady depopulation of the old rural

---

[10] P.J.O. Trist, *A Survey of the Agriculture of Suffolk* (1971), p.188 gives figures for the increase of combine-harvesters in Suffolk. They tell their own tale of steady hedgerow removal and increased field acreage. There were less than a dozen in 1938, only 118 in 1946, but by 1956 there were 2,080. These had increased to 2,940 in 1962, and then the numbers levelled out at about 3,000, an average of six per parish.

85 *Imaginative housing in Eye, with castle and church in the background.*

workers of the land. To some extent, their farmhouses and their cottages have gone. A few are still being deliberately allowed to become irreparable. But, in many cases, new occupants replace the old. In Brandeston, for instance, in 2002, there are no farmworkers, and in adjacent Otley there are only two, who commute in.

Linstead Magna and Linstead Parva are broad clay farmlands with low slopes above two of the headwaters of the Blyth. They lie between the unswerving Roman road at Cratfield and the Romano-British settlement-site at Chediston – a parish of notably rectilinear boundaries, a mile or two west of Halesworth. Sibton Abbey had a grange in Linstead Parva, and a survey of its 74 acres in 1325 shows an enclosed arable landscape closely identifiable with that of Abbey Farm today. 'Thirty perches lying detached beside le Grenemere' in 1325 probably referred to what is nowadays still called in

86 *Traditional new housing in Wetherden.*

Suffolk a 'Grimmer', a very murky green pond. (It might also be an early reference to a Green, for the pond just north of Abbey Farm does lie beside Morrell Haugh Green.) The two other Greens in Linstead Parva are of the fairly numerous, but easily overlooked, roadside-verge type, such as Hightown Green at Rattlesden. These two at Linstead Parva, Blacksmith's Green and Collipy's, lie along the fairly busy valley road, with its natural water supply. This little valley road explains why Linstead Parva, with the smaller acreage, has had the larger population at least since the Census began in 1801.

Linstead's 19th-century population rose and declined less than most of the rural parishes of the central clays. In Magna, the numbers varied between 90 and 120, reaching a peak of 134 in 1811. It has now settled down at about fifty. Parva, along the valley road, climbed to 227 in 1861, but has dwindled to a hundred or so in 1971. White's 1855 *Directory* shows something of the anatomy of this community in its Victorian heyday. Felix Godfrey, in Linstead Parva, appeared proudly as 'threshing-machine owner'. Little Linstead may be remote, but its farming industry is well abreast of the times. The other villagers then included the victualler of the *Greyhound*, the

87 *New stone circle marks the millennium at Lord de Saumarez's Shrubland Park.*

blacksmith, the tailor, the boot-and-shoe maker, and a cooper, as well as seven farmers: a community as self-contained as that very early one at West Stow, and with of course a great deal more craftsmanship and skill in working the land.

Since then, the decline in numbers may have been accompanied by a decline in sense of community. The *Greyhound* has lately reverted, through lack of business, to a private dwelling; but motor-cars and bikes had already rendered redundant the two old footpaths that converged on the *Greyhound* across the fields from far-off easterly and westerly farmsteads and hamlets. The small wooden Village Hall, close by, can hardly be reckoned a substitute. Nor is the garage, now occupying (as in so many villages) the site of the blacksmith's shop, a full replacement for the smithy of those days when the routine of the farm, and the management of the fields, were so largely centred on the horses. Tailoring and shoemaking are supplanted by the impersonal reach-me-down of the towns, and coopering has withdrawn to the big breweries. But Linstead Parva's gardens and farms are as trim and well cared for as ever they can have been, and Mr Keeble's tall roof of dark blue glazed pantiles at

Poplar Farm reflects the gleam of the sky in an unmistakable North Suffolk way. And the little medieval church at the crossroads, tucked otherwise so inconveniently into the far eastern corner of the parish, is lovingly kept even if it fills with parishioners and their friends only for the harvest festival, the one really holy time left in the Suffolk year.

The last remains of Linstead Magna's church in the fields were removed in the 1960s, and the people of both parishes speak just of 'Linstead' now, as they did in the early Middle Ages before the two parishes were created. Such regular churchgoers as there are in 'Magna' tend to go to Cratfield church, which is nearer. Otherwise Linstead holds its own. The Hall of Linstead Magna, its structure basically 16th-century, stands near the very large moat of the earlier house, and above an enormous pond, almost a lake. One of Dr St Joseph's photographs of the site shows earlier rectangular field-ditches around the Hall, that probably betray only medieval stockyard arrangements. There is no proper sense in which the site should be listed, as it is in Beresford and Hurst's book (p.203), 'a deserted medieval village': see colour illustration XXVI.

The large clay fields, deep-ditched and drained, are now farmed as part of a neighbouring estate. The countryside has changed. Even at Linstead, whose name implies that flax was grown here by its first cultivators before the coming of the Normans, and whose heavy fields would anyway turn over only for a very tough plough-team (however mechanised), the land is still fully productive. Half a mile west, the neighbouring estate, Linstead Farm, on the Cratfield boundary (which is now expunged from the maps of the egregious Ordnance Survey), is still devotedly farmed by John Horsman. It was a tremendous pleasure to be able to conclude the 1987 edition of this book by recording his outright and admirable win of, first in 1984, the Suffolk 'Farming and Conservation' Trophy sponsored by the Bury brewers, Greene King, and in 1985, the national 'Farming and Conservation' award, then sponsored by *Country Life* and presented by David Attenborough. In 2002, seven miles of hedges and a tree every ten yards are still retained on the 360 acres of this central boulder-clay farm, with ten ponds, and wild life wonderfully flourishing. To balance the positive conservation, the high output of the farm is achieved in consultation with Framlingham Farmers. Despite the appalling losses of Suffolk hedgerows recorded in the Introduction, the ancient farm-landscape of Suffolk still rewards understanding and cultivating; and, for those of us who don't farm, we try to understand; for, as John Constable said, 'we see nothing truly till we understand it'.

SELECT BIBLIOGRAPHY

Ashton, N., Healy, F., and Pettitt, P. (eds.), *Stone Age Archaeology: Essays in Honour of John Wymer* (1998).

Bruce-Mitford, R.L.S., *The Sutton Hoo Ship Burial: Vol.I* (1975)

Bruce-Mitford, R.L.S., in *P.S.I.*, Vol. XXIV (1949)

Butler, H.E. (ed.), *Chronicle of Jocelin of Brakelond* (1949)

Cam, Helen, *Liberties and Communities in Medieval England* (1944)

Cautley, H.M., *Suffolk Churches and Their Treasures* (1968)

Clarke, R. Rainbird, *East Anglia* (1960), and in *Archaeological Journal*, Vol.XCVI

Collins, Ian, *A Broad Canvas: Art in East Anglia since 1880* (1990)

Cook, Olive, *Breckland* (1956)

Darby, H.G., *The Medieval Fenland* (1949), ch.1

Davies, John, and Williamson, Tom, *Land of the Iceni* (Norwich, 1999), ch.3, 'Suffolk in the Iron Age', by Martin, Edward

Davis, R.H.C. (ed.), *The Kalendar of Abbot Samson* (1954)

Denney, A.H., *Sibton Abbey Estates, 1325-1509*, Suffolk Records Society (1959)

Dymond, D.P. (ed.), *Joseph Hodskinson's Map of Suffolk in 1783*, Suffolk Records Society (1972)

Dymond, D.P. and Northeast, P., *A History of Suffolk* (1985)

Dymond, David and Martin, Edward (eds.), *An Historical Atlas of Suffolk* (1988, revised and enlarged 1999)

Ekwall, E., *Concise Oxford Dictionary of English Place names*, 4th edn. (1960)

Evans, George Ewart, *The Horse in the Furrow* (1960)

Gardner, R., *History of Dunwich* (1754)

Glyde, John, *Illustrations of Old Ipswich* (1889)

Gransden, Antonia (ed.), *Bury St Edmunds*, B.A.A. Conference Transactions, XX (1988)

Green, Charles, 'Norfolk: Burgh Castle: Excavation by Charles Green, 1958-61', in *East Anglian Archaeology*, 20 (1983)

Harlow, C.G., Article on Ryece, *P.S.I.*, Vol.XXXII (1970)

Harper-Bill, Christopher, Rawcliffe, Carole and Wilson, Richard G. (eds.), *East Anglia's History: Studies in Honour of Norman Scarfe* (2002)

Hart, C.R., *Early Charters of Eastern England* (1966)

Hart, Cyril, *The Danelaw* (1992)

Harwood, Elain and Powers, Alan, *Tayler and Green, Architects 1938-1973* (1998)

Homans, G.C., 'The Frisians in East Anglia', *Econ. Hist. Review* (December 1957)

Ipswich: The Archaeological Implications of Development (Scole Committee, Ipswich, 1973)

Kirby, John, *The Suffolk Traveller* (1735, 2nd edn. 1764)

Margary, I.D., *Roman Roads in Britain (South)* (1955)

Martin, E.A., 'The Barrows of Suffolk' in *East Anglian Archaeology*, Report No.12 (1981)

Medieval Archaeology, Vols. III, X, XI, XIII

Oppenheim, M., 'Maritime History' in Victoria County History, *Suffolk*, Vol.II

Orford Ness: A Selection of Maps Presented to J.A. Steers (1966)

Pevsner, N., *The Buildings of England: Suffolk* (1974)

Rackham, Oliver, article in *Vernacular Architecture*, Vol.3 (1972)

Rackham, Oliver, *Trees and Woodland in the British Landscape* (1976)

Rackham, Oliver, *The History of the Countryside* (1986)

Redstone, Lilian, *Ipswich Through the Ages* (Ipswich, 1948)

Rigold, S.E., 'Further evidence about the site of Dommoc', *Journal of the British Archaeological Association* (1974)

Ryece, R., *The Breviary of Suffolk*, ed. Lord F. Hervey (1902)

Salzman, L., *Building in England to 1540* (1952)

Report of the Sandlings Project, 1983-85, Sandlings Group, Park Cottage, Saxmundham (1987)

Scarfe, Norman, *Suffolk in the Middle Ages* (1986)

Simmons, Jack, 'The Railways of Suffolk' in *The Railways of Britain* (1961), pp.197-209

Smith, A.H., *English Place-name Elements* (1970)

Suffolk Estuaries: A Report by the Suffolk Wildlife Trust (1988)

Suffolk in 1524, 'Suffolk Green Books' based on the Subsidy Returns, ed. S.H.A. Hervey (1910)

Suffolk in 1568, ditto (1909)

P.S.I. Vols.XXV, XXVI, XXVIII, XXIX, *et passim*

Thirsk, Joan and Imray, Jean, *Suffolk Farming in the Nineteenth Century*, Suffolk Records Society (1958)

Victoria County History, *Suffolk*, Vols.I (1911) and II

Wade-Martins, P., in *Norfolk Archaeology* (1969, 1970)

Warner, P., *The Origins of Suffolk* (1996)

West, S.E., in *P.S.I.*, Vol.X (1964)

West, S.E., *West Stow Anglo-Saxon Village* (1985)

West, S.E. and Plouviez, J., in *East Anglian Archaeology*, Report No.3 (1976)

Whitelock, Dorothy, *Anglo-Saxon Wills* (1930)

Wymer, J.J., *Paleolithic Sites of East Anglia* (1985)

INDEX

Roman numerals in bold refer to colour plates; bold arabic numbers indicate the page numbers of monochrome illustrations.